ROBERT S. KEEBLER, CPA, MST

The Rebirth of ROTH

A CPA's Ultimate Guide for Client Care

AMERICAN INSTITUTE OF CERTIFIED PUBLIC ACCOUNTANTS

AICPA®

Sponsored by **the Personal Financial Planning Section (PFP)**

Notice to Readers

The Rebirth of Roth: A CPA's Ultimate Guide for Client Care does not represent an official position of the American Institute of Certified Public Accountants, and it is distributed with the understanding that the author and publisher are not rendering, legal, accounting, or other professional services in the publication. If legal advice or other expert assistance is required, the services of a competent professional should be sought.

1 2 3 4 5 6 7 8 9 0 CS 0

ISBN: 978-0-87051-853-9

Publisher: Linda Prentice Cohen
Senior Managing Editor: Amy M. Stainken
Developmental Editor: Andrew Grow
Project Manager: Amy Sykes
Cover Design Direction: Nancy Karmadi
Interior designer: David McCradden

About the Author

Robert S. Keebler, *CPA, MST, AEP (Distinguished)*
Baker Tilly Virchow Krause, LLP
Certified Public Accountants & Consultants

Robert S. Keebler, CPA, MST, AEP (Distinguished) is a partner with Baker Tilly Virchow Krause, LLP. He is a 2007 recipient of the prestigious Accredited Estate Planners (Distinguished) award from the National Association of Estate Planning counsels. Mr. Keebler was named by CPA Magazine as one of the *Top 100 Most Influential Practitioners in the United States* and one of the *Top 40 Tax Advisors to Know During a Recession.* Mr. Keebler is the past Editor-in-Chief of CCH's magazine, *Journal of Retirement Planning*, and a member of CCH's Financial and Estate Planning Advisory Board. His practice includes family wealth transfer and preservation planning, charitable giving, retirement distribution planning, and estate administration. Mr. Keebler frequently represents clients before the National Office of the Internal Revenue Service in the private letter ruling process and in estate, gift and income tax examinations and appeals.

In the past 15 years, he has received over 150 favorable private letter rulings including several key rulings of "first impression." Bob is nationally recognized as an expert in estate and retirement planning and works collaboratively with other experts on academic reviews and papers, and client matters. Mr. Keebler is the author of over 75 articles and columns and editor, author, or co-author of many books and treatises on wealth transfer and taxation, including the Warren, Gorham & Lamont of RIA treatise Esperti Peterson and Keebler/ Irrevocable Trusts: Analysis with Forms.

Mr. Keebler is a member of the editorial board of the Society of Financial Service Professionals "Keeping Current" series, and Co-author of the Warren, Gorham & Lamont Treatise "Irrevocable Trusts/Analysis With Forms." He is a featured columnist for CCH's *Taxes Magazine*—"Family Tax Planning Forum," Steve Leimberg's "News of the Week Newsletter" and the Bureau of National Affairs Tax Division. Bob also had his article "Is That Your 'Final' Answer?" article published in *Tax Management Compensation Planning Journal.* Bob frequently is quoted in national publications such as *New York Times, Chicago Tribune, Baltimore Sun, Barrons, Bloomberg Wealth Manager, Financial Advisor, Forbes, Kiplinger, Lawyer's Weekly, On Wall Street, The Wall Street Journal, USA Today, Wealth Manager* and *Worth* in addition to many local and regional newspapers.

He is a frequent speaker for legal, accounting and financial planning groups throughout the United States at seminars and conferences on advanced IRA distribution strategies, estate planning and trust administration topics including the AICPA's Advanced Estate Planning, Personal Financial Planning Conference and Tax Strategies for the High Income Individual Conference.

Mr. Keebler graduated (cum laude) from Lakeland College with a degree in Accountancy and the University of Wisconsin—Milwaukee with a Masters in Taxation. Before practicing in Northeastern Wisconsin, he practiced with Price Waterhouse where he concentrated in taxation.

Robert S. Keebler, *CPA, MST, AEP (Distinguished)*
robert.keebler@bakertilly.com

Preface

Important changes have taken place since Congress created the Roth IRA in 1997. The Treasury Department finalized Roth IRA regulations and regulations governing qualified plans and all IRAs. The Economic Growth and Tax Relief Reconciliation Act of 2001 (2001 Tax Act), changed the landscape of estate planning, creating qualified Roth contribution programs, increasing annual IRA contribution limitations, and allowing additional makeup contributions for many taxpayers.

Perhaps equally important, the bull market of the 1990's finally ended, producing sharp drops in the price of many stocks. These low stock prices, make this the ideal time to make a Roth IRA conversion and should encourage those who have already made a Roth conversion to recharacterize, eliminating the tax paid on the earlier conversion and allowing them to subsequently reconvert while the value of the IRA assets is low.

Since inception, Roth conversions have been limited to those taxpayers whose AGI is under $100,000. However, due to legislation changes made in May 2006, a new door of opportunity has been opened for those interested in the Roth IRA. Beginning January 1, 2010, taxpayers will be able to convert to a Roth IRA without regard to their MAGI or filing status. Additionally, any taxable income resulting from a 2010 conversion may be spread over tax years 2011 and 2012, with 50 percent of the taxable income included in each of those two tax years.

These developments have made it necessary to reexamine our clients' existing Roth IRA planning. *The Rebirth of Roth: A CPA's Ultimate Guide for Client Care*, based on and expanded from *The Professional's Guide to Roth IRAs: Implementing the 2001 Tax Act*, brings you, the planner, up to date and offers suggestions for planning in today's changed legal and economic environment.

Acknowledgments

The author would like to thank Michelle L. Ward, JD, CSEP; Stephen J. Bigge, CPA; Jennifer L. Voigt, CPA, JD; Steven C. Lunn, CSEP; and Matthew Johnston, JD for their assistance with this project.

He would also like to thank, at the AICPA, Amy M. Stainken, JD, for overseeing the publication and Andrew Grow for his editing. We would also like to express our gratitude to Andrea Millar, CPA for her support in sharing the Roth message with the members of the PFS Division of the AICPA. Andrea's endless energy is contagious and she is a wonderful asset to the division and its members.

Finally, this book would not have been possible without a decade of support and collaboration with Natalie Choate, Mike Jones, Ed Slott and Barry Picker. The daily e-mails between this group have been a tremendous source of not only friendship but growth, insight and wisdom for which I am forever in their debt.

1-1-23 → SECURE 2.0 → RMD → 73

1-1-33 → " → RMD → 75

→ penalty for failure to withdraw ↓ 25%

1-1-24 → can rollover 35K of 529 to ROTH

1-1-24 → Roth 401k no RMDS

SECURE ACT

- defined contr. plans – restricts stretch payments
- all non qual. beneficiaries
- must be made w/in 10 yrs even if participant wasn't rec. payments yet
- on death of qual. ben. → any rem. must be paid w/in 10 yrs
- spouse can delay 10+ payment

- if participant dies after RBD
- "at least as rapidly" rule for non EDB

Table of Contents

Chapter 1: Introduction to the Roth IRA

Chapter 2: Rules and Regulations

Chapter 3: Portfolio Management Considerations

Chapter 4: Tax Planning Basics

Chapter 5: Mathematics of Traditional Compared With Roth IRAs

Chapter 6: Tax Planning Strategy

Chapter 7: Client Considerations

Chapter 8: Beneficiary Considerations

Chapter 9: Estate Planning for the Roth IRA

Chapter 10: The Roth Legacy Trust

Resources on CD-ROM

The enclosed CD-ROM contains several additional content pieces intended to heighten your understanding of Roth IRA conversions and serve as references for you and your clients. An audio file (MP3) contains a 42 minute speech by Robert Keebler meant to supplement the materials in this book. The speech is designed to guide the listener through the opportunities available to taxpayers with the elimination of the income limits on Roth conversions in 2010. In listening to the presentation, the advisor will not only learn the basics of a Roth IRA, but also the advantages of utilizing a Roth IRA and the factors that influence the decision of whether a Roth IRA conversion is advisable for a particular type of client. The PowerPoint titled "2010 Roth Conversions" provides written materials for the speech and the listener can follow along with the PowerPoint if desired.

The "Understanding Roth IRA Conversions" PowerPoint is a shorter slide presentation that advisors can use as a practical tool to create their own client presentations. These slides will help advisors show and explain to clients the concepts and mathematics of a Roth IRA conversion and some specific planning strategies. This presentation is intended to be customizable and can be modified to suit your particular client needs.

Finally, two Department of Treasury Final Rules and Regulations documents can be found in PDF format for your reference. We reference these documents many times throughout the course of this book and there is valuable source information located in these documents as well. It is recommended that the advisor familiarizes him- or herself with these important rules and regulations.

CD-ROM Contents

1999 Department of Treasury Final Rules and Regulations (PDF)
2002 Department of Treasury Final Rules and Regulations (PDF)
Understanding Roth IRA Conversions (PowerPoint Deck)
2010 Roth Conversions (PowerPoint Deck)
2010 Roth Conversions Speech (MP3)
Additional Resources (Word)

Introduction to the Roth IRA

Introduction

In the summer of 1997, Congress first introduced the concept of a tax-free, or Roth, individual retirement account (IRA). This legislation was first introduced in the Taxpayer Relief Act of 1997 (reproduced in part as appendix 1: "Taxpayer Relief Act of 1997"), explained in the Conference Committee Explanation (appendix 2: "Conference Committee Explanation"), and amended in 1998 (appendix 3: "1998 Roth IRA Amendments: Committee Report"). This tax advantaged IRA was named after the legendary Senator William Roth of Delaware. Since 1998, millions of Americans have contributed and converted to a Roth IRA. Later, Congress allowed for the Roth 401(k) to further encourage savings for a financially secure retirement. One of the more powerful financial and wealth transfer planning opportunities available today is the ability to convert a traditional IRA into a Roth IRA and, in doing so, convert future taxable income into future tax-free income. Although income tax must be paid on the converted amount, the payment of this initial tax liability can result in significant future tax savings. This chapter will focus on the basic taxation of Roth IRAs and discusses the eligibility requirements for contributing and converting to a Roth IRA along with the benefits associated with utilizing a Roth IRA.

Overview of the Roth IRA

The Roth IRA is a nondeductible IRA from which all future *qualified distributions* are free. Under certain circumstances, existing IRAs may be converted to Roth IRAs. The statutory guidance for the Roth IRA is covered under Internal Revenue Code (IRC) Section

408A. IRC Section 408A(a) provides that, except as provided under this IRC section, the traditional IRA provisions continue to apply. Further, no deduction is allowed for Roth IRA contributions,[1] and Roth IRA contributions must be made by the due date for filing the contributor's income tax return, without regard to extensions.[2]

In addition, the maximum contribution that can be made to a Roth IRA is phased out for single taxpayers with an adjusted gross income (AGI) between $105,000 and $120,000 and for joint filers with an AGI between $166,000 and $176,000.[3] The maximum contribution to a Roth IRA cannot exceed the maximum contribution permitted to a traditional IRA, which is generally $5,000, except for taxpayers in the phase-out range. Table 1-1, "Contribution Limits for Roth IRAs," outlines historic Roth IRA contribution limits.

Table 1-1: *Contribution Limits for Roth IRAs*

Taxable Years	Amount
2002–2004	$3,000
2005–2007	$4,000
2008–2009	$5,000
2010 and beyond	$5,000 (indexed to inflation)
Additional Catch-Up Contribution Allowed for Taxpayers Age 50 or Older	
Taxable Years	Amount
2004–2005	$ 500
2006 and thereafter	$1,000

Taxpayers with an AGI over the maximum contribution limitation are allowed to make traditional nondeductible IRA contributions.

Example

In 2001, John and Eva, both age 30, have an AGI of $190,000. They are still allowed to make a $5,000 ($10,000 in total) nondeductible contribution to their IRAs.

When the Roth IRA is not available to a client, you should not overlook the opportunity to create wealth within the nondeductible IRA. Table 1-2, "Nondeductible IRA Versus Taxable Account Before Estate Tax," compares a nondeductible IRA with an outside investment account based on the following example.

1 Internal Revenue Code (IRC) Section 408A(c)(1).
2 IRC Section 219(f)(3).
3 IRC Section 408A(c)(3).

Example

Gerry is 22 years old and makes $5,000 annual contributions (subject to income tax at 28 percent) for 40 years from 2009 to 2049. The invested funds grow at a 10 percent annual rate, and the gains in the taxable account are subjected to a 15 percent capital gains rate.

Table 1-2: *Nondeductible IRA Versus Taxable Account Before Estate Tax*

	Nondeductible IRA		Taxable Account		
Year	Annual Contribution*	Net to Family†	Annual Contribution	Net to Family (15%)	Net to Family (25%)
2009	$5,000	$ 5,360‡	$5,000	$ 5,425§	$ 5,375
2014	$5,000	$ 38,954	$5,000	$ 40,302	$ 38,937
2019	$5,000	$ 88,783	$5,000	$ 92,746	$ 87,119
2024	$5,000	$ 164,761	$5,000	$ 171,604	$ 156,290
2029	$5,000	$ 282,250	$5,000	$ 290,178	$ 255,595
2034	$5,000	$ 468,760	$5,000	$ 468,473	$ 398,160
2039	$5,000	$ 763,896	$5,000	$ 736,568	$ 602,830
2044	$5,000	$1,234,942	$5,000	$1,139,691	$ 896,660
2049	$ 0	$1,983,933	$ 0	$1,740,424	$1,313,117

*In all examples the contributions will be deemed to be made on the first day of the year.

†The *net to family* is an "s-if" calculation that liquidates the IRA every year subjecting it to income tax at 28 percent.

‡$5,000 annual contribution + $500 growth – 140 in tax at liquidation [($5,500 – $5,000) × 28 percent] = $5,360.

§$5,000 annual contribution + $500 growth – $75 in tax at liquidation [($5,500 – $5,000) × 15 percent] = $5,425.

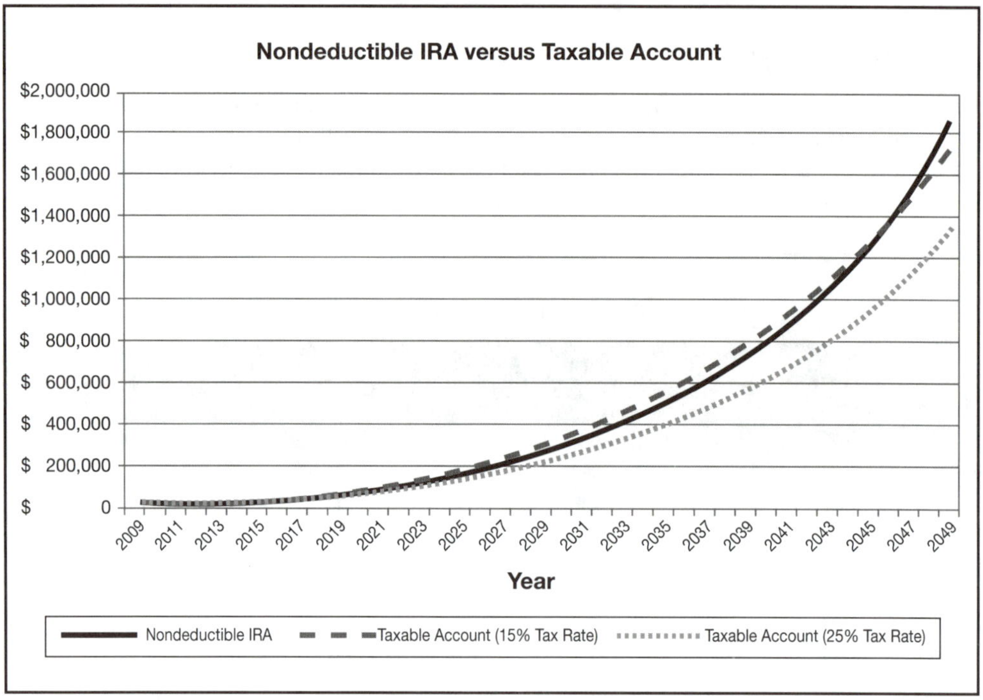

IRC Section 408A(d)(l)(A) provides that any qualified distribution from a Roth IRA is not includible in gross income. A *qualified distribution* is a distribution that meets one of the following tests:

1. It is made on or after the day on which the taxpayer reaches age 59½.
2. It is made to a beneficiary (or to the taxpayer's estate) on or after the taxpayer's death. If the distribution is made within the 5-taxable-year period beginning with the year the first contribution is made, the distribution is not a qualified distribution (see the following paragraphs).
3. It is attributable to the taxpayer's disabled condition. (See IRC Section 72(m) (7) for the definition of *disabled*.).
4. It is a qualified special-purpose distribution as defined in IRC Section 72(t)(2)(F), which discusses distributions for acquisition costs of named first time home buyers (limited to $10,000).

Even if one of the requirements in the preceding list are met, a distribution from a Roth IRA is not treated as a tax-free qualified distribution if such distribution is made within the five-taxable year period beginning with the first taxable year the individual made a contribution to a Roth IRA.

It is important to understand that both requirements (the five year holding period and satisfying one of the listed criteria) must be met for the distribution to be a qualified distribution. A distribution that meets the five year rule, but does not satisfy one of the four requirements listed above is not a qualified distribution. Similarly, a distribution that is one of the proper types, but has not been held for five years is also not a qualified distribution.

Each Roth IRA owner has one five year holding period that begins with either the year for which a contribution is first made to a Roth or the year in which the first dollar is converted from a traditional IRA to a Roth IRA. A subsequent conversion will not result in starting a new five year holding period. The five year clock starts ticking with the first conversion or contribution.[4]

Example

Marcia, age 53, is thinking about rolling her 401 (k) plan into a traditional IRA and then doing a conversion to a Roth IRA in 7 years when she retires and is in a lower income tax bracket. She makes a contribution to a Roth IRA this year to get the clock started. Then, after she retires, all distributions will immediately be tax free.

Nonqualified Distributions

Distributions that do not meet the five year holding period or are not made for one of the specified purposes are referred to as *nonqualified distributions*. Nonqualified distributions will be taxable income to the extent the distributions exceed basis.[5] *Basis* can be defined as the amount converted from a traditional IRA to a Roth IRA and contributions made to a Roth IRA. There is an ordering rule for purposes of determining what portion of a nonqualified distribution is includible in income. Under this rule, distributions are treated as made from contributions and conversions first. Thus, no portion of a distribution is treated as attributable to earnings, or includible in gross income, until the total of all distributions from the Roth IRA exceeds the amount of contributions.[6] A distribution is a nonqualified distribution if it is made within five years of the first contribution or, in the case of a conversion, if it occurs within five years of the conversion or does not otherwise meet the definition of a qualified distribution.[7]

4 Treasury Regulation Section 1.408A-6, Q&A 2 provides that the contribution is treated as occurring on January of the taxable year regardless of when the contribution actually occurs.
5 IRC Section 408A(d)(l)(B).
6 IRC Section 408A(d)(4)(B)(I).
7 IRC Section 408A(d)(3)(F).

Example

Samantha, age 28, contributes $2,000 to a Roth IRA in 2003 and another $2,000 in 2004. In 2010, Samantha withdraws $3,500 from her Roth IRA to make a down payment on a car. Although the distribution meets the 5 year holding period, it is made prior to her reaching age 59½ and is not made on account of death, disability, or as a first time home buyer expense. Thus the distribution is nonqualified. However, because the amount withdrawn ($3,500) plus the amount previously withdrawn ($0) is less than the total amount contributed ($4,000), and no conversion contributions were made, the distribution is not subject to income taxation or penalties.[8]

The *contributions withdrawn first* rule gives Roth owners greater flexibility than owners of regular nondeductible IRAs. In a regular nondeductible IRA, all withdrawals are deemed to be part earnings and part return of contributions. Roth IRA withdrawals are only subject to income tax after the amount that equals the amount contributed and converted has been withdrawn. In other words, only the earnings on Roth IRA contributions are subject to income tax at the time of a nonqualified distribution.

Table 1-3, "Contributory Roth IRA Distributions," is a brief synopsis of the type of distribution, holding period, and income tax and penalty tax consequences.

Table 1-3: *Contributory Roth IRA Distributions*

	Income Tax
Distribution After Five Years of First Conversion, plus –on or after age 59½, or –after death, or –attributable to being disabled, or –up to $10,000 for first time home purchase = Qualified Distribution*	No†
Distribution After Five Years of First Conversion, but **NOT**: –on or after age 59½, or –after death, or –attributable to being disabled, or –up to $10,000 for first time home purchase = Non-Qualified Distribution	Yes, unless distributions do not exceed basis.‡
Distribution Within Five Years of First Conversion =Non-Qualified Distribution	Yes, unless distributions do not exceed basis.‡

8 See IRC Section 72(t).

Table 1-3: *Contributory Roth IRA Distributions (continued)*

10% Early Distribution Penalty	
Distribution made after taxpayer is age 59½	No
Non-Qualified Distribution made within five years of conversion and before taxpayer is age 59½	Yes, (unless an exception to the 10% penalty applies. See IRC Sec. 72(t)) to the extent the qualified rollover contribution was includable in gross income at the time of conversion.§
Non-Qualified Distribution made after five years of conversion and before taxpayer is age 59½	Yes, (unless an exception to the 10% penalty applies. See IRC Sec. 72(t)) but only to the amount included in income.§
Qualified Distribution made before taxpayer is age 59½	No.§

*IRC Section 408A(d)(2)(A)(i).
†IRC Section 408A(d)(1).
‡Treas. Reg. Section 1.408A-6, Q&A 1(b).
§Treas. Reg. Section 1.408A-6, Q&A 5(a).

Conversion of a Traditional IRA to a Roth IRA

The conversion of a traditional IRA to a Roth IRA is treated as a distribution in which the taxpayer recognizes taxable income.[9]

Converting Nondeductible Traditional IRAs to a Roth IRA

A taxpayer who considers converting nondeductible traditional IRAs to a Roth IRA must also be concerned with a partial conversion. If all the taxpayer's IRAs are converted to a Roth IRA, there is no issue of how to calculate the taxable portion of the converted amount. If the taxpayer chooses to do only a partial conversion or chooses to convert only one of several IRAs, it is important to recognize that all IRAs are treated as one contract for tax purposes. Thus, a taxpayer may not convert only a nondeductible IRA or a portion of a nondeductible IRA and offset the basis against only that portion. Instead, the taxpayer must prorate the nondeductible amount over the total amount in all of the taxpayer's IRAs.

9 Had the taxpayer converted a traditional individual retirement account (IRA) to a Roth IRA in 1998, the opportunity was available to recognize income ratably over a 4 year period (IRC Section 408A(d)(3)(A)(iii)). Conversions occurring after 1998 are not afforded this favorable tax treatment. See, however, chapter 2, "Rules and Regulations," for the two year income spread option available for 2010 conversions.

Example

Joan has 2 traditional IRAs: a deductible IRA with a value of $10,000 and a nondeductible IRA with a value of $10,000 and a basis of $4,000 representing her nondeductible contributions. She converts only the nondeductible IRA to a Roth IRA. For tax purposes, she has one IRA with a value of $20,000 and a basis of $4,000. Because she is converting half of the aggregate value of the IRAs, the amount of basis allocated to the conversion is $2,000 (half of $4,000). Thus, she would recognize income of $8,000 ($10,000 conversion less $2,000 basis).

There is no prohibition against conversion after one's required beginning date.

Example

Sylvia, age 75, has $200,000 in her IRA. In 2010, she withdraws her 2010 required minimum distribution (RMD) and makes a conversion election.

Income on post-1998 conversions is recognized in the year of conversion.[10]

Example

Michael has $200,000 in his IRA. In 2009, he makes a conversion election and recognizes ordinary income of $200,000. The 4 year spread is not available for conversions after December 31, 1998. However, Michael could simply convert $50,000 a year for 4 years.

Existing IRAs can be converted to Roth IRAs unless (1) a taxpayer's AGI exceeds $100,000 or (2) the taxpayer is married and filing separately.[11]

In the first scenario, AGI is the taxpayer's AGI on Form 1040 (which includes application of the taxability of Social Security and the application of passive loss limitations) increased by the income from U.S. Savings Bonds used to pay higher education fees, employer-paid adoption expenses, and any foreign income excluded under IRC Section 911.[12]

10 IRC Section 408A(3)(A).
11 IRC Section 408A(c)(3)(B)(n).
12 IRC Section 408A(c)(3)(B)(I).

> **Example**
>
> Gary and Barb have AGI of $90,000 (before the conversion election). They elect to convert $500,000 of existing IRAs to a Roth IRA. Gary and Barb can elect to convert. The conversion income is not counted for purposes of the $100,000 Roth IRA conversion limitation.

In addition, a taxpayer's RMD was previously included in AGI for purposes of the $100,000 AGI limitation. Congress modified the term AGI so that it does not include RMDs, but it only applies for tax years beginning after December 31, 2004.

Note that the two limitations (such as, income and filing status) do not apply after 2009. See chapter 2, "Rules and Regulations," for more discussion of the Roth IRA in 2010.

A Roth IRA is not subject to RMDs during the taxpayer's lifetime.[13] This suspension of the RMD rules is available for Roth IRAs created with annual contributions and from Roth IRAs created by rollovers of traditional IRAs.

> **Example**
>
> Harry, age 69, converts his traditional IRA to a Roth IRA. After a Roth conversion, no minimum distributions are required during Harry's lifetime.

Taxpayers are allowed to make contributions to a Roth IRA after age 70½ if the taxpayer has earned income.[14]

> **Example**
>
> John, age 71, is still working and earning $40,000 annually. John can continue to make contributions to a Roth IRA.

Because of the $100,000 AGI limitation, proper planning can open the door to a Roth conversion election. Taxpayers can shift income into the next year, thereby reducing their AGI below $100,000. Therefore, planners should make their clients aware of this planning opportunity so they can take steps to keep their AGI below the $100,000 limit by deferring income into the following year.

13 IRC Section 408A(c)(5).
14 IRC Section 408A(c)(4).

Ideas for Managing Income

The following are available techniques and considerations that can be used to keep a taxpayer's AGI below $100,000 for tax years before 2010.

Deferring Income

The following are ways to defer income:

- Avoid regular IRA distributions.
- Convert taxable bonds to municipal bonds.
- Enter into deferred compensation agreements.
- Purchase certificates of deposits and 1 year Treasury bills (to defer income to January 2 of the following year).
- Avoid recognizing capital gains during the current year.
- Defer beginning Social Security payments.
- Purchase a tax-deferred annuity.
- Harvest or generate losses during the current year.
- Maximize contributions to pension plans.
- Establish a defined benefit plan.

Maximizing Adjustments to Income (Reduce AGI)

The following maximize adjustments to income and reduce AGI:

- Traditional IRA deductions
- Moving expenses
- One half of self-employment tax
- Self-employed health insurance deduction
- Keogh and self-employed simplified employee pension plans
- Penalty on early withdrawal of savings
- Alimony payments
- Oil and gas investments (see the following section)

Advanced Planning Opportunity—Reducing AGI

In 1986, IRC Section 469 was introduced to prevent taxpayers from reducing income by generating passive losses. However, IRC Section 469 contains a critical exception that states "the term *passive activity* shall not include any working interest in any oil or gas property which the taxpayer holds directly or through an entity which does not limit the liability of the taxpayer with respect to such interest."

Therefore, this provision allows a general partner of an oil and gas venture to invest in oil and gas and receive passive losses, which may reduce AGI for purposes of the $100,000 AGI threshold. In order for this strategy to work, the taxpayer will need to ensure that the partnership is valid and that the partnership actually incurred the drilling costs in the year the deduction is being claimed. For sophisticated investors, oil and gas investments may also be used to reduce the taxation of large post-2009 Roth IRA conversions.

Potential Problems—Resolved

Consider the following examples. Following the conversion of a traditional IRA to a Roth IRA in 2009, AGI inadvertently exceeded $100,000.

Example

Richard and Mary project their 2009 AGI to be $70,000. In January 2009, they convert their $500,000 traditional IRA to a Roth IRA. In December, Richard and Mary win the lottery, which pushes their AGI for 2009 over the $100,000 AGI limit. Richard and Mary are allowed to transfer, in a trustee-to-trustee transfer, the converted amount back to the traditional IRA by the extended due date of the taxpayer's income tax return.[15] This is termed a *recharacterization.*

The regulations allow a taxpayer to recharacterize a contribution or conversion by the extended due date of the taxpayer's income tax return. These regulations provide the following guidance with regard to the recharacterization.[16]

Example

In 2009, Individual C converts the entire amount in his traditional IRA to a Roth IRA. Individual C thereafter determines that his modified AGI for 2009 exceeded $100,000 so that he was ineligible to have made a conversion in that year. Accordingly, prior to the due date (plus extensions) for filing his federal income tax return for 2009, Individual C decides to recharacterize the conversion contribution. He instructs the trustee of the Roth IRA (first IRA) to transfer in a trustee-to-trustee transfer the amount of the contribution, plus net income, to the trustee of a new traditional IRA (second IRA). Individual C notifies the trustee of the first IRA and the trustee of the second IRA that he is recharacterizing his IRA contribution. On his federal income tax return for 2009, Individual C treats the original amount of the conversion as having been contributed to the second IRA. As a result, for federal tax purposes, the contribution is treated as having been made to the second traditional IRA and not to the Roth IRA. The result would be the same if the conversion amount had been transferred in a tax-free transfer to another Roth IRA prior to the recharacterization.

15 IRC Section 408A(d)(6).
16 Treasury Regulation Section 1.408A-5 Q&A 10.

Example

In 2009, an individual makes a $5,000 regular contribution for 2009 to his traditional IRA (first IRA). Prior to the due date (plus extensions) for filing his federal income tax return for 2009, he decides that he would prefer to contribute to a Roth IRA instead. The individual instructs the trustee of the first IRA to transfer in a trustee-to-trustee transfer the amount of the contribution, plus attributable net income, from the trustee of the first IRA to the trustee of a Roth IRA (second IRA). The individual notifies the trustee of the first IRA and the trustee of the second IRA that he is recharacterizing his $5,000 contribution for 2009. On the individual's federal income tax return for 2009, he treats the $5,000 as having been contributed to the Roth IRA for 2009 and not to the traditional IRA. As a result, for federal tax purposes, the contribution is treated as having been made to the Roth IRA for 2009. The result would be the same if the conversion amount had been transferred in a tax-free transfer to another traditional IRA prior to the recharacterization.

Example

The facts are the same as in the preceding example, except that the $5,000 regular contribution is initially made to a Roth IRA and the recharacterizing transfer is made to a traditional IRA. On the individual's federal income tax return for 2009, he treats the $5,000 as having been contributed to the traditional IRA for 2009 and not to the Roth IRA. As a result, for federal tax purposes, the contribution is treated as having been made to the traditional IRA for 2009 and not to the Roth IRA. The result would be the same if the contribution had been transferred in a tax-free transfer to another Roth IRA prior to the recharacterization, except that the only Roth IRA trustee the individual must notify is the one actually making the recharacterization transfer.

Example

In 2009, an individual receives a distribution from traditional IRA 1 and contributes the entire amount to traditional IRA 2 in an IRA rollover contribution described in IRC Section 408(d)(3). In this case, the individual cannot elect to recharacterize the contribution by transferring the contribution amount, plus net income, to a Roth IRA because an amount contributed to an IRA in a tax-free transfer cannot be recharacterized. However, the individual may convert (other than by recharacterization) the amount in traditional IRA 2 to a Roth IRA at any time, provided the rollover rules are satisfied.

Converting to a Roth IRA raises the issue of timing. Under the original proposed regulations, a taxpayer could convert to a Roth IRA, recharacterize that contribution back to a traditional IRA, and then reconvert to the Roth IRA and pay tax on the second Roth IRA conversion. This was desirable because the taxpayer could save substantial taxes by reconverting to the Roth IRA if the assets declined in value. However, the final Roth IRA regulations prohibit this type of transaction. Treasury Regulation Section 1.408A-5, Q&A 9 states the following:

> An IRA owner who converts an amount from a traditional IRA to a Roth IRA during any taxable year and then transfers that amount back to a traditional IRA by means of a recharacterization may not reconvert that amount from the traditional IRA to a Roth IRA before the beginning of the taxable year following the taxable year in which the amount was converted to the Roth IRA or, if later, the end of the thirty-day period beginning on the day on which the IRA owner transfers the amount from the Roth IRA back to the traditional IRA by means of a recharacaterization.

A full copy of the 1999 final rules and regulations from the Department of the Treasury, including Treasury Regulation Section 1.408A-5, can be found on the accompanying CD-ROM.

The essence of this provision is that if a taxpayer converts to a Roth IRA early in the year, the taxpayer will not be able to recharacterize this amount back to a traditional IRA and then convert back to a Roth IRA in the same year. This provision eliminates the opportunity to convert and reconvert in the same taxable year in order to achieve a lower tax liability. However, this recharacterization still allows a taxpayer to recharacterize a Roth conversion by the extended due date of the income tax return for any reason.

Basic Roth IRA Examples

Tom and Sue, both age 30, make nondeductible Roth IRA contributions from 2009 to 2049. Table 1-4, "The Roth IRA Versus the Traditional IRA—Net to Family Before Estate Tax," compares the Roth IRA with the traditional IRA.

When the tax bracket remains the same and distributions are *not* taken into account, there is no difference between the value of traditional IRA and the Roth IRA. However, RMDs, estate taxes, *bracket run*, and paying the conversion taxes with outside assets are all factors that make the Roth IRA more desirable.

Table 1-4: *The Roth IRA Versus the Traditional IRA—Net to Family Before Estate Tax*

		Net to Family*	
Year	Age	Roth IRA†	Traditional IRA‡
2009	30	$ 5,500§	$ 5,500µ
2014	35	$ 42,436	$ 41,839
2019	40	$ 101,921	$ 99,352
2024	45	$ 197,724	$ 190,410
2029	50	$ 352,014	$ 334,700
2034	55	$ 600,500	$ 563,532
2039	60	$1,000,689	$ 926,735
2044	65	$1,645,197	$1,503,656
2049	70	$2,677,685	$2,415,252

*This example assumes no estate tax, 28 percent federal income tax rate, no state income tax, 10 percent growth on investments inside and outside the IRAs, and a 15 percent tax on outside assets.
†This column assumes contributions of $5,000 from 2009 to 2049.
‡This column assumes contributions of $6,400 until 2049. The $6,400 contribution represents a $5,000 annual contribution to a deductible IRA plus $1,400 (5,000 × 28 percent tax rate) representing the tax savings.
§$5,000 annual contribution + $500 growth at 10 percent. No income tax on liquidation because the IRA is a Roth IRA.
µ$5,000 annual contribution + $500 growth at 10 percent – $1,540 of taxes at a 28 percent tax rate at liquidation. Because the $5,000 is a pretax contribution there is an outside balance consisting of $1,400 ($5,000 × 28 percent). The tax savings, $1,400 annual tax savings + $140 of growth at 10 percent – $21 of taxes at a 15 percent tax rate. Therefore, the IRA balance ($5,000 + $500 – $1,540) plus the outside balance ($1,400 + $140 – $21) equals net to family of $5,479. On the other hand, if the taxpayer is younger than age 59½, the 10 percent IRC Section 72(t) penalty applies.

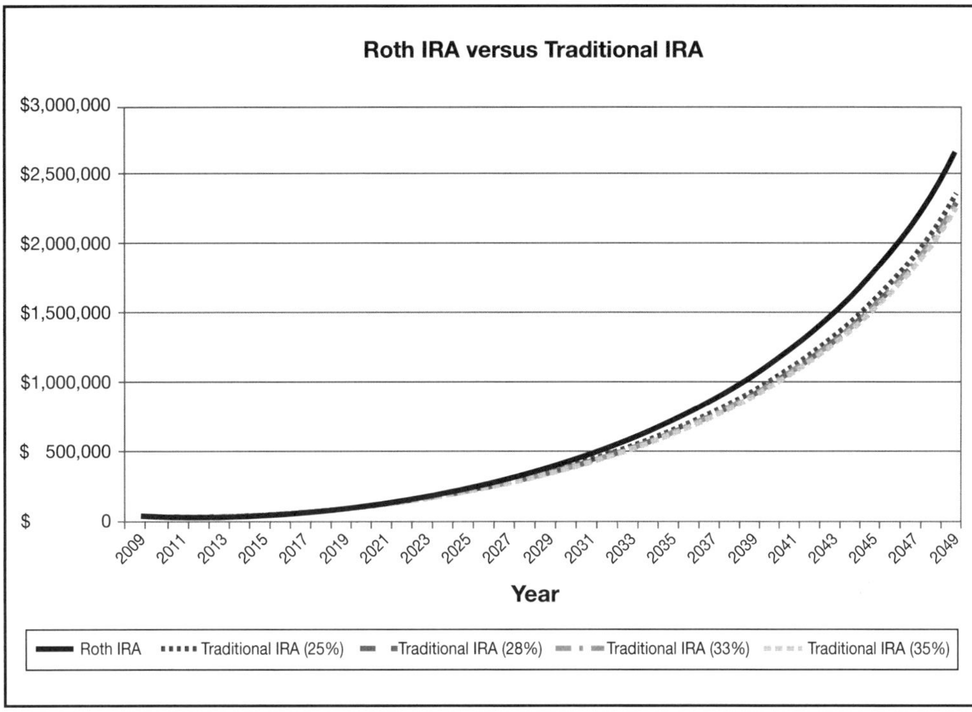

Example

Ron, age 60, makes nondeductible Roth IRA contributions from 2009 to 2018. Table 1-5, "Roth IRA," shows the value of the Roth IRA.

Table 1-5: *Roth IRA*

Year	Beginning Balance	Annual Contribution	Growth at 10 Percent	Required Distribution	Ending Balance
2009	$ 0	$5,000	$ 500	$0	$ 5,500
2010	$ 5,500	$5,000	$ 1,050	$0	$ 11,550
2011	$ 11,550	$5,000	$ 1,655	$0	$ 18,205
2012	$ 18,205	$5,000	$ 2,321	$0	$ 25,526
2013	$ 25,526	$5,000	$ 3,053	$0	$ 33,578
2014	$ 33,578	$5,000	$ 3,858	$0	$ 42,436
2015	$ 42,436	$5,000	$ 4,744	$0	$ 52,179
2016	$ 52,179	$5,000	$ 5,318	$0	$ 62,897

(continued)

Example *(continued)*

Table 1-5: *Roth IRA (continued)*

Year	Beginning Balance	Annual Contribution	Growth at 10 Percent	Required Distribution	Ending Balance
2017	$ 62,897	$5,000	$ 6,790	$0	$ 74,687
2018	$ 74,687	$5,000	$ 7,969	$0	$ 87,656
2019	$ 87,656	$ 0	$ 8,766	$0	$ 96,421
2020	$ 96,421	$ 0	$ 9,642	$0	$106,064
2021	$106,064	$ 0	$10,606	$0	$116,670
2022	$116,670	$ 0	$11,667	$0	$128,337
2023	$128,337	$ 0	$12,834	$0	$141,171
2024	$141,171	$ 0	$14,117	$0	$155,288
2025	$155,288	$ 0	$15,529	$0	$170,816
2026	$170,816	$ 0	$17,082	$0	$187,898
2027	$187,898	$ 0	$18,790	$0	$206,688
2028	$206,688	$ 0	$20,669	$0	$227,357
2029	$227,357	$ 0	$22,736	$0	$250,092
2030	$250,092	$ 0	$25,009	$0	$275,102
2031	$275,102	$ 0	$27,510	$0	$302,612
2032	$302,612	$ 0	$30,261	$0	$332,873

Economics of Paying Income Tax on Conversions

Tax Payment From Other Assets: The Preferred Solution

The most powerful way to increase wealth transfer when making a Roth IRA election is to pay the income taxes with outside assets. This allows the entire amount of the Roth IRA to remain in a tax-free investment that will not be subject to income tax in the future.

Tax Payment From Inside the Roth IRA

If a client does not have sufficient outside assets, Roth IRA funds may be the only source from which to pay taxes. It may be desirable, in limited circumstances, to pay taxes from within the Roth IRA. This should only be done if it is absolutely necessary. If a taxpayer who is older than age 59½ takes a distribution from the Roth IRA within the first 5 years, there is no 10 percent penalty.

Tax Payment From a Traditional IRA

This option is not the first choice because the distribution is taxable for the year in which it is received. Furthermore, if the client is under the age of 59½, the 10 percent penalty tax may be imposed on early withdrawals.

Partial Conversions

In many cases, it is not feasible or desirable to convert a client's entire IRA. If this is the case, the most viable solution is to do a partial conversion. The amount of the rollover depends on a number of variables, such as the availability of cash to pay the taxes, the client's age, the client's current tax bracket versus expected future tax bracket, and the client's overall estate plan.

Required Minimum Distributions

Congress recognizes that current RMDs may cause a taxpayer's AGI to be over $100,000 in the year of conversion. Its solution, however, addresses this problem. For years after 2004, RMDs are *not* included in AGI for purposes of the $100,000 limit.[17] This provision provides substantial opportunities for those taxpayers whose AGI exceeds $100,000 only because of IRA income. Beginning after the year 2004, such individuals are able to convert their traditional IRA to a Roth IRA.

The ideal candidate for a Roth IRA conversion is an individual who has outside funds to pay the taxes and will not need to take distributions after age 70½. One of the critical factors to analyze when addressing Roth IRA conversions is a change in tax brackets. For example, if a taxpayer has to overcome a change from a 28 percent to 35 percent bracket to make a Roth conversion effective, it may be difficult to justify a conversion unless other estate planning circumstances come into play.

If a client will not need the funds from a traditional IRA after age 70½, there may be some merit in converting to the Roth IRA even if the funds have to be taken from the Roth IRA or traditional IRA to pay the taxes. For example, if a client needs to fund his unified credit bypass trust with IRA assets and will not need to take funds from his traditional or ordinary IRA after age 70½, a Roth IRA conversion should be carefully analyzed.

Required Distributions Upon the Death of the Roth IRA Owner

At age 70½, the owner of a Roth IRA is not required to take a required distribution.[18] In fact, if the Roth IRA owner chooses to never take a distribution from the Roth IRA during his or her lifetime, the entire value of the Roth IRA can continue to grow tax free until the owner's death. However, Roth IRAs are subject to RMD rules upon the death of the owner unless the owner's spouse is the sole beneficiary. If the surviving spouse is the sole beneficiary upon the Roth IRA owner's death, the spouse can be treated as the owner

17 IRC Section 408A(c)(3)(C)(i)(II).
18 IRC Section 408A(c)(5).

of the inherited Roth IRA by performing a spousal rollover.[19] The benefit of having the surviving spouse treated as the owner of the Roth IRA is that the spouse, like the decedent, would not be required to take minimum distributions during his or her lifetime. Thus, the Roth IRA could continue to grow tax free during the lifetime of the surviving spouse.

If the Roth IRA owner dies and the surviving spouse is not the sole beneficiary, the entire remaining value will have to be distributed in one of the following ways:

1. By December 31 of the year of the fifth anniversary of the owner's death
2. Over the life expectancy of the designated beneficiary starting no later than December 31 of the year following the year of the owner's death

It does not appear that the failure to begin taking RMDs by December 31 of the year following the year of death forces the beneficiary to take distributions under the 5 year rule. Instead, the beneficiary should be able to pay the 50 percent penalty for the failure to withdraw the proper required distribution (see below) and thereafter take life expectancy distributions. In PLR 200811028, the IRS allowed a beneficiary to utilize the life expectancy method even when the beneficiary failed to begin taking RMDs by December 31 of the year following the year of the IRA owner's death.

A Roth IRA beneficiary who fails to take RMDs is subject to a 50 percent penalty tax on the amount that should have been withdrawn but was not.

Example

Jim passes away at age 69 with a $1,000,000 Roth IRA. Jim has a 65 year old wife and a 40 year old son. Table 1-6, "Inherited Roith IRAs," displays results from various scenarios involving changes in beneficiary designation and distribution methods.

Table 1-6: *Inherited Roth IRAs*

			Net Wealth to Family*		
Year	Spouse's Age	Child's Age	First Year Rule	Inherited By Son	Spousal Rollover†
2009	65	40	$ 1,100,000	$ 1,093,578	$ 1,100,000
2014	70	45	$ 1,258,130	$ 1,703,804	$ 1,771,561
2019	75	50	$ 1,743,591	$ 2,636,705	$ 2,853,117
2024	80	55	$ 2,621,762	$ 4,050,680	$ 4,594,973
2029	85	60	$ 4,277,320	$ 6,172,448	$ 7,400,250

19 IRC Section 401(a)(9)(B); IRS Proposed Reg. § 408A-6, Q&A-14; Form 5305-R, Article V.

Example *(continued)*

Table 1-6: *Inherited Roth IRAs (continued)*

			Net Wealth to Family*		
Year	Spouse's Age	Child's Age	First Year Rule	Inherited By Son	Spousal Rollover†
2034		65	$ 6,431,621	$ 9,318,124	$11,248,257
2039		70	$ 9,670,949	$13,911,415	$16,843,201
2044		75	$14,541,788	$20,482,193	$24,760,923

*These scenarios assume a 10 percent pretax growth rate inside the Roth along with a 28 percent ordinary income tax rate. The outside account also grows at 10 percent with 100 percent turnover and is taxed at 15 percent (effective after-tax growth rate of 8.5 percent).

†This scenario assumes that the spouse dies at age 85. The son will then take Roth IRA balance out over his life expectancy.

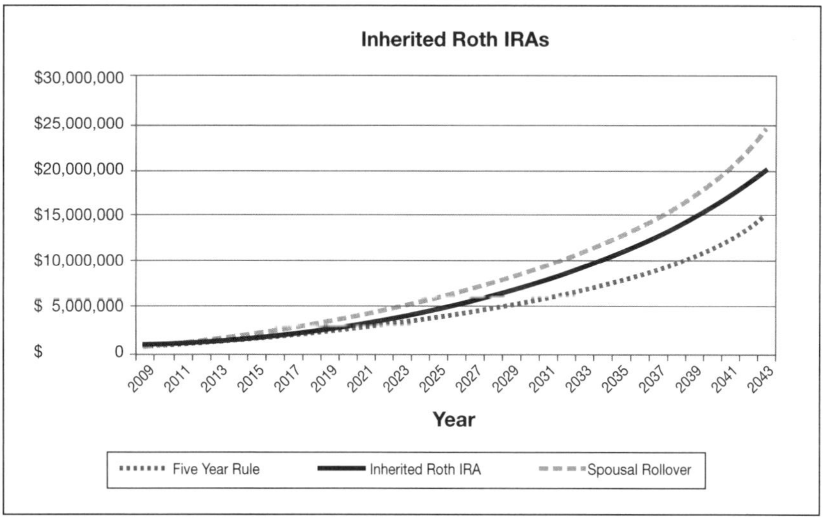

Example

Susie is the beneficiary of her deceased mother's Roth IRA. Susie is age 52 in the year 2010 (her first year of distribution), and the Roth IRA had a value of $100,000 on December 31, 2009. Susie is required to withdraw $3,096 ($100,000 divided by her remaining life expectancy of 32.3 years). Susie failed to make the withdrawal. Therefore, she is subject to a penalty tax of $1,548. If she had taken a withdrawal of an amount less than $3,096, the difference would be subject to the 50 percent federal penalty tax.

Note that the Worker, Retiree, and Employer Recovery Act of 2008 suspended the requirement to take RMDs in 2009.[20] This suspension also applies to beneficiaries of Roth IRAs.

Additional Thoughts

From an estate planning perspective, the Roth IRA has tremendous advantages, especially for taxpayers who need to fund their bypass trusts with either ordinary or Roth IRA assets. It will almost always be better to utilize a Roth IRA to fund one's bypass trust because distributions from the Roth IRA are not subject to income tax.

The revised proposed IRA distribution regulations diminished some of the benefits of a Roth IRA relative to a traditional IRA. However, in many instances, the Roth IRA will continue to be superior.

The following are some general thoughts:

1. In most cases, it is advantageous for your clients to make a partial Roth IRA conversion.
2. The best way to pay the income taxes arising from the conversion is with high-basis outside funds.
3. In many situations, only a partial conversion is acceptable from a financial or cash flow perspective.
4. Consider establishing several IRAs with different sectors or industry groupings and convert each to separate Roth IRAs. By October of the following year, it can be decided which Roth IRAs should be recharacterized, leaving intact the Roth IRAs that performed well (see chapter 6, "Tax Planning Strategy," for a further discussion of this strategy).

20 IRC Section 401(a)(9)(H).

Conclusion

Roth conversion planning is complex and advisors and CPAs must work together to determine which clients should convert and which clients should maintain their Traditional IRA. The factors that support some level of conversion generally outweigh the factors that favor no conversion. In an overgeneralization, the wealthier a person is, the greater the need to carefully study the Roth conversion question. In the next chapter, along with recent tax law changes, we will delve deeper into factors that should be considered when determining whether to perform a Roth conversion.

Rules and Regulations

Introduction

Since the introduction of Roth IRAs, there have been a number of changes to the rules governing these accounts. This chapter will outline these various amendments including the important changes to conversion eligibility beginning in 2010. A thorough discussion of the benefits of converting to a Roth IRA and the four types of conversions is also included to help guide an advisor and his or her client in making the decision of whether or not to convert to a Roth.

Expansion of the Traditional Deductible IRA

The Economic Growth and Tax Relief Reconciliation Act of 2001 (the act) expanded the amount a taxpayer can contribute to tax deductible individual retirement accounts (IRAs). For reference, the "Economic Growth and Tax Relief Reconciliation Act of 2001: Text" and "Economic Growth and Tax Relief Reconciliation Act of 2001: Committee Report" are reproduced as appendix 4 and appendix 5 at the end of this book. Table 2-1, "IRA Contribution Limits," outlines historic IRA contribution limits. Under the old law, an individual could only make tax-deductible contributions to an IRA up to the lesser of $2,000 or the individual's annual compensation.

Table 2-1: *IRA Contribution Limits*

Year	Deductible Amount
2002–2004	$3,000
2005–2007	$4,000
2008–2009	$5,000
2010 and beyond	$5,000 (indexed to inflation)

The act established a catch-up contribution for individuals who are age 50 years or older before the end of the taxable year. For these individuals, the deductible amount was increased by $500 in taxable years 2002–2005. For taxable years 2006 and beyond, the amount was increased by $1,000. Therefore, a taxpayer age 50 or over can make contributions of $6,000 in 2009 ($5,000 + $1,000 "catch-up" = $6,000). For taxable years after 2008, the contribution limits are adjusted for cost-of-living increases.

If a taxpayer, or his or her spouse, is an active participant in an employer-sponsored qualified retirement plan, the amount the participant can deduct for an IRA contribution is subject to certain adjusted gross income (AGI) limitations. The income phase-out limits increased gradually between 2001 and 2007. For taxable years beginning after 2006, the phase-out limits are subject to adjustments for inflation in increments of $1,000 (see table 2-2, "Deduction Phase-Out Limits").

Table 2-2: *Deduction Phase-Out Limits*

Year	Individuals	Joint Filers
2001	$33,000–$43,000	$53,000–$ 63,000
2002	$34,000–$44,000	$54,000–$ 64,000
2003	$40,000–$50,000	$60,000–$ 70,000
2004	$45,000–$55,000	$65,000–$ 75,000
2005	$50,000–$60,000	$70,000–$ 80,000
2006	$50,000–$60,000	$75,000–$ 85,000
2007	$52,000–$62,000	$83,000–$103,000
2008	$53,000–$63,000	$85,000–$105,000
2009 and beyond (indexed to inflation)	$55,000–$65,000	$89,000–$109,000

If a taxpayer is not considered an active participant in an employer-sponsored qualified retirement plan, but his or her spouse is and they are filing a joint return, the IRA deduction for the nonparticipant spouse is phased out when AGI is between $166,000 and $176,000. If they are filing separately, the phase-out range is up to $10,000.

The Pension Protection Act of 2006

In 2006, the Pension Protection Act of 2006 (the PPA) made some significant changes with regard to IRAs and other qualified defined contribution plans. For reference, selected portions of the PPA can be found reprinted in appendix 6: "Select Text of Pension Protection Act of 2006" at the end of this book. Following is a summary of the provisions of the act as it relates to IRA planning.

Nonspousal Rollovers of Inherited Qualified Retirement Plans

An interesting provision of the PPA is that it allows the postmortem transfer by nonspousal beneficiaries of qualified retirement plans to inherited IRAs. Generally, participants (employees) and surviving spouse beneficiaries may roll over amounts from qualified retirement plans, Internal Revenue Code (IRC) Section 403(b) annuities, and IRAs to another qualified retirement plan or IRA. Under prior law, nonspouse beneficiaries were not able roll over qualified plans into an IRA. The new law now allows nonspouse beneficiaries to roll over, via a trustee-to-trustee transfer, from a qualified retirement plan to an inherited IRA amounts inherited as a designated beneficiary. Thus, if the nonspouse beneficiary is required by the plan to take an immediate distribution, the nonspouse beneficiary can delay immediate taxation by transferring the amount to an "inherited" IRA. It is important to note that the required minimum distribution (RMD) rules for nonspouse beneficiaries remain unchanged. This new law also permits the postmortem transfer of qualified plans to inherited IRAs that are held for the benefit of qualified designated beneficiary trusts. Such a rollover can only be completed by a beneficiary who qualifies as a *designated beneficiary*. Accordingly, an estate or a trust that does not qualify as a designated beneficiary cannot transfer an inherited qualified plan to an inherited IRA.

Because many qualified plans require faster payout than otherwise allowed by the tax law, under the old rules a child (or other nonspousal beneficiary) could have been forced to take distributions of the entire retirement plan within 5 years after a parent's death or, in some cases, immediately following the parent's death. The loss of deferral typically caused a very substantial reduction in the family's overall wealth. However, under the PPA, a child who finds him- or herself in this position can transfer the retirement plan funds to an inherited IRA in the parent's name by means of a trustee-to-trustee transfer and take distributions over his or her life expectancy. Figure 2-1, "Inherited IRA Versus 5 Year Payout," illustrates the benefit of deferral created by a transfer to an inherited IRA over a 5 year payout of a $1 million qualified retirement plan balance.

Figure 2-1: *Inherited IRA Versus 5 Year Payout*

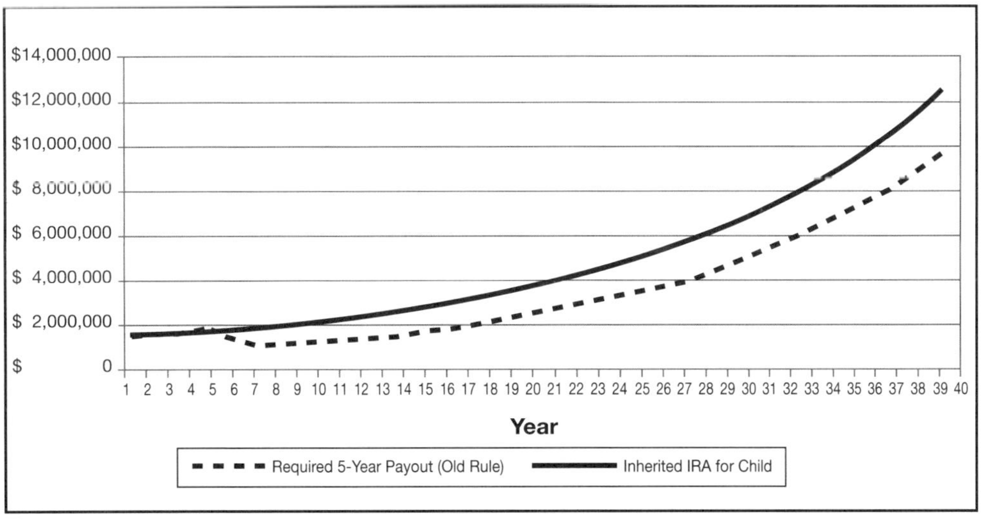

Note that care must be taken in performing the trustee-to-trustee rollover. The inherited IRA must be in the name of the owner of the original retirement account and payable to the designated beneficiary of the original account (for example, Mary Smith, Deceased IRA f/b/o Jim Smith), and the funds must pass directly from the original plan to the IRA. This provision applies to distributions made after December 31, 2006.

Notice 2007-7 was subsequently released to give guidance regarding certain provisions of the PPA. The notice, in part, indicated that a plan was not required to offer a direct rollover of a distribution to a nonspouse beneficiary. For those plans that were not amended, this meant that such beneficiaries could not take advantage of this new rollover option given by the PPA. However, beginning in 2010, all plans must be amended to allow for such nonspousal rollovers.[1]

The applicable distribution period and rollover options available to beneficiaries under this provision are summarized in the following chart.

Year of Death	Applicable Payout under the Plan	Amount Allowed to be Rolled Over	Applicable Payment Under the IRA
Before 2003	5 year rule	None	NA (no rollover permitted)
2003-2005	5 year rule	Amount not already distributed from plan as long as rollover completed before year containing fifth anniversary of death	5 year rule
All	Life expectancy	All, minus prior and current year RMDs	Life expectancy
2006 and later	5 year rule because of optional plan provision or election by beneficiary	All, minus prior and current year RMDs	Life expectancy of beneficiary **if** rollover occurs prior to the end of the year following the year of death , otherwise 5 year rule

Tax-Free Distributions from IRAs for Charitable Purposes

After years of proposals that failed, the PPA finally permitted taxpayers to make direct IRA distributions to charity without having to include the distribution in gross income. In particular, the new tax law permits up to $100,000 to be contributed each year directly to charity[2] for the 2006 and 2009 tax years. However, this direct IRA contribution is limited by the following conditions:

1. The transferor (IRA owner) must be at least age 70½ on the day of the transfer.
2. The distribution will only qualify to the extent that the distribution would have otherwise been includible in gross income.
3. The distribution must qualify under the general charitable deduction rules of IRC Section 170.

1 Housing and Economic Recovery Act of 2008.
2 As described in Internal Revenue Code (IRC) Section 170(b)(1)(A).

4. The distribution cannot be taken into account for determining the other charitable contributions to be allowed as a deduction under IRC Section 170 (in other words, the distribution cannot be added to AGI for purposes of the AGI limitations).

The transfer from the IRA to the charity must be a direct transfer in order for the distribution to qualify for the income exclusion. Thus, the trustee of the IRA must draft the check in the charity's name.

The nondeductible portion of an IRA will not need to be reduced by the amount of "basis" attributable to the distribution to charity. In other words, the distribution reduces the taxable portion of the taxpayer's IRA dollar-for-dollar.

Direct Rollovers of Qualified Retirement Plans to Roth IRAs

In the past, if taxpayers wanted to do a Roth IRA conversion, they would have to first roll the funds from the qualified retirement plan to a traditional IRA and then convert the traditional IRA to a Roth IRA. Under the PPA, taxpayers are now eligible to directly roll funds from *eligible retirement plans*[3] to Roth IRAs starting in the 2008 tax year.

Roth Conversions by Nonspouse Beneficiaries

Notice 2008-30[4] provides guidance regarding certain distribution related provisions of the PPA. Surprisingly, this notice appears to now allow beneficiaries of inherited retirement plans to convert to a Roth IRA.

Previously, only spousal beneficiaries had the option of converting to a Roth IRA because of the beneficiary's ability to perform spousal rollovers into an account in his or her own name. Nonspousal beneficiaries, however, did not have this option.[5]

Prior to amendment by the PPA, a Roth IRA could only accept a rollover contribution of amounts distributed from another Roth IRA, from a traditional or Savings Incentive Match Plan for Employees IRA, or from a designated Roth account. As noted, the law now allows taxpayers to rollover assets directly from a qualified plan to a Roth IRA without having to first go through a traditional IRA. There was no indication that this would change the prohibition of nonspousal beneficiaries converting to a Roth IRA. Q&A 7 of Section II in Notice 2008-30 expands the conversion power to nonspousal beneficiaries. The notice states that in the case of a distribution from an eligible retirement plan other than a Roth IRA, the modified adjusted gross income (MAGI) and filing status of the beneficiary are used to determine eligibility to make a qualified rollover contribution to a Roth IRA. A rollover by a nonspouse beneficiary must be made by a direct trustee to trustee transfer. A nonspouse beneficiary that is ineligible to make a qualified rollover contribution to a Roth IRA may recharacterize the contribution pursuant to IRC Sec. 408A(d)(6). A surviving spouse who makes a rollover to a Roth IRA may elect either to treat the Roth IRA as his or her own or to establish the Roth IRA in the name of the decedent with the surviving

3 As defined under IRC Section 402(c)(8)(B).

4 2008-23 Internal Revenue Bulletin 1056.

5 See IRS Publication 590 (2007), page 30, which states "If you inherited a traditional IRA from someone other than your spouse, you cannot convert it to a Roth IRA."

spouse as the beneficiary. A nonspouse beneficiary cannot elect to treat the Roth IRA as his or her own.

However, beneficiaries and their advisors should keep in mind that from a pure asset protection perspective, the exclusion of qualified plan assets from the bankruptcy estate under the Employee Retirement Income Security Act of 1974 (ERISA) generally makes it more attractive to retain funds in a qualified plan instead of converting the funds to a Roth IRA. This is true because the federal exclusion afforded ERISA plans (qualified plan assets) provides stronger protection than the exemption protection afforded IRA assets under the Bankruptcy Abuse Prevention and Consumer Protection Act of 2005. Further, in nonbankruptcy situations, asset protection for IRA assets is based on uncertain and diverse state asset protection statutes, thus strengthening the proposition that leaving assets in a qualified plan provides superior asset protection. In light of asset protection considerations, the professional must be very conscientious when analyzing the scenario of rolling over retirement plan funds from a qualified plan into a Roth IRA. The decision does not hinge purely on tax or financial planning considerations but on legal implications involving the creditor protection afforded the transferred assets. Therefore, the professional will want to encourage his or her clients to seek the counsel of qualified bankruptcy and creditor protection attorneys to ascertain whether a rollover from a qualified plan into a Roth IRA is appropriate.

Roth Conversions in the Year 2010—Choosing Whether to Convert

In the past, taxpayers who have had MAGI above $100,000 were precluded from converting a traditional IRA to a Roth IRA.[6] However, beginning with the 2010 tax year, this limitation will be lifted, thereby allowing many more taxpayers the opportunity to convert to a Roth IRA.[7] Furthermore, Roth conversions in 2010 will receive special tax treatment in that the taxable income, and therefore the resultant income tax, incurred on the Roth conversion may be spread over the 2011 and 2012 tax years.[8] However, a taxpayer may elect to report all the income on the 2010 tax return.

Benefits of Converting a Traditional IRA to a Roth IRA

There are numerous benefits associated with a Roth IRA conversion. The first and foremost is the tax-free treatment of the qualifying distributions from the Roth IRA, which, interestingly enough, includes both lifetime and postmortem distributions. Although contributions to a Roth IRA will never be tax deductible, as is the case with contributions to a traditional IRA, qualifying distributions from a Roth IRA will never be taxable. Furthermore, all growth within the Roth IRA is allowed to accumulate and compound tax free. Thus, not

6 IRC Section 408A(c)(3)(B)(i).

7 Tax Increase Prevention and Reconciliation Act of 2005.

8 For conversions executed in 2010, half of the income from the conversion is deferrable for 1 year (until 2011), and the second half of the income from the conversion is deferrable for 2 years (until 2012).

only will the tax-free growth enable the assets within the Roth IRA to accumulate more rapidly than assets in an outside taxable investment account, but the tax-free character of distributions can also result in tremendous future income tax savings to the taxpayer and his or her beneficiaries. The following two examples illustrate the benefits a Roth IRA conversion may produce for a taxpayer during his or her lifetime.

Example

Susan, age 55, converts her $1,000,000 traditional IRA to a Roth IRA. In 5 years, Susan will have reached 59½ and she will have met the 5 year holding period. Thus, any distributions from her Roth IRA will be qualified tax-free distributions. When Susan passes away, the distributions to her beneficiary, Sam, will also be tax free.

Example

Steve, age 50, converts his $1,000,000 traditional IRA to a Roth IRA. Assuming 20 years of growth at a pre-tax rate of 8 percent and a 40 percent tax rate now and in the future, the Roth IRA balance is $335,714 greater than the unconverted traditional IRA balance. In addition, the distributions from the Roth IRA are tax free.

Suspension of the Required Minimum Distribution Rules

At one's required beginning date (RBD), he or she is required to begin their RMDs. From a quantitative perspective, these RMDs reduce the future wealth accumulation within the traditional IRA. An advantage of converting a traditional IRA to a Roth IRA is that RMDs are not required to be taken from a Roth IRA during the owner's lifetime. See table 2-3, "Wealth Creation With a Traditional IRA," and table 2-4, "Wealth Creation After a Roth Conversion." These tables assume an income tax rate of 40 percent, a tax rate of 20 percent on the growth of the outside balance, and that RMDs are taken at the beginning of each year. The "Future Taxes" column represents the amount of tax on any distribution from the IRA plus the tax on the growth of the outside balance for each respective year.

Example

Mary Ann, a retired orthodontist, has a $2,000,000 IRA. She is 70 and has never touched the IRA having lived off royalties from her book "Bracing for Higher Tax Rates." The table below shows the hypothetical wealth creation if IRA RMDs were not required.

Table 2-3: *Wealth Creation With a Traditional IRA*

Mary Ann's Age	Traditional IRA	Future Taxes	Outside Balance	Total
69	$2,000,000		$ 800,000	
70	$2,119,708	($ 46,657)	$ 913,635	$ 3,033,343
75	$2,774,897	($ 78,840)	$ 1,723,233	$ 4,498,130
80	$3,473,065	($ 130,144)	$ 3,125,459	$ 6,598,525
85	$4,077,199	($ 211,198)	$ 5,495,730	$ 9,572,929
90	$4,349,271	($ 6,513,970)	$ 9,395,380	$13,744,651
Child's Age				
55	$4,622,570	($ 99,470)	$ 3,593,474	$ 8,216,044
60	$6,143,174	($ 168,973)	$ 6,261,209	$12,404,384
65	$7,797,533	($ 285,027)	$10,780,030	$18,577,563
70	$9,182,197	($ 477,985)	$18,384,424	$27,566,621
75	$9,351,248	($ 797,638)	$31,111,537	$40,462,785
Total		($16,576,823)		

Table 2-4: *Wealth Creation After a Roth Conversion*

Mary Ann's Age	Traditional IRA	Future Taxes	Outside Balance	Total
69	$ 0		$ 800,000	
70	$ 2,200,000	($ 800,000)	$ 0	$ 2,200,000
75	$ 3,543,122		$ 0	$ 3,543,122
80	$ 5,706,233		$ 0	$ 5,706,233
85	$ 9,189,946		$ 0	$ 9,189,946
90	$14,800,500	($ 6,660,225)	$ 0	$14,800,500
Child's Age				
55	$ 8,651,792	($ 5,500)	$ 297,000	$ 8,948,802
60	$11,497,819	($ 50,791)	$ 2,742,690	$14,240,509
65	$14,594,185	($ 143,411)	$ 7,744,206	$22,338,390
70	$17,185,779	($ 321,494)	$17,360,687	$34,546,466
75	$17,502,182	($ 650,786)	$35,142,468	$52,644,650
Total		($11,845,521)		

Because of the suspension of RMD rules for Roth IRAs, converting to a Roth IRA will generally result in a larger wealth transfer for the person who does not need to live off of the IRA funds. Figure 2-2, "Wealth Creation—Traditional Versus Roth IRA," tracks the differences in total wealth between a traditional and Roth IRA.

Figure 2-2: *Wealth Creation—Traditional Versus Roth IRA*

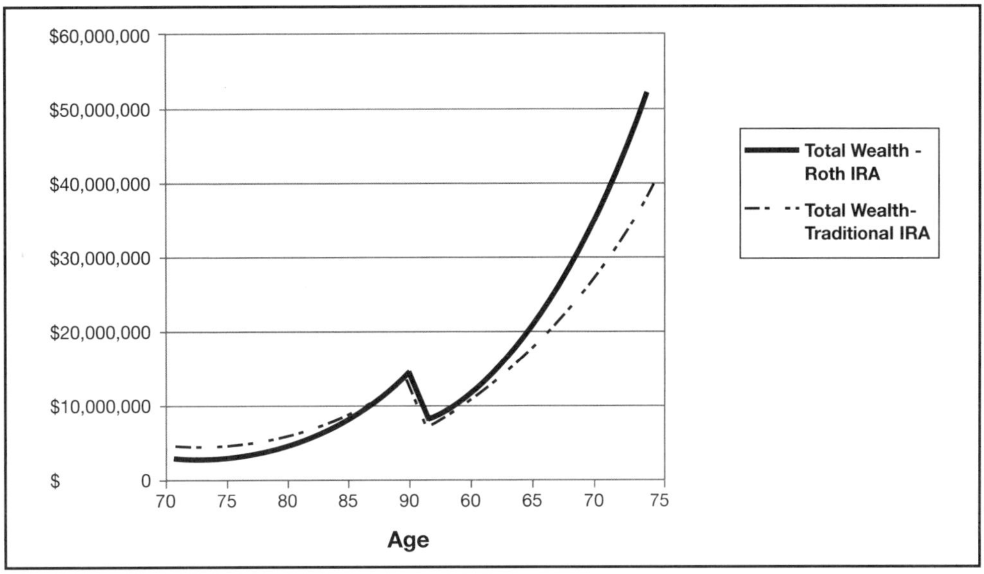

Tax Attributes

Many taxpayers can lower the effective tax rate on Roth conversions by utilizing net operating loss (NOL) and other carryforwards. By lowering the income tax rate, especially when the carryforward is about to expire (for example, a charitable carryforward), a taxpayer increases the odds of success with a Roth conversion.

> **Example**
>
> Tom's car dealership is expected to lose $500,000 in 2010 and he converts $500,000 to a Roth IRA. When timed properly, the Roth conversion is tax free.[9]

> **Example**
>
> Virginia has a $300,000 (30 percent) charitable carryforward that is about to expire. If she converts her $1,000,000 IRA to a Roth IRA, she will only pay income tax on approximately $700,000 ($1,000,000 – $300,000 = $700,000).[10]

9 In all likelihood, the net operating loss could be carried back or carried forward for future years.

10 This example is simple and does not reflect the 3 percent scaleback of itemized deductions.

> **Example**
>
> Patty, a single person, is expected to die within 6 months and has an NOL carryforward of $1,000,000. She also has a $1,000,000 traditional IRA. Patty, on the advice of her estate planning lawyer, visits you to evaluate a Roth conversion. You advise her that the Roth conversion will be tax free.

In addition to the benefit of tax-free growth and distributions, there are least ten reasons why a taxpayer can benefit from a conversion to a Roth IRA:

1. To take advantage of favorable tax attributes (such as charitable deductions carryforwards, NOL carryforwards, and investment tax credits)
2. Suspension of the lifetime RMD rules
3. The payment of income tax prior to the imposition of estate tax allows for greater wealth to be transferred to future generations (due to the fact that no income tax deduction is allowed for state death taxes levied on IRAs)
4. Greater growth potential, to the extent that outside sources (taxable brokerage account) are used to pay for the taxes due on the Roth IRA conversion
5. To better utilize an IRA owner's unified credit and goods and services tax exemption
6. To reduce the taxable estate of the IRA owner
7. To hedge against the projected increase in tax rates when a first spouse dies
8. To take advantage of a high basis IRA
9. Post-mortem required minimum distributions are tax free if they are qualified distributions
10. The recharacterization privilege creates a powerful advantage for the taxpayer

The Four Types of Roth IRA Conversions

We believe there are four distinct types of Roth IRA conversions:

1. *Strategic conversions* are conversions performed to take advantage of the long term wealth transfer objectives of the taxpayer.
2. *Tactical conversions* are conversions performed to take advantage of investor-specific, short term, federal income tax attributes that may be nearing expiration.
3. *Opportunistic conversions* are conversions performed to take advantage of short term stock market volatility, rotation in asset classes, and sector rotation.
4. *Hedging conversions* are conversions performed to take advantage of projected future events that may result in the taxpayer incurring higher income tax rates in the near future.

Strategic Conversions

The objectives behind this type of IRA conversion are generally motivated by wealth transfer. Considering that Roth IRA owners are not required to take RMDs from their IRA account when they reach age 70½, transferring traditional IRA assets into a Roth IRA will allow the assets to experience continued, compounded tax-free growth that may allow wealth to accumulate for future generations. An ideal candidate for strategic conversion is one who (1) possesses "outside funds" (for example, nonqualified investment accounts) from which to pay the tax on the conversion, (2) anticipates being in the same or higher marginal income tax bracket in the future, (3) does not need to make withdrawals from the Roth IRA to meet his or her annual living needs, and (4) desires to leave a tax-free asset to his or her children or grandchildren.

Tactical Conversions

This type of Roth IRA conversion is executed to take advantage of unused, short-term, special tax attributes that the taxpayer may otherwise not be able to utilize. A nonexhaustive list of these types of tax attributes includes NOL carryforwards, current year ordinary losses, unused charitable contribution carryforwards, nonrefundable tax credits, as well as alternative minimum tax credit carryovers. Due to the fact that the taxpayer typically needs to incur taxable income in order to utilize these special tax attributes, a Roth IRA conversion is executed to produce taxable income, which will in essence free up the unrealized favorable tax attributes. In addition to the utilization of the tax attribute, the taxpayer may benefit by executing a Roth IRA conversion while paying little to no income tax on the conversion.

Opportunistic Conversions

The motivation behind the execution of this type of Roth IRA conversion is to take advantage of economic conditions that are short term and expected to reverse over time. For example, a taxpayer whose traditional IRA contains stock that is expected to incur immense growth in the near future may benefit from executing a Roth IRA conversion. As opposed to holding the stock in a traditional IRA, holding the stock in a Roth IRA would allow the stock's sizeable growth to occur completely tax free. The concept of converting by asset class to multiple Roth IRAs with the tactic of recharacterizing the underperforming asset classes is another example of an opportunistic conversion.

Hedging Conversions

This type of Roth IRA conversion is generally executed to "hedge against" a future tax increase. Hedging conversions can be further subdivided into two types or categories of conversions, namely an income tax hedging conversion and an estate tax hedging conversion. Both categories of Roth IRA conversions are generally executed to hedge against some future event that may result in the individual incurring higher income taxes or estate taxes. The highest marginal rate is expected to return to 39.6 percent plus a healthcare surtax, if any, recommend by the House.[11]

11 H.R. 3200, America's Affordable Health Choices Act of 2009.

Factors in Deciding Whether to Convert

To arrive at an optimum scenario, it is generally a good idea to develop several spreadsheet that analyze the many variables of a Roth IRA conversion. In addition, we have found that the following key factors need to be identified and addressed in order to best analyze whether a Roth IRA conversion is appropriate:

1. Asset mix (that is, qualified versus nonqualified, liquid versus illiquid)
2. Traditional IRA balance
3. Time horizon
4. Current and future cash flow needs
5. Current marginal tax rate versus projected future marginal tax rate
6. Wherewithal to pay the income tax with nonqualified funds
7. Estate planning objectives

Mathematics For and Against Roth Conversions

Now that we have reviewed the benefits of converting and the four types of conversions, we should review the math that supports the case for and against Roth conversions.

Principle Number One

A Roth conversion within a taxpayer's same tax bracket, using funds from within the IRA itself, is tax neutral.

Example

David, age 40 and married, is considering converting $100,000 to a Roth IRA. At the present time, David and his wife are in the 25 percent tax bracket and expect to be in that tax bracket for all future tax years. Given these assumptions, the amount of IRA assets available for David in 30 years is as follows.

	Traditional IRA	Roth IRA	Difference ($)	Difference (%)
Pre-Tax Account Balance (Current)	$ 100,000	$ 100,000		
Less: Income Tax on Roth IRA Conversion @ 25%	—	(25,000)		
After-Tax Account Balance (Current)	$ 100,000	$ 75,000	$(25,000)	–25.00%
Growth Factor	400%	400%		
Pre-Tax Account Balance (Year 30)	$ 400,000	$ 300,000		
Less: Income Tax on IRA Withdrawal @ 25%	(100,000)			
After-Tax Account Balance (Year 30)	$ 300,000	$ 300,000	—	—

Principle Number Two

The law of diminishing returns.

Setting aside the conversion by asset classes, in mathematical theory, each additional dollar of a Roth conversion can only provide an equal or lesser benefit than the dollar immediately before it. In other words, the 15 percent bracket conversion is more efficacious than a 25 percent bracket conversion; the 25 percent bracket conversion is more efficacious than a 28 percent bracket conversion, and so on. Further, a conversion using outside funds is more effective than a conversion using IRA funds themselves. Lastly, a conversion using funds that will never be withdrawn is more efficacious than a conversion using IRA funds that will have to be used for future cash flow needs.

Tax Bracket	Amounts converted at a lower tax bracket produces greater result.
Source of Funds to Pay Tax	Outside, high basis funding produces a greater result.
Future Spending	Amounts converted that will be held until death produce a greater result.

Principle Number Three

A Roth conversion within a taxpayer's same tax bracket, using funds from outside the IRA, is generally tax favorable.

A critical factor in analyzing strategic conversions is the ability to use outside funds to pay the income tax liability on a Roth IRA conversion. If a client has outside funds for which to pay the income tax liability on a Roth IRA conversion, he or she will be in a better economic position than if he or she had kept all the funds within the traditional IRA.

Example

Olivia, age 72 and single, has a $2,000,000 traditional IRA and $700,000 in a taxable brokerage account (*outside funds*). Olivia is normally in the 35 percent tax bracket each year and in 2010 is eligible to convert to a Roth IRA. Ignoring the impact of required RMDs from the traditional IRA and assuming an income tax rate on the conversion of 35 percent, a pretax growth rate in the IRA of 9 percent and an after-tax growth rate of 7.5 percent in the taxable brokerage account, the amount of wealth Olivia will have in 10 years under both scenarios is as follows.

(continued)

Example *(continued)*

	Do Nothing			Roth IRA Conversion				
	Traditional IRA	Brokerage Account	Total	Roth IRA	Brokerage Account	Total	Difference ($)	Difference (%)
Pre-Tax Account Balance (Current)	$ 2,000,000	$ 700,000	$ 2,700,000	$2,000,000	$ 700,000	$2,700,000		
Less: Income Tax on Roth IRA Conversion at 35%	—	—	—	—	(700,000)	(700,000)		
Less: "Built-In" Income Tax at 35%	(700,000)	—	(700,000)	—	—	—		0.00%
After-Tax Account Balance (Current)	$ 1,300,000	$ 700,000	$ 2,000,000	$2,000,000	$ —	$2,000,000	$ —	
Pre-Tax Account Balance (Year 10)	$ 4,734,727	$1,442,722	$ 6,177,449	$4,734,727	$ —	$4,734,727		
Less: "Built-In" Income Tax at 35%	(1,657,155)	—	(1,657,155)	—	—	—		
Afer-Tax Account Balance (Year 10)	$ 3,077,573	$1,442,722	$ 4,520,295	$4,734,727	$ —	$4,734,727	$214,432	4.74%

Figure 2-3, "Roth IRA Conversion Using Outside Funds," illustrates the advantage of doing a Roth IRA conversion with outside funds versus doing nothing.

Figure 2-3: *Roth IRA Conversion Using Outside Funds*

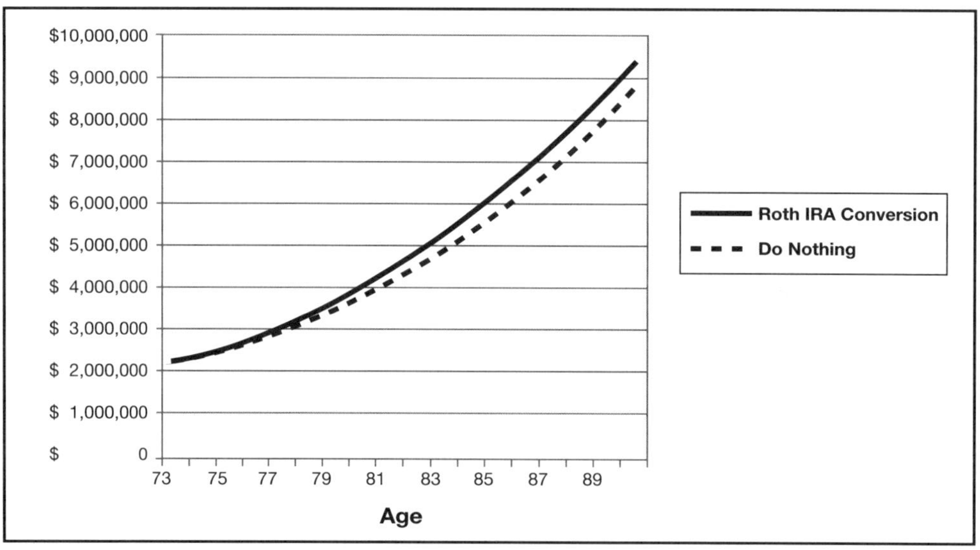

Principle Number Four

The longer the time frame, the better the economic result.

Another factor in analyzing strategic conversions is the client's time horizon. Obviously, the more time funds can grow in a tax-free environment, the better the economic result. Even in cases when the client expects to be in a lower tax bracket in the future, if the client has outside funds to pay the income tax on a Roth IRA conversion and has a long time horizon, it is possible that a Roth IRA conversion would be effective. See figure 2-4, "Impact of Time."

Figure 2-4: *Impact of Time*

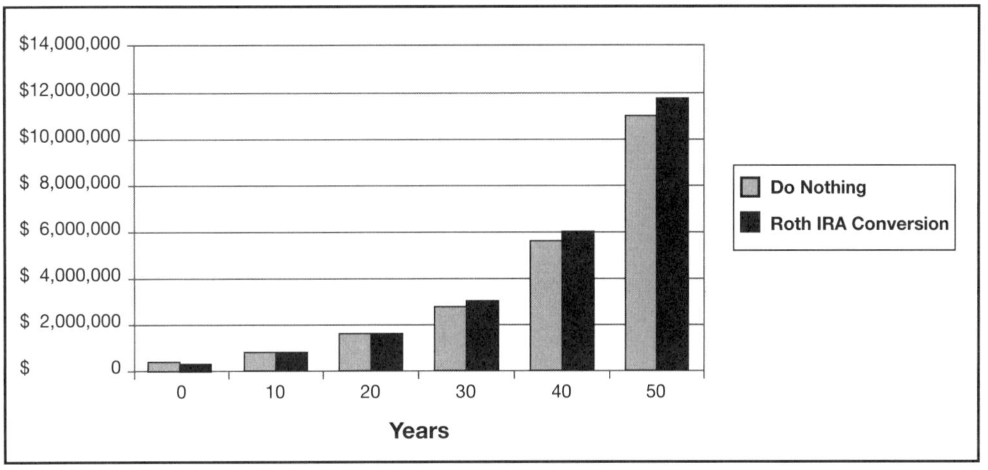

Example

Paul, age 45 and single, has a $400,000 IRA and $112,000 of nonqualified liquid assets. Right now, Paul is in the 28 percent tax bracket and expects to be in the 25 percent tax during his retirement years. Ignoring the impact of RMDs from the traditional IRA and assuming a pretax growth rate in the IRA of 7 percent and an after-tax growth rate of 6 percent in the taxable brokerage account, the amount of wealth Paul will have in the future is as follows.

	Do Nothing			Roth IRA Conversion				
	Traditional IRA	Brokerage Account	Total	Roth IRA	Brokerage Account	Total	Difference ($)	Difference (%)
Pre-Tax Account Balance (Current)	$ 400,000	$ 112,000	$ 512,000	$ 400,000	$ 112,000	$ 512,000		
Less: Income Tax on Roth IRA Conversion at 28%	—	—	—	—	(112,000)	(112,000)		
Less: "Built-In" Income Tax at 25%	(100,000)	—	(100,000)	—	—	—		
After-Tax Account Balance (Current)	$ 300,000	$ 112,000	$ 412,000	$ 400,000	$ —	$ 400,000	$ (12,000)	–3.00%
Pre-Tax Account Balance (Year 10)	$ 786,861	$ 200,575	$ 987,435	$ 786,861	$ —	$ 786,861		
Less: "Built-In" Income Tax at 25%	(196,715)	—	(196,715)	—	—	—		
Afer-Tax Account Balance (Year 10)	$ 590,145	$ 200,575	$ 790,720	$ 786,861	$ —	$ 786,861	$ (3,860)	–0.49%
Pre-Tax Account Balance (Year 20)	$ 1,547,874	$ 359,199	$ 1,907,073	$1,547,874	$ —	$ 1,547,874		
Less: "Built-In" Income Tax at 25%	(386,968)	—	(386,968)	—	—	—		
Afer-Tax Account Balance (Year 20)	$ 1,160,905	$ 359,199	$ 1,520,105	$1,547,874	$ —	$ 1,547,874	$ 27,769	1.83%
Pre-Tax Account Balance (Year 30)	$ 3,044,902	$ 643,271	$ 3,688,173	$3,044,902	$ —	$ 3,044,902		
Less: "Built-In" Income Tax at 25%	(761,226)	—	(761,226)	—	—	—		
Afer-Tax Account Balance (Year 30)	$ 2,283,677	$ 643,271	$ 2,926,948	$3,044,902	$ —	$ 3,044,902	$ 117,954	4.03%

Principle Number Five

Because married couples have lower tax rates than single taxpayers, Roth conversions within the same tax bracket will almost always be desirable for couples over age 65.

Example

Carl and Nancy, ages 75 and 70, respectively, have been retired for several years and have had the following sources of income and deductions on a year-by-year basis:

Interest	$ 3,600
IRA distributions	60,000
Social Security (gross)—Carl	16,500
Social Security (gross)—Nancy	7,500
State income taxes	2,000
Real estate taxes	1,500
Charitable contributions	1,500

In addition, Carl and Nancy had the following retirement assets:

Traditional IRA	$850,000
Roth IRA	150,000
Taxable investment account	250,000

In 2007, Carl was diagnosed with a medical condition whereby he is not expected to live much more than 3 years. Because of this situation, Carl and Nancy sought the advice of their CPA and financial advisor to learn what actions should be taken from an income tax perspective.

Upon reviewing Carl and Nancy's financial position and their cash flow needs, the CPA calculated the taxable income and income tax liability on a premortem and postmortem basis based on the assumption that Nancy would continue to withdraw $48,000 per year from Carl's IRA after he passes away.

	Before Carl's Death	After Carl's Death
Interest	$ 3,600	$ 3,600
IRA distributions	48,000	48,000
Social Security (taxable)—Carl	14,025	0
Social Security (taxable)—Nancy	6,375	6,375
Adjusted gross income	$ 72,000	$ 57,975
Less: Standard deduction	(12,800)	(6,650)
Less: Personal exemptions	(6,800)	(3,400)
Taxable Income	$ 52,400	$ 47,925
Income tax liability	$ 7,078	$ 8,405
Effective tax rate	13.5%	17.5%
Marginal tax rate	15%	25%

(continued)

Example *(continued)*

Seeing that a significant portion of the $48,000 IRA distribution after Carl's death would be subject to the 25 percent marginal income tax rate, the CPA and financial advisor suggested to Carl that he consider converting $10,000 per year from his traditional IRA to a Roth IRA. By converting only $10,000 per year, all of the Roth IRA conversion income would be taxed at Carl and Nancy's marginal income tax rate of 15 percent.

From 2007 until his death in 2009, Carl converted $10,000 to his Roth IRA each year, paying $1,500 ($10,000 × .15) of additional income tax on each conversion. After Carl's death, Nancy only took $38,000 from Carl's traditional IRA and $10,000 from Carl's Roth IRA, both of which were rolled over to her own IRA. By converting to a Roth IRA before death, Carl and Nancy saved over $3,000 in income taxes during a period of 6 years. This can be shown as follows.[12]

	2007	2008	2009	2010	2011	2012	Total
$10,000 Roth IRA conversion	$8,578	$8,578	$8,578	$5,905	$5,905	$5,905	$43,449
No Roth IRA conversion	$7,078	$7,078	$7,078	$8,405	$8,405	$8,405	$46,449

The same principal would also apply to much larger, more substantial Roth conversions.

Principle Number Six

In those states that collect a separate state inheritance or "pick-up" estate tax, a predeath Roth conversion is highly desirable when compared to dying with a regular IRA.

Like an income tax hedging conversion, an estate tax hedging conversion hedges against the possibility that the combined income and estate tax on a traditional IRA will be higher than converting to a Roth IRA. Currently, the federal tax law imposes an estate tax on taxable estates in excess of $3,500,000, and many states also impose their own version of an estate or inheritance tax.

In the context of traditional IRAs, qualified retirement plans, and Roth IRAs, the gross value of these assets will be included in the decedent's gross estate. However, even though these assets are included in a decedent's gross estate, these assets will not receive a step-up in basis because they are deemed to be income in respect of a decedent (IRD).

12 For sake of simplicity and comparability, all tax liabilities were determined by reference to the tax law in effect during the 2007 tax year.

Where an estate tax has been imposed upon the same funds that are subject to income tax, an income tax deduction for the federal estate tax paid on IRD is designed to help mitigate the effect of double taxation. This is commonly referred to as an "IRC Section 691(c) deduction."

The calculation in the following table outlines this concept.

Total Value of IRA Included in Taxable Estate	$1,000,000
Gross Federal Estate Tax at 45%	$ (450,000)
State Death Tax at 10%	(100,000)
Total Estate Taxes	$ (550,000)
Total IRA Value	$1,000,000
Less: IRC §691(c) Deduction	(450,000)
Taxable IRA Value	$ 550,000
Total Income Tax at 40%	$ (220,000)
Total IRA Value	$1,000,000
Less: Federal Estate Tax	(450,000)
Less: State Death Tax	(100,000)
Less: Income Taxes	(220,000)
Net IRA Value	$ 230,000
% of IRA Lost to Taxes	77.00%

Even if a client expects to be in the same income tax bracket in the future as he or she is today, it generally is better for him or her to convert to a Roth IRA today and pay the income tax on the conversion. At first blush, this may not seem reasonable. However, when you factor in federal and state estate taxes, the reason for doing an estate tax hedging conversion becomes more evident.

Under general mathematical principles, it would first appear that doing a Roth IRA conversion prior to death would not have any impact on the client from an income tax perspective. This would be true if a federal income tax deduction were allowed for the entire amount of estate taxes (both federal and state) paid on the traditional IRA. However, the federal tax law does not allow an income tax deduction for any state estate taxes paid on IRD. Because of this, the taxpayer is losing a part of the IRA balance to state estate taxes for which the beneficiaries are not receiving a corresponding deduction on their income tax returns. Conversely, the client's estate would be reduced by all income taxes (both federal and state) paid prior to death. Accordingly, it is more tax efficient to incur an income tax before incurring an estate tax.

The following table illustrates this point.

	Traditional IRA	Roth IRA	Tax Savings
Total IRA Balance	$ 2,000,000	$ 2,000,000	
Less: Income Taxes Paid on Roth IRA Conversion (35%)	—	(700,000)	
IRA Balance Subject to Estate Tax	$ 2,000,000	$ 1,300,000	
Federal Estate Tax (45%)	$ 900,000	$ 585,000	
State Estate Tax (10%)	200,000	130,000	
Total Estate Tax	$ 1,100,000	$ 715,000	
Total IRA Balance	$ 2,000,000		
Less: IRC §691(c) Deduction	(900,000)		
IRA Balance Subject to Income Tax	$ 1,100,000		
Federal Income Tax (35%)	$ 385,000	$ 700,000	
Total Taxes	$ 1,485,000	$ 1,415,000	$70,000

Principle Number Seven

Roth IRA distributions, like regular IRA distributions, can be paid out over the life expectancy of the beneficiary. However, Roth distributions retain their income-tax-free character.

When determining whether to convert to a Roth IRA, one must take into consideration the fact that Roth IRAs are not subject to the RMD rules like traditional IRAs. Beneficiaries of Roth IRAs, however, *are* subject to the RMD rules. Nevertheless, the distributions the beneficiaries take from the Roth IRA will generally not be subject to income tax. Thus, depending on the size of the client's IRA, his or her life expectancy, and the ages of the beneficiaries, the total amount of additional wealth that can be created by the client converting to a Roth IRA can be staggering.

Example

Mark, age 69 and single, is considering converting $100,000 to a Roth IRA. At the present time, Mark is in the 25 percent tax bracket and expects to be in the 25 percent tax bracket for the foreseeable future. In addition, Mark has named his son, Chris (age 42), as beneficiary of his traditional IRA. It is expected that Chris will also be in the 25 percent tax bracket when he inherits Mark's IRA.

The following are the other pertinent facts and assumptions:

Mark's assumed age at death	86
Taxable investment account	$25,000
Yield rate (dividends and interest)	2.00%
Growth rate	7.00%
Ordinary income tax rate	25.00%
Capital gains tax rate	15.00%

As evidenced by the following charts, Chris would have over $80,000 more assets in 30 years if Mark were to convert $100,000 to a Roth IRA during the current year.

	Traditional IRA	Roth IRA	
Yr	Total Assets	Total Assets	Difference
1	$106,781	$107,000	$ 219
5	$138,670	$140,255	$ 1,585
10	$191,390	$196,715	$ 5,325
15	$262,867	$275,903	$13,036
20	$359,346	$386,851	$27,505
25	$489,818	$539,357	$49,539
30	$666,096	$746,622	$80,526

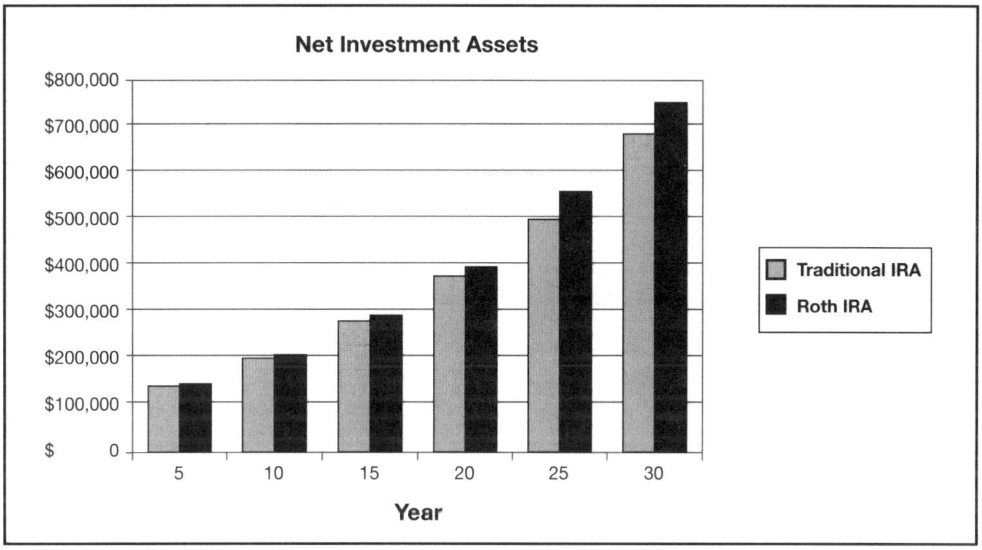

Using the same assumptions in the preceding example, except that the growth rate is 9 percent, Chris would have over $150,000 more assets in 30 years if Mark were to convert $100,000 to a Roth IRA. This is shown as follows.

	Traditional IRA	Roth IRA	
Yr	Total Assets	Total Assets	Difference
1	$ 108,744	$ 109,000	$ 256
5	$ 151,871	$ 152,862	$ 1,991
10	$ 229,435	$ 236,736	$ 7,301
15	$ 344,715	$ 364,248	$ 19,534
20	$ 515,164	$ 560,249	$ 45,085
25	$ 767,376	$ 856,239	$ 88,864
30	$1,140,001	$1,298,079	$158,077

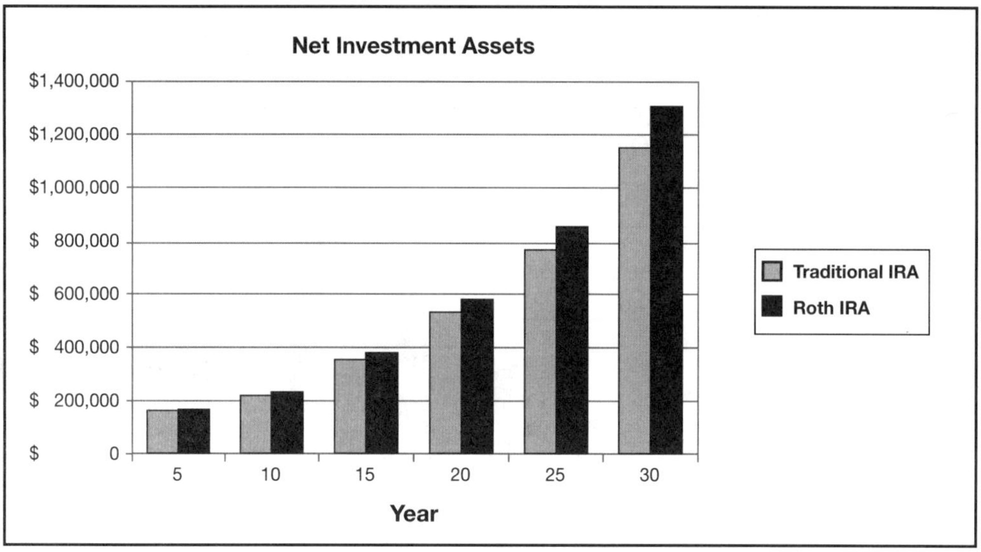

Determining the Proper Amount to Convert

After a taxpayer has identified that a Roth IRA conversion would be beneficial for them, they must then determine how much of his or her traditional IRA to convert and when to perform the conversion. Although there is no bright line rule or optimum conversion amount for all taxpayers, considering that each taxpayer's financial, income tax, and wealth situations are different, there are a few general rules of thumb or principles to follow when executing a Roth IRA conversion. These principles include the following:

- To the extent that the taxpayer's current marginal income tax rate is equivalent to or lower than his or her projected future marginal income tax rate, little harm can be done in executing a Roth IRA conversion.
- Convert an amount that will allow as much of the conversion income as possible to remain in the taxpayer's current marginal income tax bracket (in other words, the more the taxpayer's marginal income tax bracket increases due to the conversion, the more financially harmful the conversion may be).
- The ability to utilize funds from outside of the traditional IRA to finance the conversion will afford the taxpayer a more beneficial result (in other words, if at all possible, avoid "reaching into the IRA" to pay for the conversion).

Therefore, although there is an interplay of factors affecting the decision as to whether to perform a Roth IRA conversion and the amount of the traditional IRA to convert, the driving force behind these determinations is generally the taxpayer's current and projected future marginal income tax rates, his or her ability to finance the conversion with funds from outside of the IRA, and his or her ability to defer distributions after age 70½.

Assume for a moment that the assets within a traditional IRA are only expected to grow at around 5 percent. In this situation, an opportunistic conversion is out of the question. Accordingly, the decision to convert now becomes more strategic and driven by long term economics. Given these assumptions, a conversion of the entire traditional IRA to a Roth IRA would be imprudent. In this case, the optimum conversion amount will be somewhere between a 100 percent conversion and no conversion at all.

The key to finding the optimum conversion amount will depend on the client's current and future projected income tax rates and spending needs. As discussed, to the extent that the client expects the future tax rate to be the same or higher than the current tax rate, little to no harm can be done by converting to a Roth IRA.

In many cases, the client will be in a higher income tax bracket in the future. The primary reason for this is that, upon reaching age 70½, RMDs must come from the traditional IRA. Depending on the size of the client's traditional IRA and the other income generated outside of the IRA (for example, taxable dividends and interest and Social Security), the client will most likely be in a higher tax bracket once RMDs begin. Thus, in choosing the optimum amount to convert to a Roth IRA, the client most likely would convert an amount that would be taxed at a rate that would be the same or less than the client's projected future tax rate, including RMDs.

Example

Linda, age 50 and married, has $100,000 in a traditional IRA that she is considering converting to a Roth IRA. At the present time, Linda and her husband are in the 25 percent tax bracket and expect to be in the 28 percent tax bracket once her RMDs begin. Assuming a brokerage account balance of $25,000 generating an after-tax growth rate of 7 percent, 9 percent, or 11 percent, respectively, and a pretax growth rate of 8 percent for the IRA, the amount of wealth Linda will have in the future is as follows.

(continued)

Example *(continued)*

After-Tax Growth Rate of 7%	Do Nothing			Roth IRA Conversion				
	Traditional IRA	Brokerage Account	Total	Roth IRA	Brokerage Account	Total	Difference ($)	Difference (%)
Pre-Tax Account Balance (Current)	$ 100,000	$25,000	$ 125,000	$ 100,000	$ 25,000	$ 125,000		
Less: Income Tax on Roth IRA Conversion at 25%	—	—	—	—	(25,000)	(25,000)		
Less: "Built-In" Income Tax at 25%	(25,000)	—	(25,000)	—	—	—		
After-Tax Account Balance (Current)	$ 75,000	$25,000	$ 100,000	$ 100,000	$ —	$ 100,000	$ —	0.00%
Pre-Tax Account Balance (Year 10)	$ 215,892	$49,179	$ 265,071	$ 215,892	$ —	$ 215,892		
Less: "Built-In" Income Tax at 25%	(53,973)	—	(53,973)	—	—	—		
Afer-Tax Account Balance (Year 10)	$ 161,919	$49,179	$ 211,098	$ 215,892	$ —	$ 215,892	$ 4,794	2.27%
Pre-Tax Account Balance (Year 20)	$ 466,096	$96,742	$ 562,838	$ 466,096	$ —	$ 466,096		
Less: "Built-In" Income Tax at 28%	(130,507)	—	(130,507)	—	—	—		
Afer-Tax Account Balance (Year 20)	$ 335,589	$96,742	$ 432,331	$ 466,096	$ —	$ 466,096	$33,765	7.81%

Example *(continued)*

After-Tax Growth Rate of 9%	Do Nothing			Roth IRA Conversion				
	Traditional IRA	Brokerage Account	Total	Roth IRA	Brokerage Account	Total	Difference ($)	Difference (%)
Pre-Tax Account Balance (Current)	$ 100,000	$ 25,000	$ 125,000	$ 100,000	$ 25,000	$ 125,000		
Less: Income Tax on Roth IRA Conversion at 25%	—	—	—	—	(25,000)	(25,000)		
Less: "Built-In" Income Tax at 25%	(25,000)	—	(25,000)	—	—	—		
After-Tax Account Balance (Current)	$ 75,000	$ 25,000	$ 100,000	$ 100,000	$ —	$ 100,000	$ —	0.00%
Pre-Tax Account Balance (Year 10)	$ 215,892	$ 59,184	$ 275,077	$ 215,892	$ —	$ 215,892		
Less: "Built-In" Income Tax at 25%	(53,973)	—	(53,973)	—	—	—		
Afer-Tax Account Balance (Year 10)	$ 161,919	$ 59,184	$ 221,103	$ 215,892	$ —	$ 215,892	$(5,211)	2.36%
Pre-Tax Account Balance (Year 20)	$ 466,096	$140,110	$ 606,206	$ 466,096	$ —	$ 466,096		
Less: "Built-In" Income Tax at 28%	(130,507)	—	(130,507)	—	—	—		
Afer-Tax Account Balance (Year 20)	$ 335,589	$140,110	$ 475,699	$ 466,096	$ —	$ 466,096	$(9,603)	–2.02%

(continued)

Example *(continued)*

After-Tax Growth Rate of 11%	Do Nothing			Roth IRA Conversion				
	Traditional IRA	Brokerage Account	Total	Roth IRA	Brokerage Account	Total	Difference ($)	Difference (%)
Pre-Tax Account Balance (Current)	$ 100,000	$ 25,000	$ 125,000	$ 100,000	$ 25,000	$ 125,000		
Less: Income Tax on Roth IRA Conversion at 25%	—	—	—	—	(25,000)	(25,000)		
Less: "Built-In" Income Tax at 25%	(25,000)	—	(25,000)	—	—	—		
After-Tax Account Balance (Current)	$ 75,000	$ 25,000	$ 100,000	$ 100,000	$ —	$ 100,000	$ —	0.00%
Pre-Tax Account Balance (Year 10)	$ 215,892	$ 70,986	$ 286,878	$ 215,892	$ —	$ 215,892		
Less: "Built-In" Income Tax at 25%	(53,973)	—	(53,973)	—	—	—		
Afer-Tax Account Balance (Year 10)	$ 161,919	$ 70,986	$ 232,905	$ 215,892	$ —	$ 215,892	$(17,012)	–7.30%
Pre-Tax Account Balance (Year 20)	$ 466,096	$201,558	$ 667,654	$ 466,096	$ —	$ 466,096		
Less: "Built-In" Income Tax at 28%	(130,507)	—	(130,507)	—	—	—		
Afer-Tax Account Balance (Year 20)	$ 335,589	$201,558	$ 537,147	$ 466,096	$ —	$ 466,096	$(71,051)	–13.23%

Conclusion

Roth IRA conversion planning is still relatively new and only a relatively modest number of people have taken advantage of this planning thus far. As 2010 quickly approaches, more and more clients will seek professional advice to determine the feasibility of a Roth IRA conversion. While quite complex, with a good understanding of the basic mathematical principles behind Roth IRA conversions, one will be able to convey the power of tax-free deferral to his or her client. If the decision is made to utilize a Roth IRA, the client's portfolio structure will need to be considered. The next chapter is meant to assist the advisor in determining a client's overall portfolio composition.

Portfolio Management Considerations

Introduction

CPAs are well versed in the art of financial planning and understand the importance of growing and managing retirement assets for retirement. Although the importance of managing the nest egg during the accumulation years is understood, what many may not realize is that management of the nest egg, including the positioning of retirement assets during the distribution years and the order and mix in which withdrawals are made, is just as important and can have a profound impact on the duration of the client's withdrawals and the longevity of their retirement assets.

Therefore, this chapter will explore investment alternatives as well as tax-efficient withdrawal strategies, including the importance of a distribution portfolio and the building blocks of tax-deferred growth and tax-sensitive asset allocation.

IRA Investments

Although a wide variety of investments can be utilized within an individual retirement account (IRA), there are certain assets that an IRA cannot own. An IRA is not allowed to own any collectible (that is, any work of art, any rug or antique, any metal or gem, any stamp or coin, any alcoholic beverage, and any other tangible personal property so designated by the Secretary of the Treasury). If the IRA does obtain a collectible, the collectible will be treated as a distribution from the IRA in the amount equal to the cost to the IRA of the collectible.

There is an exception, however, in that IRAs are allowed to own certain United States platinum, silver, or gold coins or coins issued under the laws of any state.[1] IRAs also are not allowed to invest in life insurance.[2] Owning real estate in an IRA, however, is not barred under any section of the Internal Revenue Code (IRC) or regulations.

Prohibited Transactions

Even though one can own real estate in an IRA, it is imperative to make sure that by doing so, one does not run afoul of the prohibited transaction rules. IRC Section 4975 imposes a tax on prohibited transactions. These taxes, however, do not apply to IRAs; instead, the IRA is disqualified if it engages in a prohibited transaction.[3] If an IRA is disqualified, the entire IRA is deemed to be distributed, and income taxes and other applicable excise taxes (such as the early distribution penalty of IRC Section 72(t)) will be due. The same rules apply to Roth IRAs.[4] The term *prohibited transaction* includes, but is not limited to, lending of money, any direct or indirect sale or exchange, or leasing of any property between a plan and a disqualified person.

A *disqualified person* includes but is not limited to a person who is a fiduciary; an employer whose employees (any or all) are covered by the plan; or a corporation, partnership, or trust or an estate of which (or in which) 50 percent or more is owned directly or indirectly or held by any of the preceding; or a member of the IRA owner's family (spouse, ancestor, lineal descendant, and any spouse of a lineal descendant).

If there is any question that owning the real estate within the IRA will violate the prohibited transaction rules, it is highly recommended that an exemption be requested from the Department of Labor.[5] Prudence would also suggest that a private letter ruling be requested from the IRS. In order to grant an exemption, the Department of Labor must find that the exemption is administratively feasible, in the interests of the plan and of its participants and beneficiaries, and protective of the rights of participants and beneficiaries of the plan.

Obtaining an exemption and private letter ruling provides the client, the advisor, and the custodian with an assurance that their proposed transaction will not cause disqualification of the IRA.

Unrelated Business Taxable Income

Even if a taxpayer gets over the prohibited transaction hurdle, advisors need to be aware that investing in real estate could subject the client's IRA to unrelated business taxable income (UBTI) under IRC Section 511. The UBTI rules were established to even the playing field when exempt organizations engage in a business typically engaged in by for-profit organizations. For example, if a charity begins selling greeting cards in competition with Hallmark, the income earned on the cards would be subject to UBTI.

---

1 Internal Revenue Code (IRC) Section 408(m)(3). Under Notice 87-16, 1987-1 CB 446, however, coins that are made into jewelry are treated as collectibles.

2 IRC Section 408(a)(3).

3 IRC Section 408(e)(2)(A).

4 Treasury Regulation Section 1.408A-1, Q&A 1(b). A full copy of the 1999 final rules and regulations from the Department of the Treasury, including Treasury Regulation Section 1.408A-1, can be found on the accompanying CD-ROM.

5 The Secretary of Labor has the power to grant a prohibited transaction exemption under IRC Section 4975(c)(2).

An IRA is exempt from taxation and is therefore subject to the taxes imposed by the UBTI rules. *Unrelated trade or business* is defined as, in the case of an IRA subject to IRC Section 511, any trade or business regularly carried on by such IRA or by a partnership of which it is a member. The UBTI rules also apply to a Roth IRA. Income from an activity carried on by the IRA would be subject to UBTI if the activity constitutes a "trade or business," the activity is "regularly carried on" by the IRA, and the conduct of the activity is "not substantially related" (other than through the production of funds) to the IRA's tax-exempt purpose.[6]

Although rental income generally is excluded from UBTI, if the real estate that is producing the rental income is debt financed, such income is not excluded from UBTI. Therefore, unless the real estate in the IRA is completely paid for, the rent will most likely be subject to UBTI.

Other Considerations

Aside from the potential tax traps mentioned in the preceding paragraphs, there are a number of other important factors that should be considered. When a taxpayer owns real estate in an IRA, he or she loses his or her ability to take depreciation deductions against other income. The fact that property taxes will be due on the property is another factor that should not be overlooked. Such taxes will, of course, need to be paid from IRA funds if the property is held within an IRA.

On the flip side, any capital gains involving the real estate will be tax free inside the IRA. However, when distributions are taken from the IRA, ordinary income tax will be due. Depending on the client's tax bracket, the ordinary income tax rate most likely will be higher than any capital gain rate, thus causing an increase in tax liability. This, of course, does not apply to Roth IRAs because qualified distributions from Roth IRAs are income tax free. Consequently, owning real estate in a Roth IRA potentially could help the client avoid capital gains taxes.

Finding an IRA custodian who will accept real estate as an investment vehicle also can be difficult, although such custodians certainly do exist. It is important to find a reputable custodian who specializes in holding real estate in an IRA.

Thought should also be given to the fact that real estate is not a liquid asset. If the client is near or at his or her required beginning date, the following question should be asked: "Will the IRA contain enough liquid assets to take the required minimum distributions?" Because real estate is not a liquid asset, when outside assets exist, many real estate experts believe there is no good reason to purchase real estate in an IRA.

Portfolio Management

A key consideration in portfolio design is which portion of the investment pyramid (from the riskiest at the pinnacle to the safest at the base) should be invested within the qualified retirement plan, traditional IRA, or Roth IRA, and which portion belongs outside of the qualified plan, IRA, or both.

6 See IRC Sections 501(c)(7), 501(c)(9), and 501(c)(17).

Your clients may ask you about which asset classifications they should acquire for which retirement portfolio. For example, the questions may be, "Should my aggressive commitments be placed in my 401(k) plan, my traditional IRA, my Roth IRA, or positioned outside of my qualified plans?" These could be difficult questions for you and the client's investment advisers to answer.

Diversifying Investments

Analogous to the executive who holds a portfolio comprised predominantly of company stock, the taxpayer who does not diversify assets and investments may be faced with the same uncertainty and investment risks.

As taxpayers age, their investments tend to become more conservative due to the fact that their focus changes from accumulation and growth to sustainable income and withdrawal strategies. When a taxpayer is not diversified and holds a concentration of assets in one investment, accomplishing a relatively conservative investment strategy and a sustainable income can be difficult. Additionally, due to the lack of diversification, the professional will be subject to investment risk, which may include the following:

- *Lack of diversity in the portfolio.* This may lead to lack of growth and ultimately limit the overall level of return.
- *Lack of risk management.* The taxpayer will be unable to limit his or her downside risk potential due to the lack of diversification.
- *Lack of liquidity.* Some professional firms may be highly leveraged, which may make it hard for the exiting professional to withdraw funds upon departure from the firm.

In order to help guard against these investment risks and facilitate the retiring taxpayer's accomplishment of a conservative investment portfolio and a withdrawal strategy providing for a sustainable income, the advisor needs to be cognizant of the dangers inherent in a taxpayer's lack of diversification.

Increasing Wealth by Improving Tax Structures

As a general axiom of financial planning, most investors will achieve a stronger financial position and increase their overall wealth faster if they invest in tax-deferred or tax-free accounts prior to investing in taxable accounts. By and large, this is predominantly true because assets in tax-favored account tax structures, such as traditional and Roth IRAs, grow faster than assets in outside taxable accounts due to the deferral of income tax on the appreciation and earnings in these accounts. Stated another way, due to the tax drag that encumbers outside taxable accounts, assets in tax-favored accounts accumulate faster than assets in outside taxable accounts.

The *tax drag* that burdens outside taxable accounts can fundamentally be defined as the reduction in the portfolio's rate of return for the annual income tax liability imposed on the growth and earnings in the account. For example, assume that an investor has a stock portfolio that has an 8 percent rate of return and that the investor is in the 25 percent marginal income tax bracket. Therefore, in this example, the tax drag on the investment portfolio is 2 percent (8% × 25%). Furthermore, the after-tax rate of return of the investment is 6 percent (8% – 2%). By understanding the after-tax rate of return an investment is earning, an advisor can truly compare apples to apples. With this knowledge, the advisor is better equipped to ascertain which retirement vehicles will allow the professional to increase his or her wealth and position him- or herself favorably in structuring a distribution portfolio.

Advantages of Investments Within the Qualified Plan, Traditional IRA, or Roth IRA

The advantages of investing through qualified plans include the following:

- Growth and earnings are tax-deferred.
- An income tax advantage is often available when the plan or IRA is established.
- Tax rates may decrease before distributions.
- There are certain favorable tax treatments for distributions, for instance, IRC Section 408 rollovers and forward averaging.
- Qualified plan assets are afforded additional protection in bankruptcy.

Advantages of a Roth IRA

The advantages of investing through a Roth IRA include the following:

- Qualified distributions are tax free.
- Contributions can be withdrawn on a tax-free, first-in, first-out basis.
- Roth IRA distributions are not considered income for determining whether Social Security benefits are taxable.

Disadvantages of Investments Within a Qualified Plan or IRA

The disadvantages of investing through a qualified plan or IRA include the following:

- There is no step-up in basis at death.
- Tax rates may increase before distributions.

Disadvantages of a Roth IRA

The disadvantages of investing through a Roth IRA include the following:

- There is no up-front deduction.
- Income is recognized on conversion of a traditional IRA to a Roth IRA.
- Income recognized on conversion may affect the taxation of Social Security benefits.

Overall Portfolio Theory

When planning a client's investment portfolio, all investments, including any qualified plan or IRA investments and investments outside of such plans, should be managed as one portfolio from an investment and tax perspective. In essence, this means looking at proper asset allocation and tax strategies and other investment considerations on a comprehensive basis rather than a subportfolio-by-subportfolio basis.

When putting portfolio theory to work for a client, you should keep the following in mind:

- Qualified distributions from a Roth IRA are not subject to income tax.
- The maximum federal tax rate for individuals is 35 percent (in 2009) compared with a 15 percent capital gains rate.
- For married individuals with incomes of greater than $372,950, a tax rate of 35 percent (in 2009) exists.
- A portion of many clients' Social Security benefits are subject to federal income tax, as follows:
  - Married clients earning more than $32,000 (for single clients, the threshold is $25,000) will pay tax on 50 percent of their Social Security benefits (IRC Section 86).
  - Married clients earning more than $44,000 (for single clients, the threshold is $34,000) will pay tax on 85 percent of their Social Security benefits.

Investment Allocation

A client should consider dividing his or her investment securities between qualified plans and nonqualified plans. To the extent that the client has a security that appreciates in value, the step-up in basis at death and capital gains rates are available. Alternatively, if a security goes down in value, capital losses are available. In the context of a qualified plan or IRA, securities that appreciate substantially can be sold on a tax-free basis and repositioned within other investments. Further, the tax rate differential between ordinary income and capital gains could make holding growth equities outside of a qualified plan more attractive.

For many clients, placing a portion (for example, 40 percent) of their investment in an investment account and putting the remaining portion (for example, 60 percent) in an IRA or qualified plan may be appropriate. If the plan appreciates in value, the securities within the IRA can be sold on a tax-free basis, without tax erosion.

Municipal Bonds

Because municipal bonds are not subject to federal income tax, these investments are inappropriate for a traditional IRA or Roth IRA. There is no advantage to placing the asset in a Roth IRA account, and if the asset were placed in a traditional IRA, the favorable tax-free treatment would be lost.

U.S. Government Securities

Because of the conservative nature of U.S. government securities, they may well be appropriate for investment in an IRA. Further, under the tax law of many states, IRA distributions, to the extent that earnings represent income from U.S. government securities, are not subject to tax.

Corporate Bonds

Corporate bonds may also be an appropriate investment for an IRA in that the earnings from the bonds are free of income tax until distribution from the IRA.

High Yield Equities

High yield equities may be an appropriate investment for an IRA or Roth IRA because the earnings from the equities are free of income tax until distribution.

Growth Equities

Although generally appropriate for an IRA investment, certain blue chip investments that are considered to be *hold* investments may be best suited for investing outside of an IRA. The reason for this is the step-up in basis available at death and the applicable capital gains rate. The taxpayer should consider dividing *hold* investments between qualified and non-qualified funds.

Speculative Equities

Although often appropriate for an IRA, speculative investments, by their very nature, result in more losses (in addition to more gains), and holding these investments so the losses can be used to offset other capital gains may be appropriate. Further, balancing speculative investments in a particular issue between individual investments and IRA investments may be appropriate. In this regard, when certain growth objectives are obtained, the stock either outside the IRA or inside the IRA can be sold, leaving the other assets in the portfolio.

It is also important to consider your client's years remaining until retirement when including speculative investments in a portfolio. By their nature, speculative investments might not be ripe for liquidation when needed to generate retirement cash flow. Thus, the closer your client is to retirement, the less attractive speculative investments become regardless of whether they are in an IRA or held directly by the client.

Real Estate

Nonleveraged real estate is an acceptable investment for an IRA, and the income will be sheltered from tax in future years. Leveraged real estate may be more appropriately positioned outside a client's IRA because losses (subject to the passive loss rules under IRC Section 469) are tax deductible. Further, with older clients, a step-up in basis or death may be a related estate planning consideration.

Low income housing credit partnerships (under IRC Section 42) are more appropriately held outside of an IRA. These credits are of no benefit when held within an IRA.

Care must be taken not to violate the prohibited transaction rules under IRC Section 4975 when investing in nontraditional assets inside an IRA. See the "Prohibited Transactions" section in this chapter for a detailed explanation of these rules.

Options

Covered-call writing is allowed under the rules governing IRAs. Generally, other option positions, however, will have to be used outside the IRA.

Wash Sales

In Revenue Ruling 2008-5, the IRS ruled that if an individual sells stock or securities for a loss and causes his or her IRA to purchase substantially identical stock or securities within 30 days before or after the sale, the loss on the sale of the stock or securities is disallowed under

IRC Section 1091 (the Wash Sale rule). The taxpayer's basis in the IRA or Roth IRA was not increased by virtue of IRC Section 1091(d).

Utilizing Tax-Deferred Funds to Manage Income Tax Brackets

In order to manage income tax brackets and minimize overall income tax, taxpayers could first withdraw funds from their tax-deferred accounts up to, but not exceeding, an amount that fills up their 15 percent federal income tax bracket and then focus the remainder of withdrawals on taxable accounts. However, for those taxpayers who have higher taxable incomes, they may benefit by instead withdrawing sufficient funds from their tax-deferred accounts to fill up their 25 percent federal income tax bracket. The advisor should be aware that the benefits of utilizing this strategy may be decreased or lost altogether if the taxpayers withdraw funds from their tax-deferred account in amounts exceeding the 15 percent or 25 percent marginal income tax brackets.

The benefit of this strategy is derived through the payment of income tax on the distributions at the lowest marginal income tax rates and the maximization of the lowest marginal income tax brackets. By allowing the retired taxpayer to be taxed currently on the distributions at lower income tax rates instead of being taxed in the future on the distributions at higher income tax rates, the taxpayer is able to minimize his or her overall income tax liability. Thus, this strategy is especially effective for taxpayers who anticipate a large increase in their future projected marginal income tax rates. For example, if a taxpayer is currently in the 15 percent marginal income tax bracket and is anticipating an increase in his or her marginal income tax rate to 25 percent due to the onset of RMDs, the taxpayer would benefit and effectively minimize his or her overall tax liability by withdrawing funds currently and paying tax at the 15 percent tax rate instead of the higher 25 percent tax rate in the future.

Although this strategy will be most effective in the short term, for the strategy to be effective in the long term, the taxpayer will generally want to reinvest the withdrawn funds into a taxable account instead of consuming them. Additionally, the advisor should note that generally only tax-deferred funds and not tax-free funds (those from a Roth IRA) should be utilized in the execution of this strategy. Roth funds should generally not be utilized for this purpose because, due to the fact that Roth distributions are not subject to income tax, there is no incentive to withdraw the funds currently to take advantage of lower marginal income tax rates. Furthermore, although income tax brackets may be managed by the utilization of nominal Roth funds in unison with tax-deferred funds, the use of larger portions of Roth funds for this purpose is generally not prudent. This is because the opportunity cost of forgoing the compounded tax-free growth generally outweighs the tax benefit achieved through the use of tax-free funds in the management of income tax brackets. Therefore, the prudent taxpayer will adhere to the general principle that tax-free funds should be withdrawn last.

Blending Theory With Practice

Overall portfolio theory provides some good guidelines for investment advisers. Therefore, unless you are an investment advisor, you should work closely with the advisor that fills that role for your client. It is very important that you understand your client's financial objectives and the nature of the underlying investments. Communication among members of the client's planning team is critical.

Two of the key guidelines in evaluating the overall portfolio theory are the age and health of the client and spouse. If a client's death (and therefore a step-up in basis) is foreseeable in the near future (for example, advanced age or severe illness), you should consider holding a larger portion of the growth portfolio outside of an IRA and keeping more of the conservative assets within a traditional IRA.

When choosing the investments for traditional and Roth IRAs, you should consider holding high growth assets in the Roth IRA; assets with lower growth potential should be held in the traditional IRA. Although neither IRA pays tax on current earnings or growth, the lack of a withdrawal tax for the Roth IRA would minimize the tax erosion on the part of the portfolio that experienced the better return.

For newly retired clients for whom a portion of their Social Security benefits are subject to federal income tax, you should consider holding foundation investments (for example, bonds) in an IRA, especially if distributions are not required, and holding the growth portfolio outside of the IRA.

For clients in community-property states, at the death of the first spouse, a complete step-up in basis occurs on the property held outside of an IRA. This is an important factor to consider when determining which assets should be held within a qualified environment versus outside of the qualified environment.

Portfolio theory also becomes important for clients leaving a retirement plan. Many clients have a substantial portion of their portfolio in the stock of their employer. Allowing this stock, which has been held in a qualified plan for many years, to move into a safer portfolio is a difficult decision for clients. As a possible solution, it may be appropriate to sell the stock over a period of time, using hedging strategies (generally outside of the IRA) to assure your client that value is preserved. It may also be possible to reposition the portfolio by reinvesting dividends in other stocks and market sectors.

Conclusion

The way a taxpayer manages their retirement nest egg during retirement is just as important as the way they manage their nest egg while planning for retirement. Through the integration of tax-deferred growth and tax-sensitive asset allocation, a taxpayer will be positioned to capitalize on the benefits of employing a tax-sensitive withdrawal strategy. By following the general principle of taxable first, tax-deferred second, and tax-free last; the taxpayer may effectively extend the duration of their withdrawals and the longevity of their retirement assets.

Tax Planning Basics

Introduction

For many, qualified retirement assets represent a substantial portion of their wealth. The benefits afforded by allowing assets to grow in a tax-deferred environment have given rise to tremendous wealth accumulation during the life of the owner and if structured properly, will give rise to tremendous wealth accumulation for the owner's family. This chapter will discuss and illustrate the power of allowing retirement assets to grow in a tax-deferred environment and how retirement assets can be structured to provide the greatest benefit. This chapter will also introduce the reader to the inherited IRA concept. The key advantage of the inherited IRA concept is that it allows the owner's family to keep IRAs intact in an income tax-deferred environment and take withdrawals from the inherited IRA over their own life expectancies. If properly executed and funded, this strategy can create substantial wealth transfer opportunities.

Tax Planning for the Roth IRA Funded With Annual Contributions

Under current law,[1] taxpayers with adjusted gross income (AGI) below $166,000[2] (subject to a phase-in provision) are allowed to make annual contributions totaling $5,000 in 2009[3] to the Roth individual retirement account (IRA). Also, a husband and wife are able to make annual contributions of $10,000.

> **Example**
>
> Ron and Lynn are both employed and have been contributing to nondeductible IRAs. Instead, Ron and Lynn will now begin to contribute to a Roth IRA that has a 10 percent annual return. In 15 years, their $10,000 annual contributions will have grown from their initial investment of $150,000 to approximately $322,000. Under the Roth IRA, the growth will never be subject to income tax provided the distributions are qualified.

Employees may make contributions to a qualified Roth contribution program established under a 403(b) plan or a 401(k) plan. See Internal Revenue Code (IRC) Section 402A.[4] Employees may elect to make Roth contributions in lieu of all or a portion of elective deferrals that the employee is otherwise eligible to make under the applicable retirement plan. Unlike deferrals to a 403(b) plan and a 401(k) plan, elective deferrals to a qualified Roth contribution program are not income tax excludable.

If a client is currently making contributions to a nondeductible IRA, the decision to make the same contributions to a Roth IRA is relatively straightforward, unless the client plans on retiring or using the funds before age 59½.

Generally, the Roth IRA creates considerably more wealth than a traditional IRA, as shown in table 4-1, "Roth IRA Versus Traditional IRA—Net to Family at Death After Income and Estate Tax." Lynn, age 30, contributes $5,000 to her IRA at the end of each year for 35 years starting in 2009. The $5,000 annual contribution to the traditional IRA produces tax savings of $1,750 ($5,000 × 35 percent = $1,750), which is invested in an outside account. Assume a 35 percent federal income tax rate, a 45 percent estate tax rate, no state income or estate tax, an IRC Section 691(c) income in respect of a decedent (IRD) deduction, 100 percent growth on investments inside and outside the IRAs, 100 percent turnover on outside assets, and a 15 percent gains tax on outside assets. Required minimum distributions (RMDs) from the traditional IRA are taken at the end of each year starting in

1 Annual contributions to Roth individual retirement accounts (IRAs) are limited to $5,000 less any deductible IRA contributions. (See Internal Revenue Code (IRC) Section 408A(c)(2).) There is no prohibition on making Roth IRA contributions after attaining age 70.5. (See IRC Section 408A(c)(4).)

2 The maximum contribution that can be made to a Roth IRA is phased out for individual taxpayers with AGIs between $105,000 and $120,000 and for joint filers whose adjusted gross income (AGI) is between $166,000 and $176,000. (See IRC Section 408A(c)(3)(C).)

3 See the Economic Growth and Reconciliation Act of 2001. Reproduced as appendix 4 "Economic Growth and Tax Relief Reconciliation Act of 2001: Text" at the end of this book.

4 Beginning in 2006.

2049 when Lynn reaches age 70½. Figure 4-1, "Net to Family at Death," plots the differences between traditional and Roth IRA net distributions to family at death.

Table 4-1: *Roth IRA Versus Traditional IRA—Net to Family at Death After Income and Estate Tax*

	Net to Family at Death	
Year	Traditional IRA + Outside Balance	Roth IRA
2009	$ 2,750	$ 2,750
2014	$ 20,942	$ 21,218
2019	$ 49,579	$ 50,961
2024	$ 94,706	$ 98,862
2029	$ 165,888	$ 176,007
2034	$ 278,279	$ 300,250
2039	$ 455,905	$ 500,344
2044	$ 734,142	$ 819,849
2049	$1,160,840	$1,320,375
2054	$1,828,005	$2,126,476
2059	$2,857,149	$3,424,712
2064	$4,432,352	$5,515,532

Figure 4-1: *Net to Family at Death*

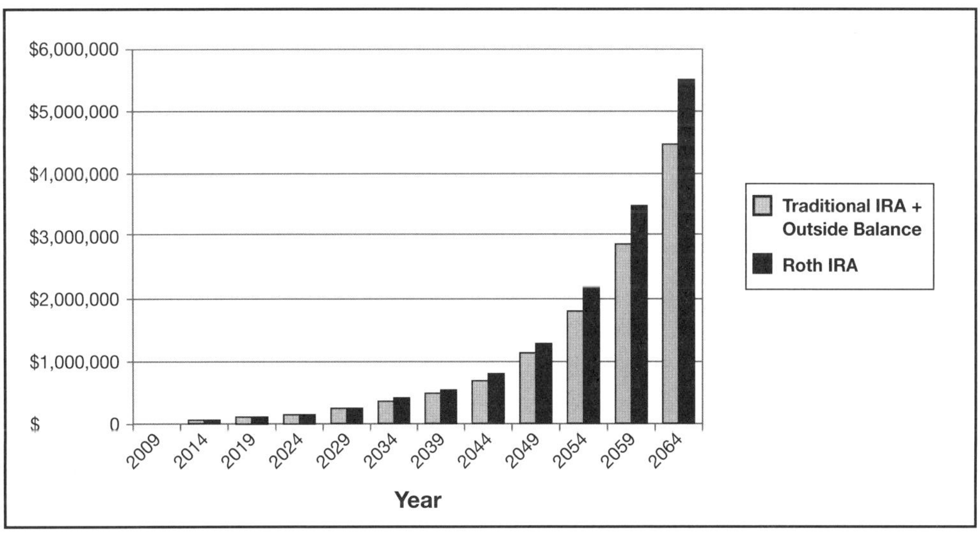

Penalty Tax

Younger taxpayers' main problem with the Roth IRA is that Roth IRA distributions before age 59½ will be *nonqualified distributions* taxable as ordinary income to the extent they exceed basis. Thus, if a taxpayer takes a distribution before age 59½, the taxpayer is subject to a 10 percent penalty excise tax.[5] If a taxpayer is fairly sure that he or she will not need the funds before age 59½, the Roth IRA represents a strong opportunity to accumulate funds for retirement. The taxpayer will be able to avoid the 10 percent penalty by taking substantially equal periodic payments.

Note that the 10 percent penalty tax also applies to the nonqualified distributions of after tax return of basis if either of the following occurs:

1. Any portion of the distribution is allocable to a rollover contribution created by the conversion of a traditional IRA.
2. The distribution occurs within a 5 year taxable period beginning with the contribution.[6]

Conversion of Existing IRAs to Roth IRAs—Spinning Straw Into Gold

For many taxpayers, converting to a Roth IRA is the modern day equivalent of "spinning straw into gold." However, the conversion of existing IRAs to Roth IRAs is one of the most complex issues confronting planners. To completely understand the options available to your clients, you should start with a review of the IRC provisions governing the conversion of a traditional IRA to a Roth IRA.

Before this provision is eliminated in 2010, the most cumbersome requirement is the $100,000 AGI limitation.[7] If a taxpayer's AGI is either definitely going to be under $100,000 or can be kept under $100,000 (or AGI is no longer a factor as is the case starting in 2010) through planning, a conversion to a Roth IRA should be considered.

Managing Investment Portfolio Income to Reduce Taxation

For conversions before 2010, there are planning strategies that can be utilized to decrease a taxpayer's AGI below the $100,000 threshold. As discussed in chapter 1, "Introduction to the Roth IRA," there is an opportunity for a taxpayer who is a general partner in an oil and gas venture. Tax law allows a general partner in an oil and gas venture to deduct the amount of intangible drilling costs in the year these expenses are incurred. Therefore, a taxpayer could reduce his or her AGI for purposes of a Roth IRA conversion using this technique. At the end of this chapter, appendix A: "Roth IRA Conversion Checklist" provides some practical guidance on the tasks involved with Roth IRA conversion planning.

---

5 IRC Section 72(t).

6 IRC Section 408A(d)(3)(F).

7 See IRC Section 408A(c)(3)(B)(I). Under this provision, actual AGI is increased by specified IRC Section 911 foreign-income items, and the exclusions for U.S. Savings Bond interest used for educational expenses and employer-paid adoption assistance.

At first glance, many taxpayers apparently cannot make the election to convert their traditional IRA to a Roth IRA. However, if your careful analysis of your client's income shows that it is possible to shift income from the current year to the next, your client may decide to do so. This involves traditional income tax shifting techniques that many planners have used over the years. The following is an outline of a number of ideas that may be helpful to reduce a client's AGI:

- Avoid regular IRA distributions.
- Convert taxable bonds to tax-free municipal bonds.
- Modify or create deferred-compensation agreements.
- Purchase certificates of deposit or one year Treasury bills designed to defer income to January of the following year.
- Avoid capital gains.
- Defer beginning Social Security.
- Set up pension and deferred benefit plans.
- Harvest capital losses.
- Invest in oil and gas ventures.

Example

Brian, age 60, is retired and expects to have a 2009 income of approximately $120,000. Included in this income will be $60,000 of taxable bond interest income. To reduce Brian and his wife's income for 1 year, they may wish to convert their existing bond holdings to municipal bonds.

Example

Assume the preceding example, except Brian is currently negotiating a postretirement deferred-compensation agreement. Structuring the postretirement deferred-compensation agreement to defer income beyond 2009 would work to keep Brian's income below $100,000.

Another choice facing planners and their clients is the advisability of converting all or a portion of an existing IRA to a Roth IRA. A taxpayer need not convert 100 percent of his or her current IRAs to Roth IRAs. Although it can be a somewhat complex mathematical puzzle, this option allows the taxpayer to optimize a percentage of his or her existing IRA that should be converted to a Roth IRA. Among the considerations regarding the amount to convert are the following:

- The taxpayer's current income tax situation and projected income tax situation for the next five years
- The impact on the taxation of current and future Social Security benefits
- The impact on estate planning
- The need or lack of need to fund the family trust (for example, a unified credit bypass trust) with IRA assets

- The outside assets available to fund the tax liability incurred by making a Roth IRA election
- Converting before beginning to receive Social Security benefits

The following six distinct estate and income tax planning considerations support converting to a Roth IRA:

1. The taxpayer has a special tax attribute available. For example, he or she may have charitable deduction carryforwards or investment tax credits.
2. Taxpayers who can pay the income tax resulting from a Roth IRA election from non-IRA funds will benefit greatly from the Roth IRA. See table 4-2, "Traditional IRA Versus Roth IRA—No Estate Tax or Required Minimum Distributions (Use of Outside Funds)."
3. The payment of income tax before the imposition of estate tax (when a Roth IRA election is made) compared with the available IRD deduction when a traditional IRA is subject to estate tax provides a moderate benefit.[8]
4. Suspension of the minimum distribution rules at age 70½ provides a considerable advantage to the Roth IRA holder. See figure 4-2, "Traditional IRA Versus Roth IRA—No Estate Tax or Required Minimum Distribution (Outside Funds)."
5. Taxpayers who need to use IRA funds to fund their applicable exclusion bypass trust are well advised to consider electing a Roth IRA for that portion of their overall IRA funds used to fund the trust.
6. Taxpayers who make the Roth IRA election during their lifetimes will reduce their overall estates, thereby lowering the effect of higher estate tax rates.

Table 4-2: *Traditional IRA Versus Roth IRA—No Estate Tax or Required Minimum Distributions (Use of Outside Funds)**

	Traditional IRA			Roth IRA		
Year	Ending IRA and Outside Fund Balance	Taxes on IRA ($140,000)	Net to Family	Ending IRA and Outside Fund Balance	Taxes on IRA	Net to Family
Jan. 1, 2009	$ 750,000	($ 140,000)	$ 610,000	$ 750,000	($140,000)	$ 610,000
Dec. 31, 2009	$ 821,250	($ 154,000)	$ 667,250	$ 669,350	$ 0	$ 669,350
Dec. 31, 2014	$ 1,293,647	($ 248,019)	$ 1,045,629	$ 1,065,242	$ 0	$ 1,065,242
Dec. 31, 2019	$ 2,039,850	($ 399,436)	$ 1,640,414	$ 1,696,407	$ 0	$ 1,696,407
Dec. 31, 2024	$ 3,219,667	($ 643,296)	$ 2,576,371	$ 2,703,246	$ 0	$ 2,703,246
Dec. 31, 2029	$ 5,086,767	($1,036,035)	$ 4,050,732	$ 4,310,248	$ 0	$ 4,310,248
Dec. 31, 2034	$ 8,044,123	($1,668,545)	$ 6,375,578	$ 6,876,503	$ 0	$ 6,876,503
Dec. 31, 2039	$12,732,347	($2,687,208)	$10,045,139	$10,976,649	$ 0	$10,976,649

*This assumes the Roth IRA election is made on January 1, 2009, and the entire tax liability for that year is withdrawn from the outside account. It also assumes growth of 10 percent; income tax of 28 percent; and capital gains rates of 15 percent; a 100 percent turnover of outside investments, and that there are no required minimum distribution or estate taxes incorporated in this example.

8 IRC Section 691(c).

Figure 4-2: *Traditional Versus Roth IRA—No Estate Tax or Required Minimum Distribution (Outside Funds)*

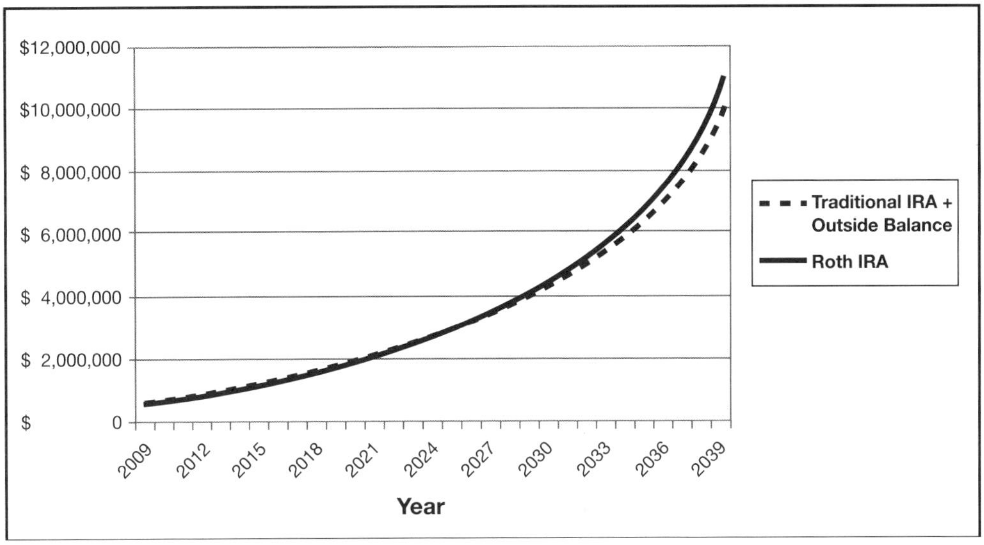

As already discussed, taxpayers who need to use retirement assets to fund a unified credit trust are well advised to consider the following strategy: to the extent that their overall income tax rate will not be unduly increased, the taxpayer should consider converting up to the applicable exclusion amount of a traditional IRA to a Roth IRA. The amount in the Roth IRA can then be used to fund the taxpayer's unified credit bypass trust. Table 4-3, "Roth IRA Versus Traditional IRA After the Death of Account Holder," provides an example of using a Roth IRA (from which taxes have already been paid) compared with a traditional IRA. The computation assumes

- a $675,000 beginning balance with a beneficiary who is age 50;
- distributions from the IRAs begin in 2009 and are based on a 34.2 year life expectancy; and
- growth both inside and outside the IRA is 10 percent, with the outside growth being subject to capital gains tax at 15 percent and a 28 percent federal income tax rate.

There is no federal income tax on qualified Roth IRA distributions, which will be especially helpful if distributions are made to a trust.

Table 4-3: *Roth IRA Versus Traditional IRA After the Death of Account Holder*

	Ending Outside and IRA Balance	
Year	Roth IRA	Traditional IRA*
2009	$ 742,500	$ 534,387
2014	$ 1,195,804	$ 853,931
2019	$ 1,925,854	$ 1,351,734
2024	$ 3,101,607	$ 2,119,937
2029	$ 4,995,169	$ 3,293,519
2034	$ 8,044,769	$ 5,066,629
2039	$12,956,181	$ 7,712,078
2044	$20,866,059	$11,616,856

*The IRC Section 691(c) deduction is not available because a federal estate tax has not been incurred.

Whether to Convert From a Traditional IRA to a Roth IRA

Making the decision to convert is more than a mathematical or analytical question; it must be addressed holistically, taking into account a client's financial, retirement, income tax, and estate planning. Having analyzed the Taxpayer Relief Act of 1997 (reproduced in part as appendix 1: "Taxpayer Relief Act of 1997" at the back of this book) and the related computations during the time since passage, the author is reasonably certain that most individuals with more than $250,000 in their plans should convert a portion of that plan to a Roth IRA. This holds true to an even greater extent for individuals who have in excess of $1 million in their plan and, to a lesser but still significant degree, for those taxpayers with smaller IRAs.

To understand the conversion analysis, you should begin with the basic computations.

> **Example**
>
> Sue has $750,000 in her IRA, which could remain a traditional IRA from the years when Sue is age 60 to age 90, or it could be fully converted to a Roth IRA. For ease of analysis, the assumption is that the dollars will be taxed at 28 percent in both instances. As table 4-4, "A Traditional IRA Versus Roth IRA—Same Tax Rate (Use of Inside Funds)" shows, there is no difference between converting or not converting when inside funds are used to pay the conversion tax and the income rate remains the same.

Example *(continued)*

Table 4-4: *Traditional IRA Versus Roth IRA—Same Tax Rate (Use of Inside Funds)**

	Traditional IRA			Roth IRA		
Year	Ending IRA and Outside Fund Balance	Taxes on IRA	Net to Family	Ending IRA and Outside Fund Balance	Taxes on IRA	Net to Family
Jan. 1, 2009	$ 750,000	($ 140,000)	$ 610,000	$ 750,000	($140,000)	$ 610,000
Dec. 31, 2009	$ 821,250	($ 154,000)	$ 667,250	$ 667,250	$ 0	$ 667,250
Dec. 31, 2014	$ 1,293,647	($ 248,019)	$ 1,045,629	$ 1,045,629	$ 0	$ 1,045,629
Dec. 31, 2019	$ 2,039,850	($ 399,436)	$ 1,640,414	$ 1,640,414	$ 0	$ 1,640,414
Dec. 31, 2024	$ 3,219,667	($ 643,296)	$ 2,576,371	$ 2,576,371	$ 0	$ 2,576,371
Dec. 31, 2029	$ 5,086,767	($1,036,035)	$ 4,050,732	$ 4,050,732	$ 0	$ 4,050,732
Dec. 31, 2034	$ 8,044,123	($1,668,545)	$ 6,375,578	$ 6,375,578	$ 0	$ 6,375,578
Dec. 31, 2039	$12,732,347	($2,687,208)	$10,045,139	$10,045,139	$ 0	$10,045,139

*This assumes the Roth IRA election is made on January 1, 2009, and the entire tax liability for that year is withdrawn from the Roth IRA. It also assumes growth of 10 percent; income tax of 28 percent; and capital gains rates of 15 percent; a 100 percent turnover of outside investments, and that there is no estate tax.

Because there is no difference, are there other factors that may drive the conversion? When you look deeper into this analysis, you will see that the suspension of minimum distributions at age 70½, using non-IRA funds to pay the tax on the Roth conversion, and the potential for reducing the overall combined estate and income tax will all drive your clients' decisions.

The Roth IRA is a superior vehicle to create wealth because once a taxpayer reaches age 70½, no minimum distributions are required. The most powerful variable you should take into account when analyzing whether to convert from a traditional IRA to a Roth IRA is whether your clients can use outside funds (that is, funds not currently invested in IRAs) to fund the income tax associated with the conversion to a Roth IRA. The mathematical advantage of rolling funds into a Roth IRA and using outside funds is quite staggering, as table 4-2 shows.

Table 4-5, "Traditional IRA Versus Roth IRA—No Estate Tax (Use of Outside Funds)," shows the effect of the required minimum distribution rules that apply to a traditional IRA during a participant's lifetime. To understand the Roth IRA conversion analysis, you should reconcile the analysis of the example illustrated in table 4-4, in which no benefit occurred, to the analysis illustrated in table 4-5, in which an overwhelming difference is illustrated. See figure 4-3, "Traditional IRA Versus Roth IRA Using Inside or Outside Funds to Pay Taxes on Conversions."

Table 4-5: *Traditional IRA Versus Roth IRA—No Estate Tax (Use of Outside Funds)**

	Traditional IRA			Roth IRA		
Year	Ending IRA and Outside Fund Balance	Taxes on IRA ($140,000)	Net to Family	Ending IRA and Outside Fund Balance	Taxes on IRA	Net to Family
Jan. 1, 2009	$ 750,000	($140,000)	$ 610,000	$ 750,000	($140,000)	$ 610,000
Dec. 31, 2009	$ 821,250	($154,000)	$ 667,250	$ 669,350	$ 0	$ 669,350
Dec. 31, 2014	$ 1,293,647	($248,019)	$1,045,629	$ 1,065,242	$ 0	$ 1,065,242
Dec. 31, 2019	$ 2,029,494	($386,184)	$1,643,310	$ 1,696,407	$ 0	$ 1,696,407
Dec. 31, 2024	$ 3,107,730	($515,350)	$2,592,380	$ 2,703,246	$ 0	$ 2,703,246
Dec. 31, 2029	$ 4,723,843	($659,825)	$4,064,018	$ 4,310,248	$ 0	$ 4,310,248
Dec. 31, 2034	$ 7,126,939	($796,759)	$6,330,181	$ 6,876,503	$ 0	$ 6,876,503
Dec. 31, 2039	$10,677,754	($883,635)	$9,794,119	$10,976,649	$ 0	$10,976,649

*This assumes the Roth IRA election is made on January 1, 2009, and the entire tax liability for that year is withdrawn from the outside account. It also assumes growth of 10 percent; income tax of 28 percent; and capital gains rates of 15 percent; a 100 percent turnover of outside investments, and that there is no estate tax incorporated in this example. However, it is important to know that the impact of required minimum distributions has been included.

Figure 4-3: *Traditional Versus Roth IRA Using Inside or Outside Funds to Pay Taxes on Conversion*

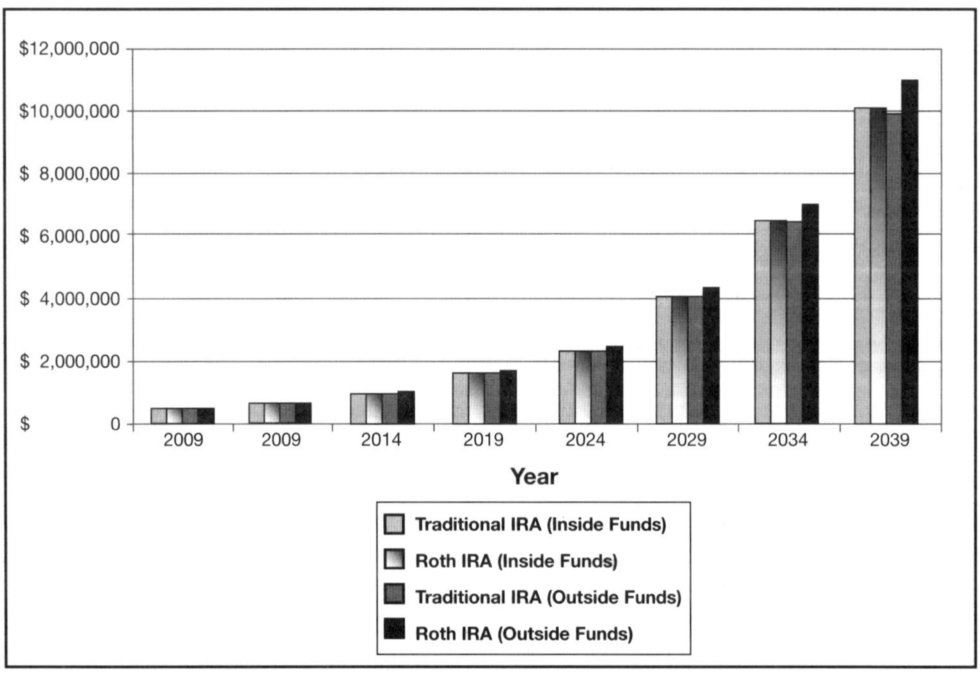

The total advantage over 30 years of converting to a Roth IRA using outside funds versus keeping your retirement savings in a traditional IRA is $1,182,530. Figure 4-4, "Total Advantage of Roth IRA Over 30 Years," shows that $251,020 of this advantage is attributable to not having to pay out RMDs and that $931,510 of the benefit is attributable to paying the income tax on the conversion with outside funds.

Figure 4-4: ***Total Advantage of Roth IRA Over 30 Years***

Initial advantage based on conversion in one year, no tax rate differential	$ 0
Advantage attributable to deferral of RMDs at age 70½	251,020
Advantage attributable to paying the tax liability with funds from outside of the IRA	931,510
Total advantage of Roth IRA over 30 years	$1,182,530

The advantage is even more powerful when estate tax implications are taken into account. See chapter 9, "Estate Planning for the Roth IRA," for a detailed discussion of the estate planning considerations.

Tax Planning at the Death of the First Spouse

At the death of the first spouse, the surviving spouse is confronted with the following choices:

- Roll the traditional IRA or Roth IRA funds over into his or her own name.
- Disclaim the funds.
- Leave the funds in an inherited IRA.

These choices are primarily driven by estate and income tax planning concerns and, to a lesser extent, legal and asset protection issues. When providing advice to a client at the death of the first spouse, you should move quickly to determine what beneficiary designations are currently in place and to determine whether disclaimers are needed. The plan document should always be reviewed soon after a client dies. The steps to follow are listed in figure 4-5, "A Checklist for Minimum Distributions Upon Death for Traditional IRAs."

Figure 4-5: *A Checklist for Minimum Distributions Upon Death for Traditional IRAs*

		Yes	No
1.	Is there a beneficiary?	☐	☐
2.	If there is no named beneficiary, does the IRA contract call for a default beneficiary?	☐	☐
3.	Is the spouse the sole beneficiary?	☐	☐
4.	Are there multiple beneficiaries?	☐	☐
	a. Do all of the beneficiaries qualify as a designated beneficiary?	☐	☐
	b. Is the spouse one of the beneficiaries?	☐	☐
5.	Did death occur before on or after the required beginning date?	☐	☐

Because Roth IRAs are not subject to RMDs during the IRA owner's lifetime, the required beginning date in the preceding checklist is not relevant for Roth IRAs. Therefore, a checklist for minimum distributions upon death of a Roth IRA owner would not include question 5, "Did death occur before or after the required beginning date," from the checklist. The distribution rules upon death of a Roth IRA owner are the same as those that apply to traditional IRAs if death occurs before the required beginning date.[9]

When meeting with a surviving spouse, one of your first roles is to determine whether sufficient resources exist to fund the unified credit exemption. If a spouse is named as the primary beneficiary of an IRA, he or she may need to disclaim all or a portion of the IRA to help fund the bypass trust. This is accomplished by having the trust as contingent beneficiary, and it should be in place prior to the IRA owner's death.

Tax Planning When the IRA Passes to the Spouse

The surviving spouse may make several elections at the death of a spouse with regard to both a traditional IRA and a Roth IRA.

The surviving spouse may elect to roll the IRA over into either a new or existing IRA in his or her own name.[10] Unlike the rules that apply to traditional IRAs, the rules that apply to Roth IRAs do not require distributions during the Roth IRA owner's lifetime.

Example

Harold dies at age 74. Following Harold's death, his wife, Julie, age 73, rolls both his traditional IRA and Roth IRA into newly established traditional and Roth IRAs in her own name and establishes new beneficiaries. Because Julie has already attained the required beginning date, she must begin distributions from the traditional IRA. However, no distributions are required from Julie's rollover Roth IRA until her death.

If the deceased spouse had not reached the required beginning date, the surviving spouse may continue to maintain the traditional IRA in the deceased spouse's name, deferring distributions until the year in which the deceased spouse would have attained the required beginning date had death not occurred.[11]

9 Treasury Regulation Section 1.401 (a)(9)-3.
10 10 IRC Section 408A(c)(6)(A) and IRC Section 408A(c).
11 Treasury Regulation Section 1.401(a)(9)-3, Q&A 3(b).

> **Example**
>
> Marvin dies at age 68. His wife, Maria, does not roll over the IRA; she maintains it in Marvin's name. Maria is not required to begin distributions until Marvin would have obtained age 70½. However, as a practical matter, if Maria does not roll the IRA over into an IRA in her own name, she will not be allowed to name a new beneficiary for tax purposes. In other words, the inherited IRA concept will not be available upon Maria's death.

Spousal Disclaimers

Under the property law of most states, the surviving spouse is allowed to disclaim assets passing under a beneficiary designation form. When a surviving spouse executes a disclaimer, the funds within a traditional IRA or Roth IRA pass to the next beneficiary as if the disclaiming spouse predeceased the owner. The next beneficiary is often a trust for the benefit of the surviving spouse, the children of the couple, or both. The new beneficiary or beneficiaries resulting from the disclaimer are able to utilize their life expectancy(ies) to determine RMDs.

Tax Planning When a Roth IRA Passes to a Nonspousal Beneficiary

When a Roth IRA passes to a designated beneficiary who is not the spouse, distributions are based on the beneficiary's life expectancy and must begin by December 31 of the year following the year of the owner's death. The designated beneficiary's life expectancy is determined in the year following the year of the owner's death and is reduced by 1 year for each year thereafter. If there are multiple beneficiaries and all qualify as designated beneficiaries and separate accounts have been established by December 31 of the year following the year of death, then each beneficiary can take distributions based on his or her individual life expectancy. If separate accounts have not been established, then distributions to all beneficiaries must be based on the oldest beneficiary's life expectancy.

> **Example**
>
> Alan dies when his child, the named beneficiary of his IRA, has a 47.5 year life expectancy for the year following the year of Alan's death. Distributions are made during the 47.5 years. Distributions do not have to begin until December 31 of the year following the year of Alan's death. There is a beginning balance of $1 million and a projected 10 percent growth rate. This is illustrated in table 4-6, "Distributions After Alan's Death."
>
> *(continued)*

Example

Table 4-6: *Distributions After Alan's Death*

Year	Pension Fund Beginning Value	Life Expectancy	Annual Distribution
2001	$1,000,000	47.5	$ 21,053
2002	$1,076,842	46.5	$ 23,158
2003	$1,159,053	45.5	$ 25,474
2004	$1,246,937	44.5	$ 28,021
2005	$1,340,807	43.5	$ 30,823
2006	$1,440,983	42.5	$ 33,905
2007	$1,547,785	41.5	$ 37,296
2008	$1,661,538	40.5	$ 41,026
2009	$1,782,563	39.5	$ 45,128
2010	$1,911,179	38.5	$ 49,641
2011	$2,047,691	37.5	$ 54,605
2012	$2,192,395	36.5	$ 60,066
2013	$2,345,562	35.5	$ 66,072
2014	$2,507,439	34.5	$ 72,679
2015	$2,678,236	33.5	$ 79,947
2016	$2,858,117	32.5	$ 87,942
2017	$3,047,193	31.5	$ 96,736
2018	$3,245,502	30.5	$106,410
2019	$3,453,001	29.5	$117,051

If a trust is the beneficiary and it is a qualified trust, distributions to the trust will be based on the oldest trust beneficiary's life expectancy. If the trust is not a qualified trust, distributions to the trust will be made under the 5 year rule unless the participant dies after his or her required beginning date (all Roth IRA owners are deemed to die before their required beginning date). In that case, distributions of the IRA must be taken for the year of death based upon the owner's age in the year of death according to the Uniform Lifetime Table.[12] For succeeding years, the life expectancy factor is determined by referencing the owner's age in the year of death using the Single Life Table under Treasury Regulation Section 1.401(a)(9)-9, Q&A 1. This factor is reduced by 1 for every year thereafter. A full copy of the 2002 final rules and regulations from the Department of the Treasury, including Treasury Regulation Section 1.401(a)(9), can be found on the accompanying CD-ROM.

12 IRS Annual Publication 590, appendix C, Table III "Uniform Lifetime Table."

Trust as a Beneficiary

When a trust is the designated beneficiary of a Roth IRA, distributions are then made over the life expectancy of the oldest trust beneficiary as long as the trust qualifies as a designated beneficiary under Treasury Regulation Section 1.401(a)(9)-4, Q&A 5. See chapter 8, "Beneficiary Considerations," for additional discussion.

> **Example**
>
> Lou dies at age 72, naming an irrevocable trust for the benefit of his wife, Martha, age 70, and his daughter, Lydia, age 40. Distributions are made over Martha's life expectancy.

Generally, when multiple beneficiaries are named, distributions are based on the life expectancy of the oldest beneficiary. If, however, separate shares are created by December 31 of the year following the year of death, each beneficiary can use his or her own life expectancy for determining distributions from his or her respective share. Such separate share treatment is not available when a trust is named beneficiary of an IRA, even if the trust and IRA are divided into separate shares upon the death of the grantor or IRA owner. There is a way around this rule, however. If, instead of simply naming the main trust as beneficiary of the IRA, the separate trust shares are named specifically as beneficiaries, the separate share rule is available to trust beneficiaries.[13]

Gifts to Charity

Clients with charitable intentions should leave their traditional IRAs to a charity, retaining their other assets and Roth IRAs for the benefit of their families. If a traditional IRA is left to charity, the IRA will not be subject to either income or estate tax. Because the charity is tax-exempt, no income tax will be paid with regard to the IRA, and Section 2055 charitable estate tax deduction will also be obtained. If a Roth IRA were to pass to charity, the income tax advantage is lost.

The Inherited-IRA Concept

The inherited-IRA concept considers the effect of arranging a client's affairs so that the balance in a large IRA (or qualified retirement plan) can be inherited intact by the client's children upon the death of the surviving spouse or upon the death of the client if unmarried at the time of death. This concept can also be used even if the client has no children but wishes to leave the IRA to other beneficiaries such as nieces, nephews, brothers, or sisters. The key advantage of this strategy is that it allows the beneficiaries to keep the IRA assets intact in an income tax deferred environment and take withdrawals from the inherited IRA over their own life expectancies. If properly executed and funded, this strategy can create substantial wealth-transfer opportunities for clients.

---

13 See Private Letter Ruling 200537044.

Ordinarily, the IRA distribution strategy that provides for the greatest benefit to a family is the strategy that provides the greatest deferral of taxes. Deferring withdrawals from the IRA or qualified retirement plan for as long as possible usually results in the greatest family wealth transfer.

To permit this long term deferral strategy to work, there must be sufficient liquidity, from a source other than the IRA, to pay the estate and excise taxes that would be due. Typically, if the client is married, the surviving spouse will roll over IRA assets into a new IRA in his or her name. The estate tax is deferred until the surviving spouse's death, at which time the estate taxes due on the total taxable estate are payable within nine months of the surviving spouse's death. Unless the estate taxes can be paid from another source, the IRA is invaded to pay these taxes.

When beneficiaries must withdraw funds from a traditional IRA to pay the estate taxes, the amount withdrawn is subject to income tax. This results in a *negative tax spiral*, ultimately resulting in a total tax loss of up to 70–80 percent of the original traditional IRA balance, leaving only 20–30 percent of the funds for the client's heirs.

Example

Gene dies at age 75, naming his wife, Amy, as the beneficiary of his traditional IRA. Subsequent to Gene's death, Amy rolls the funds over into an IRA in her own name, naming their only child as the beneficiary. Later, at Amy's death, the child's adjusted life expectancy is 40 years. Distributions will be made over the life expectancy of the beneficiary. If, for example, the balance of the IRA was $2 million at Amy's death and the beneficiary had a 40 year life expectancy, only $50,000 need be withdrawn in the first year. However, funds also need to be withdrawn to pay estate taxes along with income taxes. This negative tax spiral is shown in table 4-7, "Negative Tax Spiral."

Table 4-7: *Negative Tax Spiral*

Account	Amount	Percent
IRA balance	$2,000,000	100%
Estate tax	(900,000)	45.00%
Income tax	(385,000)	19.25%
Net to heirs	$ 715,000	
Percetage to heirs		35.75%
Percentage to taxes		64.25%

To prevent this devastating depletion of wealth, the source of funds to pay the estate taxes should come from outside the IRA. In a number of circumstances, other liquid assets may be available for this purpose. However, the IRA assets commonly represent the bulk of an estate. Therefore, it may be appropriate to consider the purchase of life insurance to provide the liquidity needed to keep the IRA intact.

In practice, this strategy is implemented by establishing an irrevocable life insurance trust with your client's heirs as beneficiaries. The trustee purchases a survivorship life insurance policy or, in the case of a surviving spouse or unmarried client, a single life policy. Upon the death of the insured, the life insurance proceeds are paid to the trust. To the extent needed to pay estate taxes, cash could be loaned to the estate, used to purchase estate assets, or distributed to the beneficiaries of the trust. This prevents the need for beneficiaries to withdraw funds from the IRA to pay the taxes. Upon death of the IRA owner, the beneficiaries can receive distributions over their life expectancies.

See chapter 9, "Estate Planning for the Roth IRA," for additional discussion of the inherited-IRA concept.

Roth Conversions at First Death

A potential planning opportunity for a Roth IRA conversion occurs after the death of the original traditional IRA owner. In many situations, the surviving spouse will roll over the traditional IRA into his or her own IRA. At this point, there may be a large IRA balance and a modest need for the IRA funds. In addition, there may also be liquid, high basis assets available to pay the Roth IRA conversion taxes because the typical planning will take advantage of the unified credit with the remaining assets passing to the surviving spouse, avoiding estate tax at the first death. Even though there will be no estate tax at the first death, there may be an estate tax at the second death. If this is the case, serious consideration should be given to making a Roth IRA conversion because of the many estate tax advantages of utilizing a Roth IRA.

The Art of Recharacterizations

In time, conversions, by asset class, and recharacterizations will be viewed as an intersection of finance and tax law. Previously, we have discussed the tax law associated with recharacterizations and provided some thoughts with regard to recharacterization by asset class. However, accountants and planners need to be aware of a troubling issue when a taxpayer takes advantage of the two year spread of income.

Example

Melissa and Charlie, a married couple, convert Charlie's $1,000,000 traditional IRA into a Roth IRA in 2010. Understanding the time value of money, they recognize income in 2011 and 2012, paying their taxes on the 2011 income on April 15, 2012 (for instance, by virtue of protective estimates), and their 2012 taxes on the quarterly estimate dates in 2012 and January 2013. This seems simple enough until you study the situation carefully and realize there is a substantial problem.

The last date to recharacterize is October 15, 2011; however, none of the taxes have been paid at that point in time. If the funds to pay the taxes are invested in the securities market and the securities market were to decrease in value after October 15, 2011, Charlie and Melissa (assuming they did not recharacterize) would still owe $400,000 of tax on the conversion. For example, if the market were to collapse by 50 percent (similar to 2008), then they would need to take the $400,000 of taxes from the $500,000 remaining value in the Roth IRA, leaving only $100,000 of value. To overcome this situation, your clients have three choices:

- Move enough cash to cover the tax liability to short term investments on or before October 15, 2011
- Buy put options to provide enough cash to pay taxes in the event of a market collapse
- Reserve a portion in cash and buy deep-in-the-money put options to protect the remaining exposure

Recharacterization strategies continue to develop. Many sophisticated practitioners are now recommending that if an account has decreased in value by November 30 of the year of conversion (for instance November 30, 2010, for a January 1, 2010 conversion) that it be immediately recharacterized to the traditional IRA for the last 31 days of 2010 followed by an immediate "reconversion" in January of 2011. Table 4-8, "Sample Conversion Chart," shows conversions A-E with an explanation of how each conversion, recharacterization, and reconversion could be addressed.

Conclusion

Ordinarily, the IRA distribution strategy that provides the greatest benefit to the taxpayer's family is the strategy under which the greatest deferral of taxes occurs. In other words, deferring withdrawals from the IRA for as long as possible usually results in the greatest family wealth transfer. The next chapter will explore the mathematics of utilizing a Traditional IRA versus a Roth IRA and the variables in the decision process.

Table 4-8: *Sample Conversion Chart*

	1/1/10	Action	11/30/10	Action	1/1/11	Action	4/15/11	Action	10/15/11	Action	11/30/11	Action	1/1/12	Action
A	$100,000	Original Conversion 1/1/10	$125,000	Hold	$130,000	Hold	$130,000	Hold	$135,000	Hold	$130,000	N/A	$130,000	N/A
B	$100,000	Original Conversion 1/1/10	$120,000	Hold	$120,000	Hold	$120,000	Hold	$120,000	Hold	$125,000	N/A	$130,000	N/A
C	$100,000	Original Conversion 1/1/10	$100,000	Hold	$100,000	Hold	$ 95,000	Recharac-terize 4/15/11	$ 80,000	Reconvert 5/16/11	$ 85,000	Hold	$ 90,000	Hold
D	$100,000	Original Conversion 1/1/10	$ 75,000	Recharac-terize 11/30/10	$ 80,000	Reconvert 1/1/11	$ 85,000	Hold	$ 85,000	Hold	$ 90,000	Hold	$ 95,000	Hold
E	$100,000	Original Conversion 1/1/10	$ 75,000	Recharac-terize 11/30/10	$ 90,000	Reconvert 1/1/11	$ 85,000	Hold	$ 90,000	Hold	$ 75,000	Recharac-terize 11/30/11	$ 80,000	Reconvert 1/11/12

Appendix A
Roth IRA Conversion Checklist

Initial Planning

- Send initial letter to client outlining benefits of Roth IRA conversions
- Set up meeting with client to discuss the fundamentals of Roth IRAs and the efficacy of converting to a Roth IRA
  - Use Roth IRA client presentation (MS PowerPoint)
  - Use basic analysis to explain the mathematical principles behind Roth IRA conversions
  - Obtain relevant data from client
    - Prior year tax returns
    - Investment account balances and risk profile
    - Annual income and expense detail
    - Estate planning and charitable goals
- Send engagement letter

Comprehensive Analysis

- Determine modified adjusted gross income (MAGI) for conversions
- Prepare comprehensive Roth IRA conversion analysis
- Set up meeting with client and financial professionals (if the client deems appropriate) to go over results of comprehensive Roth IRA conversion analysis
- Make revisions (if needed) to comprehensive Roth IRA conversion analysis
- Set up follow up meeting and/or telephone conferences to go over revised comprehensive Roth IRA analysis results
- Assist client with making the final decision as to whether or not to convert to a Roth IRA and how much to convert

Implementation of Plan

- Develop timeline and list of action steps
- Work with client and his/her financial advisor(s) in setting up different traditional IRAs prior to conversion (i.e. "Roth IRA Segregation Conversion Strategy")
- Review rollover paperwork and amounts to be converted to ensure proper execution of the Roth IRA conversion
- Convert separate traditional IRAs to Roth IRAs

Follow Up

- Review investment performance periodically during the year
- Review client's income during the year to determine if the Roth IRA conversion decision is materially impacted
- Prepare federal and state income tax projections and quarterly income tax estimates (if needed)
  - Determine the impact (if any) of the alternative minimum tax (AMT)

Finalizing the Plan

- **Late-March/Early-April (year following year of conversion)**—Review investment performance of new Roth IRA to determine approximately how much of the prior year Roth IRA conversion to keep (*Note:* Only a rough estimate needs to be done at this time as to how much Roth IRA conversion to keep. Nevertheless, the advisor should have a pretty good idea of this so that the client isn't paying in too much or too little with his or her tax return extension)
  - The amount of the Roth IRA conversion to keep will be based on the following factors:
    - The incremental income tax to be paid on the conversion (versus what the client expects to pay on distributions in later years)
    - Current tax law (versus what changes may occur within the near future)
    - Investment performance of each Roth IRA
    - The ability to use non-IRA funds to pay the income tax due on the conversion
- **April 15th or earlier (year following year of conversion)**—File an extension for the prior year income tax return
- **Late-September (year following year of conversion)**—Review investment performance, revise comprehensive Roth IRA analysis to determine effectiveness of prior year Roth IRA conversions and assist client in making final decision as to which Roth IRA conversions to keep
- **First week of October (year following year of conversion)**—Assist client with recharacterizing the unwanted portion of the prior year Roth IRA conversion back to a traditional IRA
- **October 15th or earlier (year following year of conversion)**—Finalize and file the prior year income tax return

Mathematics of Traditional Compared With Roth IRAs

Introduction

In January 2010, the world of IRA planning will change dramatically. As we near this date, when qualifying income limitations are eliminated, more clients will be proffering the same question: "Should I convert to a Roth IRA?" In order to be competitive, CPAs will need to help their clients answer this multi-faceted question. In this chapter, we will analyze the mathematical aspects of the Traditional IRA compared to the nondeductible IRA and the Roth IRA.

The Mathematics of the Traditional IRA Compared to the Nondeductible IRA and the Roth IRA

The tables in this chapter show the computations of the traditional individual retirement account (IRA), the nondeductible IRA, and the Roth IRA. Table 5-1, "Roth IRA Versus Traditional IRA Versus Nondeductible IRA—No Estate Tax," compares the results of 3 individuals investing $5,000 annually into a Roth IRA, traditional IRA with tax savings accumulating in an outside account, and a nondeductible IRA. As figure 5-1, "Net to Family Comparison," illustrates, the Roth produces the best result, followed by the traditional IRA and outside balance, followed by the nondeductible IRA.

Example

John, Jane, and Marie, all age 30, are in the 28 percent tax bracket and make IRA contributions until age 64. John contributes $5,000 annually to a Roth IRA, and his wife, Jane, contributes $5,000 annually to a traditional IRA. Jane receive a $1,400 annual tax savings on her $5,000 deductible contribution ($5,000 × 28% = $1,400). Jane invests these tax savings into an outside account, which is subject to a 15 percent capital gains tax. Jane's cousin, Marie, contributes $5,000 annually to a nondeductible IRA. See the results in table 5-1, "Roth IRA Versus Traditional IRA Versus Nondeductible IRA—No Estate Tax."

Table 5-1: *Roth IRA Versus Traditional IRA Versus Nondeductible IRA—No Estate Tax*

		Net to Family		
Year	Age	Roth IRA	Traditional IRA + Outside Balance	Nondeductible IRA
2009	30	$ 5,000	$ 5,000	$ 5,000
2014	35	$ 38,578	$ 38,177	$ 36,176
2019	40	$ 92,656	$ 90,647	$ 82,112
2024	45	$ 179,749	$ 173,704	$ 151,819
2029	50	$ 320,012	$ 305,294	$ 259,809
2034	55	$ 545,909	$ 513,951	$ 429,454
2039	60	$ 909,717	$ 845,078	$ 693,396
2044	65	$1,490,634	$1,365,970	$1,091,080

Figure 5-1: *Net to Family Comparison*

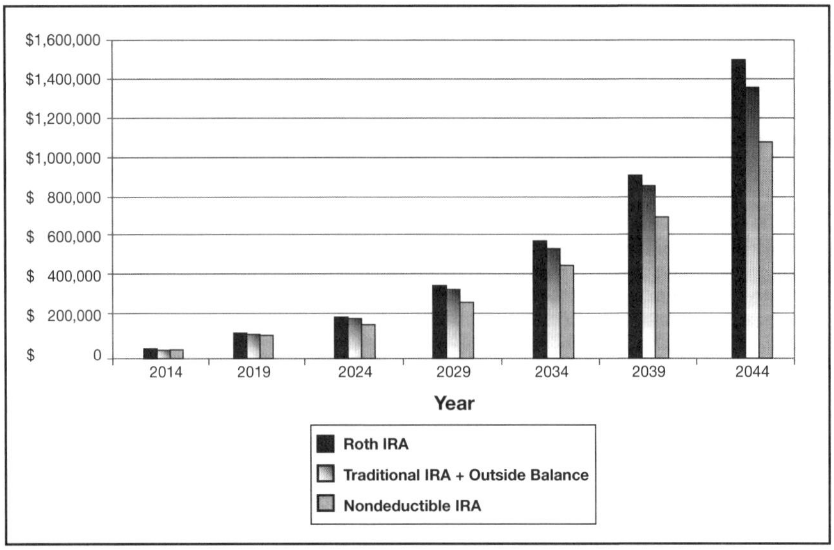

Example

Jordan has $100,000 in his IRA and asks you to compare (1) allowing his IRA to remain as a traditional IRA with (2) converting it to a Roth IRA. Table 5-2, "Basic Roth Conversion Analysis," shows the basic Roth conversion analysis, without taking into account the estate tax implications or the rules concerning required minimum distributions (RMDs) that apply at age 70½.

Table 5-2: *Basic Roth Conversion Analysis*

	Traditional IRA	Roth IRA
2009 value	$100,000	$100,000
Less tax at 28%	0	(28,000)
Subtotal	$100,000	$ 72,000
Growth over 20 years at 7%	$286,968	$206,617
Balance	$386,968	$278,617
Less tax at 28%	(108,351)	0
Net to family before taxes	$278,617	$278,617

Interestingly enough, these tables show that there is actually no value to using the government's money over the 20 year period. Mathematically, whether the asset basis is reduced by 28 percent at the front end (in the case of the Roth IRA) or later upon distributions, the result is the same. However, if the client and the planner provide foresight, they may be able to determine whether the taxpayer's retirement income is likely to be greater or smaller than his or her current income.

Example

A young CPA or lawyer would likely benefit more from funding a Roth IRA than a deductible IRA. The deductible IRA may provide an immediate tax benefit of 15 percent or 28 percent and then be subject to a much higher rate when withdrawn. This is shown in table 5-3, "Basic Roth Conversion Analysis."

Table 5-3: *Basic Roth Conversion Analysis*

	Traditional IRA	Roth IRA
2009 value	$100,000	$100,000
Less tax at 28%	0	(28,000)
Subtotal	$100,000	$ 72,000
Growth over 20 years at 7%	$286,968	$206,617
Balance	$386,968	$278,617
Less tax at 35%	(135,439)	0
Net to family before taxes	$251,529	$278,617

In this instance, the wealth transfer is decreased by $27,000 because of the increased tax rate. For those taxpayers who are currently in a 28 percent tax bracket but expect their tax brackets to increase substantially when RMDs start, the Roth IRA may be a feasible alternative. By recognizing income today, a smaller absolute amount of taxable income is recognized, minimizing "bracket creep." Additionally, the Roth IRA provides the advantage of no RMDs at age 70½ and, as discussed in this chapter, income from a Roth IRA will not affect taxation of the taxpayer's Social Security benefits.

Alternatively, a client in later years of employment may be in the high earning years, earning just below the threshold for the deductible IRAs. If the client anticipates that the retirement income needed from taxable investments will be substantially less than the income in the client's highest earning years, he or she should use the traditional IRA.

Example

Lenny is currently a middle manager with a large corporation. In 2009, he expects to earn approximately $48,000. During the next ten years, he expects to retire and anticipates needing an annual income (including Social Security benefits) of approximately $25,000. For Lenny, the deductible IRA would provide a greater tax benefit by providing an immediate deduction of 28 percent and (potentially) later be subject to tax at a much lower rate.

In analyzing the Roth IRA versus the traditional IRA, you must also take into account that when a taxpayer reaches age 70½, RMDs apply to the traditional IRA, whereas they are not required from the Roth IRA.[1] Because of this, once a taxpayer reaches age 70½, the Roth IRA begins to become the superior wealth-creation vehicle. Table 5-4, "Roth IRA Versus Traditional IRA Net to Family—No Estate Tax, Impact of Minimum Distribution," which compares the Roth with the traditional IRA on an after-income tax basis, shows the impact of wealth creation using a $500,000 traditional versus a $360,000 Roth IRA at age 70½.

1 See Internal Revenue Code (IRC) Section 408(d) for the tax treatment of distributions from a traditional individual retirement account (IRA). See IRC Section 408A(c)(5) for the tax treatment of the Roth IRA at age 70½.

Table 5-4: *Roth IRA Versus Traditional IRA Net to Family—No Estate Tax, Impact of Minimum Distribution*

Age	Year	Roth IRA*	Traditional IRA & Outside Balance†
70	2009	$ 396,000	$ 396,000
71	2010	$ 435,600	$ 435,403
72	2011	$ 479,160	$ 478,513
73	2012	$ 527,076	$ 525,658
74	2013	$ 579,784	$ 577,197
75	2014	$ 637,762	$ 633,514
76	2015	$ 701,538	$ 695,026
77	2016	$ 771,692	$ 762,185
78	2017	$ 848,861	$ 835,480
79	2018	$ 933,747	$ 915,438
80	2019	$1,027,122	$1,002,631
81	2020	$1,129,834	$1,097,674
82	2021	$1,242,818	$1,201,232
83	2022	$1,367,099	$1,314,022
84	2023	$1,503,809	$1,436,816
85	2024	$1,654,190	$1,570,447

*Assume a beginning balance of $360,000 with no RMDs and a 10 percent growth rate.
†Assume a $500,000 beginning balance with RMDs starting in 2001, a 10 percent growth rate, a 28 percent income tax rate on distributions, and a 15 percent tax rate on the outside account. The RMDs are taken on December 31 of each year.

Table 5-4 illustrates that the Roth IRA has increased to $1,654,190, whereas the funds from the traditional IRA have only grown to $1,570,447. This is because at age 70½ a taxpayer is required to begin taking distributions from his or her traditional IRA. Therefore, these distributions will be in a taxable environment (meaning, invested in bonds, stocks, or mutual funds). On the other hand, if the taxpayer does not need the funds for retirement, he or she can continue the tax-free deferral in the Roth IRA because there are no RMDs during the taxpayer's lifetime.

Taxpayers With Nondeductible IRAs

A number of clients may have made nondeductible IRA contributions.[2] In most instances, clients who have substantial basis in their IRAs may be wise to convert to a Roth IRA. By converting to the Roth IRA, all future growth of the IRA is not subject to income tax. If a nondeductible IRA is converted to a Roth IRA, income tax will only be paid on the fair market value in excess of basis.[3]

> **Example**
>
> Dave's only IRA is valued at $42,000, and it has a basis of $22,000. If this IRA were converted to a Roth IRA, $20,000 ($42,000 – $22,000) of income would be recognized.

Even if Dave were in a 28 percent tax bracket, the effective rate on this conversion will only be 13 percent[4] because of his basis in the IRA. Again, to the extent that the account grows in the future, 100 percent of the distributions will be tax free, and at age 70½, the RMD rules will not be imposed. If Dave has other IRAs, it is not clear whether the amount of income subject to tax is determined on an IRA-by-IRA basis or on an aggregate basis.

The Intricacies of Analyzing the Conversion, Revisited

To understand whether a client should convert his or her existing IRA to a Roth IRA, you should begin by examining the situation of a client who is currently in the 28 percent tax bracket.

2 See IRC Section 408(o) for general discussion of nondeductible IRA contributions.
3 See IRC Section 408A(c)(3)(D).
4 Total tax liability of $5,600 divided by total value of $42,000 equals 13 percent.

Example

Laura currently has an IRA valued at $500,000. Her 2009 adjusted gross income is expected to be $85,000. She consults with you about whether to convert her existing IRA to a Roth IRA. Because of the scheduled increases in the unified credit, Laura says that she does not expect to incur an estate tax and wants your insight on this decision. She further indicates that she would like you to use a 28 percent income tax bracket for each year, ignoring the minimum distribution rules because she assumes she will be taking distributions from either IRA during the course of her retirement. Table 5-5, "A Traditional IRA Versus a Roth IRA—No Estate Tax or Required Minimum Distribution," compares the two IRAs.

Table 5-5: *A Traditional IRA Versus a Roth IRA—No Estate Tax or Required Minimum Distribution**

	Traditional IRA			Roth IRA		
Year	Ending IRA and Outside Fund Balance†	Taxes on IRA	Net to Family	Ending IRA and Outside Fund Balance	Taxes on IRA	Net to Family
Jan. 1, 2009	$ 750,000	($ 140,000)	$ 610,000	$ 750,000	($140,000)	$ 610,000
Dec. 31, 2009	$ 821,250	($ 154,000)	$ 667,250	$ 667,250	$ 0	$ 667,250
Dec. 31, 2014	$ 1,293,647	($ 248,019)	$ 1,045,629	$ 1,045,629	$ 0	$ 1,045,629
Dec. 31, 2019	$ 2,039,850	($ 399,436)	$ 1,640,414	$ 1,640,414	$ 0	$ 1,640,414
Dec. 31, 2024	$ 3,219,667	($ 643,296)	$ 2,576,371	$ 2,576,371	$ 0	$ 2,576,371
Dec. 31, 2029	$ 5,086,767	($1,036,035)	$ 4,050,732	$ 4,050,732	$ 0	$ 4,050,732
Dec. 31, 2034	$ 8,044,123	($1,668,545)	$ 6,375,578	$ 6,375,578	$ 0	$ 6,375,578
Dec. 31, 2039	$12,732,347	($2,687,208)	$10,045,139	$10,045,139	$ 0	$10,045,139

*This assumes the Roth IRA election is made on January 1, 2009, and the entire tax liability for that year is withdrawn from the Roth IRA. It also assumes growth of 10 percent; income tax of 28 percent, capital gains rates of 15 percent, a 100 percent turnover of outside investments, and that there is no estate tax.

†Assumes a 2008 ending IRA balance of $500,000 and an outside balance of $250,000.

Example

Because she is an engineer, Laura asks you to return to the first example, except she would like you to illustrate the tax being paid from outside funds. This is in addition to Laura's IRA balance. Table 5-6, "Traditional Versus Roth IRA—No Estate Tax or Required Minimum Distributions (Use of Outside Funds)," illustrates this situation.

Table 5-6: *Traditional Versus Roth IRA—No Estate Tax or Required Minimum Distributions (Use of Outside Funds)**

	Traditional IRA			Roth IRA		
Year	Ending IRA and Outside Fund Balance†	Taxes on IRA	Net to Family	Ending IRA and Outside Fund Balance	Taxes on IRA	Net to Family
Jan. 1, 2009	$ 750,000	($ 140,000)	$ 610,000	$ 750,000	($140,000)	$ 610,000
Dec. 31, 2009	$ 821,250	($ 154,000)	$ 667,250	$ 669,350	$ 0	$ 669,350
Dec. 31, 2014	$ 1,293,647	($ 248,019)	$ 1,045,629	$ 1,065,242	$ 0	$ 1,065,242
Dec. 31, 2019	$ 2,039,850	($ 399,436)	$ 1,640,414	$ 1,696,407	$ 0	$ 1,696,407
Dec. 31, 2024	$ 3,219,667	($ 643,296)	$ 2,576,371	$ 2,703,246	$ 0	$ 2,703,246
Dec. 31, 2029	$ 5,086,767	($1,036,035)	$ 4,050,732	$ 4,310,248	$ 0	$ 4,310,248
Dec. 31, 2034	$ 8,044,123	($1,668,545)	$ 6,375,578	$ 6,876,503	$ 0	$ 6,876,503
Dec. 31, 2039	$12,732,347	($2,687,208)	$10,045,139	$10,976,649	$ 0	$10,976,649

*This assumes the Roth IRA election is made on January 1, 2009, and the entire tax liability for that year is withdrawn from the outside account. It also assumes growth of 10 percent, income tax of 28 percent, capital gains rates of 15 percent, a 100 percent turnover of outside investments, and that there are no required minimum distribution or estate taxes incorporated in this example.

†Assumes a 2008 ending IRA balance of $500,000 and an outside balance of $250,000.

Example

Assume the preceding example, except that Laura has asked you to determine the impact of the RMD rules on your analysis. Table 5-7, "Traditional IRA Versus Roth IRA—No Estate Tax, Income Tax Paid With Outside Funds," illustrates this example.

Example *(continued)*

Table 5-7: *Traditional IRA Versus Roth IRA—No Estate Tax, Income Tax Paid With Outside Funds**

	Traditional IRA			Roth IRA		
Year	Ending IRA and Outside Fund Balance	Taxes on IRA	Net to Family	Ending IRA and Outside Fund Balance	Taxes on IRA	Net to Family
Jan. 1, 2009	$ 750,000	($140,000)	$ 610,000	$ 750,000	($140,000)	$ 610,000
Dec. 31, 2009	$ 821,250	($154,000)	$ 667,250	$ 669,350	$ 0	$ 669,350
Dec. 31, 2014	$ 1,293,647	($248,019)	$1,045,629	$ 1,065,242	$ 0	$ 1,065,242
Dec. 31, 2019	$ 2,029,494	($386,184)	$1,643,629	$ 1,696,407	$ 0	$ 1,696,407
Dec. 31, 2024	$ 3,107,730	($515,350)	$2,592,380	$ 2,703,246	$ 0	$ 2,703,246
Dec. 31, 2029	$ 4,723,843	($659,825)	$4,064,018	$ 4,310,248	$ 0	$ 4,310,248
Dec. 31, 2034	$ 7,126,939	($796,759)	$6,330,181	$ 6,876,503	$ 0	$ 6,876,503
Dec. 31, 2039	$10,677,754	($883,635)	$9,794,119	$10,976,649	$ 0	$10,976,649

*This assumes the Roth IRA election is made on January 1, 2009, and the entire tax liability for that year is withdrawn from the outside account. It also assumes growth of 10 percent, income tax of 28 percent, capital gains rates of 15 percent, a 100 percent turnover of outside investments, and that there is no estate tax incorporated in this example. However, it is important to know that the impact of required minimum distributions has been included.

Moreover, the following computation shows the total advantage of the Roth IRA over 30 years.

Initial advantage based on conversion, no tax rate differential	$ 0
Advantage attributable to deferral of distributions at age 70	251,020
Advantage attributable to paying funds from outside of the IRA	931,510
Total advantage of Roth IRA over 30 years	$1,182,530

When a client does not expect to be subject to estate tax, the analysis of whether to convert from a traditional IRA to a Roth IRA is based on the following factors:

- Any changes in marginal income tax rates
- Whether taxes generated by the conversion can be funded from a source outside of the traditional IRA
- The benefit of avoiding RMD rules applicable at age 70½
- The impact on the taxation of Social Security benefits
- The growth during the recharacterization period

Another consideration is the investment portfolio design the taxpayer is using. See chapter 3, "Portfolio Management Considerations," for a detailed discussion of portfolio considerations.

Taxation of Social Security Benefits

Many taxpayers need to take into account how the Roth IRA conversion election affects the taxation of their Social Security benefits. See chapter 7, "Client Considerations," for an explanation of the impact of an IRA conversion on the taxation of Social Security benefits.

The Impact of Future Estate Tax on the Conversion Decision

Example

John has a $3 million stock portfolio in addition to his $2.5 million IRA. Assume that at the time of his death, his IRA will be exposed to a 45 percent estate tax.

In John's case, his wealth transfer is enhanced by paying the income tax before paying the estate tax. See table 5-8, "IRC Section 691(c) Deduction Compared to Paying Income Tax." This occurs because the IRC Section 691(c) income in respect of a decedent deduction allows only for the deduction of federal estate tax. (The state estate tax is not deductible in determining federal taxable income.)

Table 5-8: *IRC Section 691(c) Deduction Compared to Paying Income Tax*

	Estate Tax First Traditional IRA	Income Tax First Roth IRA
IRA balance	$ 2,500,000	$ 2,500,000
Less federal and state income tax at 40%	0	(1,000,000)
Less federal estate tax at 45%	(1,125,000)	(675,000)
Less state estate tax at 10%	(250,000)	(150,000)
Total taxes	(1,375,000)	(1,825,000)
Net to family	$ 1,125,000	$ 675,000
IRA balance subject to income tax	$ 2,500,000	
Less IRC Section 691(c) deduction	(1,125,000)	
Balance subject to income tax	1,375,000	
Less federal and state income tax at 40%	(550,000)	
Net to family	$ 575,000	$ 675,000

The IRC Section 691(c) income tax deduction for estate tax paid is not subject to the two percent adjustment to itemized deductions.[5]

Conclusion

Roth conversion planning is complex and CPAs must determine which clients should convert and which clients should maintain their traditional IRA. The factors that support some level of conversion generally outweigh the factors that favor no conversion. While complex, an understanding of the mathematical principles discussed above will allow advisors to illustrate the power of tax-free deferral to their clients and their client's families.

5 IRC Section 67(b)(7).

Tax Planning Strategy

Introduction

Often, clients do not seek tax advice until an error has already occurred. This chapter outlines some of the relief available to taxpayers who find themselves facing unfavorable tax consequences regarding their traditional or Roth individual retirement account (IRA).

In addition, this chapter will address a number of asset protection issues involving IRAs. In light of today's increasingly litigious society, asset protection planning has recently come to the forefront as an important issue. While families and individuals can choose from an array of strategies ranging from sophisticated to the more fundamental, an individual should seek the counsel of an asset protection attorney to tailor their asset protection plan to their unique situation.

Practice and Procedure

Excess Accumulation Excise Tax Waiver

Although distributions from a Roth IRA are not required during an owner's lifetime, beneficiaries of a Roth IRA are required to begin annual distributions.[1] The failure to take annual required minimum distributions (RMDs) results in an excise tax imposed equal to 50 percent of the RMD not distributed for the applicable year.[2] The excise tax may be waived, however, if the individual establishes to the satisfaction of the Secretary that the shortfall in the amount distributed was due to reasonable error and that reasonable steps are being taken

1 Exceptions apply to spouse beneficiaries.
2 Internal Revenue Code (IRC) Section 4974(a).

to remedy the shortfall.[3] To request a waiver, the taxpayer should complete a Form 5329 for each applicable year and attach a letter requesting a waiver explaining the reasonable error and showing that reasonable steps are being taken to remedy the shortfall.

Sixty Day Rollover Waiver

Amounts distributed from an IRA are included in income unless they are transferred to an eligible retirement plan no later than the sixtieth day following the day of receipt of the distribution.[4] Internal Revenue Code (IRC) Section 408(d)(3)(I), however, was added for distributions beginning in 2002 as a means to provide relief for some taxpayers who missed this 60 day rollover deadline. Under this IRC section, the Secretary may waive the 60 day requirement.

Revenue Procedure 2003-16[5] provides guidance on applying to the IRS for a waiver of the 60 day rollover requirement. A taxpayer must apply for a hardship exception to the 60 day rollover requirement using the same procedure as that outlined in Revenue Procedure 2009-4 for letter rulings, accompanied by the user fee set forth in Revenue Procedure 2009-8.

The IRS will issue a ruling waiving the 60 day rollover requirement in cases in which the failure to waive such requirement would be against equity or good conscience, including casualty, disaster, or other events beyond the reasonable control of the taxpayer. In determining whether to grant a waiver, the IRS will consider all relevant facts and circumstances, including

1. errors committed by a financial institution;
2. inability to complete a rollover due to death, disability, hospitalization, incarceration, restrictions imposed by a foreign country or postal error;
3. the use of the amount distributed (for example, in the case of payment by check, whether the check was cashed); and
4. the time elapsed since the distribution occurred.

No application to the IRS is required if (1) a financial institution receives funds on behalf of a taxpayer prior to the expiration of the 60 day rollover period, (2) the taxpayer follows all procedures required by the financial institution for depositing the funds into an eligible retirement plan within the 60 day period (including giving instructions to deposit the funds into an eligible retirement plan), and (3) the funds are not deposited into an eligible retirement plan within the 60 day rollover period solely due to an error on the part of the financial institution. Automatic approval is granted only

1. if the funds are deposited into an eligible retirement plan within one year from the beginning of the 60 day rollover period and
2. if it would have been a valid rollover had the financial institution deposited the funds as instructed.

---

3 IRC Section 4974(d).
4 IRC Section 408(d)(3).
5 Revenue Procedure 2003-16, 2003-1 CB 359.

The IRS has previously been relatively lenient in granting waivers of the 60 day rollover period. See Private Letter Rulings (PLRs) 200406050, 200405013, 200610030, and 200616044. However, recently the IRS has narrowed their position by only granting relief if the taxpayer's fact pattern falls squarely under one of the examples listed in Revenue Procedure 2003-16 (that is, errors committed by a financial institution, death, disability, hospitalization, incarceration, restrictions imposed by a foreign country, or postal error). See PLRs 200738027, 200736036, and 200730023.

Late Roth Recharacterization

Except as otherwise provided by the Secretary, a taxpayer may elect to recharacterize an IRA contribution made to a type of IRA as having been made to another type of IRA by making a trustee-to-trustee transfer of the IRA contribution, plus earnings, to the other type of IRA.[6] In such a recharacterization, the IRA contribution is treated as having been made to the transferee IRA and not the transferor IRA. A recharacterization election generally must occur on or before the date prescribed by law, including extensions, for filing the taxpayer's federal income tax return for the year of contribution (October 15 of the year following the year of the Roth conversion).[7]

If a taxpayer misses the deadline for recharacterizing a Roth IRA back to a traditional IRA, permission for a late recharacterization can be requested through the private letter ruling process. Treasury Regulation Section 301.9100-2(b) generally provides for an automatic extension of six months from the due date of a return, excluding extensions, to make elections that otherwise must be made by the due date of the return or the due date of the return plus extensions, provided

1. the taxpayer's return was timely filed for the year the election should have been made and
2. the taxpayer takes appropriate corrective action within this six month period.

Treasury Regulation Section 301.9100-3 permits the IRS to grant an extension of time to make a regulatory election, when such extension does not meet the requirements of Treasury Regulation Section 301.9100-2. The IRS ruled that a recharacterization constitutes a regulatory election.[8] An application for relief will be granted when the taxpayer provides sufficient evidence to establish that (1) the taxpayer acted reasonably and in good faith and (2) granting relief would not prejudice the interests of the government.

A taxpayer will be deemed to have acted reasonably and in good faith if

1. its request for relief is filed before the failure to make a timely election is discovered by the IRS;
2. the taxpayer inadvertently failed to make the election because of intervening events beyond the taxpayer's control;

---

6 IRC Section 408A(d)(6) and Treasury Regulation Section 1.408A-5. A full copy of the 1999 final rules and regulations from the Department of the Treasury, including Treasury Regulation Section 1.408A-5, can be found on the accompanying CD-ROM.

7 *Ibid.*

8 Announcement 99-57, 1999-24 Internal Revenue Bulletin 50.

3. the taxpayer failed to make the election because, after exercising reasonable diligence, the taxpayer was unaware of the necessity for the election;
4. the taxpayer reasonably relied upon the written advice of the IRS; or
5. the taxpayer reasonably relied on a qualified tax professional, including a tax professional employed by the taxpayer, and the tax professional failed to make, or advise the taxpayer to make, the election.

Ordinarily, the IRS will not grant relief when tax years that would have been affected by the election had it been timely made are closed by the statute of limitations before the taxpayer's receipt of a ruling granting relief under this section. For examples of when the IRS has granted an extension to recharacterize, see PLRs 200925045, 200924062, and 200921036.

Private Letter Ruling Requests

A private letter ruling request is a written submission to the IRS asking for a ruling regarding a specific tax matter. For example, a taxpayer may ask the IRS for permission to take RMDs from an inherited IRA over the life expectancy of a trust beneficiary. A letter ruling interprets the tax laws and applies them to the taxpayer's specific set of facts.

The IRS ordinarily does not issue a letter ruling for the following situations:

1. Matters involving an issue under examination or consideration or litigation.
2. Issues that are only part of an integrated transaction.
3. Certain areas because of the factual nature of the problem involved or for other reasons. Revenue Procedure 2009-3[9] and Revenue Procedure 2009-7[10] provide a list of these areas.
4. Regarding which of two entities under common law rules applicable in determining the employer-employee relationship is the employer, when one entity is treating the worker as an employee.[11]
5. To business, trade, or industrial associations or to similar groups concerning the application of the tax laws to members of the group.
6. Regarding the tax consequences of a transaction for taxpayers who are not directly involved in the request if the requested letter ruling or determination letter would not address the tax status, liability, or reporting obligations of the requester.
7. To foreign governments or their political subdivisions about the U.S. tax effects of their laws.
8. On the effect of a tax treaty on the tax laws of a treaty country for purposes of determining the tax of the treaty country.
9. On a matter involving the federal tax consequences of any proposed federal, state, local, municipal, or foreign legislation.
10. If the request presents an issue that cannot be readily resolved before a regulation or any other published guidance is issued.

---

9 2009-1 Internal Revenue Bulletin (IRB) 107.
10 2009-1 IRB 226.
11 Section 4.01(52) of Revenue Procedure 2001-3, 2001-1 IRB 111.

11. On frivolous issues. A *frivolous issue* is one without basis in fact or law or one that asserts a position that courts have held frivolous or groundless.
12. With respect to an issue that is clearly and adequately addressed by statute, regulations, decisions of a court, revenue rulings, revenue procedures, notices, or other authority published in the Internal Revenue Bulletin.
13. On alternative plans of proposed transactions or on hypothetical situations.
14. On the replacement of involuntarily converted property, whether or not the property has been replaced, if the taxpayer has already filed a return for the taxable year in which the property was converted.

The procedure for obtaining a private letter ruling is outlined in the first revenue procedure of each year.[12] Among other requirements, each request for a letter ruling must contain the following:

1. Names, addresses, telephone numbers, and taxpayer identification numbers of all interested parties
2. The annual accounting period and the overall method of accounting for maintaining the accounting books and filing the federal income tax return of all interested parties
3. A description of the taxpayer's business operations
4. A complete statement of the business reasons for the transaction
5. A detailed description of the transaction
6. An analysis of facts and their bearing on the issue or issues (if documents attached to a request contain material facts, they must be included in the taxpayer's analysis of facts in the request rather than merely incorporated by reference)
7. If the taxpayer advocates a particular conclusion, the taxpayer must include an explanation of the grounds for that conclusion and the relevant authorities to support it
8. A deletions statement indicating the information to be deleted when the ruling is open to public inspection
9. A penalties of perjury statement
10. A checklist, which can be found in Revenue Procedure 2009-1

Generally, it takes over six months to get a response back from the IRS on a ruling request. Depending on the issues involved and the caseload of the IRS attorney, it can take well over a year to obtain a ruling. A taxpayer can, however, ask for expedited handling. Although expedited handling is granted only in rare and unusual cases, expedited handling may be available for those taxpayers with a compelling need to have a request processed ahead of those requests received before it.

Currently, the IRS submission fees for a ruling request are as follows (Revenue Procedure 2009-8 is the fee schedule that should be used for ruling requests involving IRA matters):

12 See Revenue Procedure 2009-1, 2009-1 IRB 1.

Revenue Procedure 2009-1

Reduced User Fee for Taxpayers with Income Below $250,000	$ 625
Substantially Identical Letter Rulings	$ 1,200
Standard Letter Ruling Request	$11,500

Revenue Procedure 2009-8

Reduced User Fee for Taxpayers with Income Below $250,000	Not Available
Substantially Identical Letter Rulings	Not Available
Standard Letter Ruling Request	$9,000

60 Day Rollover Waivers

Waivers of 60 Day Rollover Period—Rollover less than $50,000	$ 500
Waivers of 60 Day Rollover Period—Rollover equal to or greater than $50,000 but less than $100,000	$1,500
Waivers of 60 Day Rollover Period—Rollover equal to or greater than $100,000	$3,000

Asset Protection

From a pure asset protection perspective, the exclusion of qualified plan assets from the bankruptcy estate under The Employee Retirement Income Security Act of 1974 (ERISA) generally makes it more attractive to retain funds in a qualified plan instead of converting the funds to a Roth IRA. This is true because the federal exclusion afforded ERISA plans (qualified plan assets) provides stronger protection than the exemption protection afforded IRA assets under the Bankruptcy Abuse Prevention and Consumer Protection Act of 2005 (BAPCPA). Further, in nonbankruptcy situations, asset protection for IRA assets is based on uncertain and diverse state asset protection statutes, thus strengthening the proposition that leaving assets in a qualified plan provides superior asset protection. The complexity of this area requires the assistance of bankruptcy counsel to walk your client through this statutory labyrinth.

The following section provides a summary of the basic asset protection principles regarding qualified plans and IRA assets in bankruptcy and nonbankruptcy situations.

The Basics of Asset Protection in Bankruptcy: Exclusion Versus Exemption

Debtors that have filed for bankruptcy generally have two means through which to protect their retirement plan assets from attachment by creditors. The debtor can either seek to claim an exclusion from the bankruptcy estate for their retirement assets or an exemption from the bankruptcy estate.

The most favorable treatment an asset can achieve is exclusion from the bankruptcy estate. This is because retirement assets qualifying for exclusion are never brought into the bankruptcy estate and are therefore never subject to the claims of creditors. Although less favorable, an exemption from the bankruptcy estate may also provide creditor protection for assets in bankruptcy. Assets that are ineligible for exclusion are included in the bankruptcy estate but may nonetheless find protection from creditor's claims through an exemption. At the end of this chapter, appendix A: "IRA Creditor Protection Against Claims of Parents' Creditors and Beneficiary's Creditors" illustrates the potential claims possibilities for both parents and different beneficiaries against creditors.

Analysis of the Federal Laws Providing Creditor Protection for Qualified Plans in Bankruptcy Situations

The two main bodies of federal law providing protection for retirement plan assets are ERISA[13] and BAPCPA.[14]

ERISA is the primary federal law under which retirement plan assets receive exclusion from the federal bankruptcy estate. ERISA provides virtually impenetrable protection for assets within covered employer retirement plans by excluding the plan assets from the debtor's bankruptcy estate. However, ERISA protection is not all encompassing. A retirement plan must fall under the scope of ERISA regulation in order to be afforded its protection.

The covered employee retirement plans that are afforded ERISA protection include 401(k) and 403(b) plans, defined benefit plans, money-purchase plans, and profit-sharing plans.[15] Most noticeably absent from this list are traditional IRAs and Roth IRAs. These retirement plans are not covered by ERISA and are therefore not excluded from the debtor's bankruptcy estate. However, these retirement plan assets are currently afforded protection in the form of an exemption under BAPCPA.

BAPCPA is the second body of federal law that confers protection upon retirement plan assets in bankruptcy proceeding. Under BAPCPA, protection in the form of a specific exemption is now provided for "retirement assets to the extent that those funds are in a fund or account that is exempt from taxation under section 401,[16] 403,[17] 408,[18] 408A,[19] 414,[20] 457,[21] or 501(a)[22] of the Internal Revenue Code of 1986."[23] Therefore, even though ERISA still provides protection for the covered retirement assets, the all-encompassing provision of

13 The Employee Retirement Income Security Act of 1974 (ERISA), Section 4.

14 The Bankruptcy Abuse Prevention and Consumer Protection Act of 2005 (BAPCPA) (P.L. 109-8). Signed into law on April 20, 2005.

15 Note that plans covering only the owner and the owner's spouse are not afforded protection under ERISA.

16 Qualified pension, profit-sharing, and stock bonus plans.

17 Employee annuities.

18 IRAs.

19 Roth IRAs.

20 Multiemployer annuities.

21 Deferred compensation plans of state and local governments and tax-exempt organizations.

22 Tax-exempt organizations.

23 BAPCPA Section 224 of P.L. 109-8, *supra* note 2.

BAPCPA now generally controls the issue of creditor protection for both ERISA and non-ERISA (IRA and Roth IRA) retirement plans.

Protection Afforded IRAs in Bankruptcy Situations

Through BAPCPA, creditor protection is now afforded to all IRA accounts regardless of state bankruptcy laws. Currently, unlimited exemption protection is provided for rollover IRAs, and a contributory IRA (traditional IRA or a Roth IRA) is afforded limited protection in the form of a $1,000,000 exemption. To the extent a contributory traditional or Roth IRA exceeds the $1,000,000 limitation, excluding funds from qualified plan rollovers,[24] the amounts above the $1,000,000 cap will not receive exclusion and will be subject to creditor claims in bankruptcy.

Therefore, due to the $1,000,000 limitation placed on contributory IRA protection, qualified plan accounts should not be rolled over into, or otherwise commingled with, an existing contributory IRA. Instead, the assets should be rolled into a new IRA set up specifically for the purpose of receiving the rolled over funds.

Protection of Retirement Assets in Nonbankruptcy Situations

ERISA protection generally applies consistently between bankruptcy and nonbankruptcy situations. However, protection afforded non-ERISA retirement plan assets (IRA assets) in nonbankruptcy situations is heavily dependent on state law. This is because BAPCPA generally only applies to debtors who have filed for bankruptcy. Therefore, investors in nonbankruptcy situations will need to consult state asset protection laws for protection of their IRA assets.

In light of asset protection considerations, the professional must be very conscientious when analyzing the scenario of rolling over retirement plan funds from a qualified plan into a Roth IRA. The decision does not hinge purely on tax or financial planning considerations; it hinges on legal implications involving the creditor protection afforded the transferred assets. Therefore, the professional will want to encourage his or her clients to seek the counsel of qualified bankruptcy or creditor protection attorneys to ascertain whether a rollover from a qualified plan into a Roth IRA is appropriate.

Roth Conversion Segregation Strategy

When you convert a traditional IRA to a Roth IRA, you may always eliminate the entire tax liability associated with the Roth IRA conversion by recharacterizing the entire Roth IRA back to a traditional IRA by October 15 of the year following the year of the conversion. However, one cannot recharacterize a portion of the Roth IRA by singling-out only those stocks that decline in value due to the "anti-cherry-picking" rules.[25] The anti-cherry-picking rules were specifically designed to prevent an individual who performed a Roth IRA conversion from thereafter recharacterizing only those stocks that declined in value.

24 Rollover contributions under IRC Sections 402(c), 402(e)(6), 403(a)(4), 403(a)(5), and 403(b)(8).
25 IRS Notice 2000-39.

The effect of the rules is to prorate all gains and losses to the entire Roth IRA, regardless of the actual stock or fund recharacterized.

Example

On January 2, 2009, when Nick's traditional IRA was worth $1,000,000, he converted the entire amount to a Roth IRA. Nick will owe ordinary income tax on the entire $1,000,000. The IRA consisted of 50 percent ABC Fund ($500,000) and 50 percent XYZ Fund ($500,000). As of April 15, 2010, the ABC Fund had declined in value to $350,000, and the XYZ Fund had increased in value to $550,000. Thus, the total value of the IRA account declined in value to $900,000. Nick would like to recharacterize all of his ABC Fund back to a traditional IRA. Changes to Nick's IRA are summarized in the following table.

	Initial Value on Date of Conversion	Value on Date of Recharacterization	Relative Percentages of overall Roth IRA on Date of Recharacterization	Increase or Decrease in Value
ABC Fund	$ 500,000	$350,000	38.89%	$(150,000)
XYZ Fund	$ 500,000	$550,000	61.11%	$ 50,000
Total	$1,000,000	$900,000	100.00%	$(100,000)

Without the anti-cherry-picking rules, Nick could reconvert only those assets that dropped in value (ABC Fund) and eliminate $500,000 of taxable income. However, the anti-cherry-picking rules require that the gains and losses of the entire Roth IRA be applied on a pro-rata basis for income tax purposes. Thus, the application of the anti-cherry-picking rules to Nick's situation is summarized as follows:

1. Calculate the value of the ABC Fund as a percentage of the total value of the IRA as of the recharacterization date. In the example above, this amounts to 38.89 percent ($350,000/$900,000).
2. Multiply the percentage (38.89 percent), as determined in the first step, by the entire Roth IRA conversion value ($1,000,000) at the time of conversion. This amounts to $388,900.
3. The difference between the recomputed recharacterized amount ($388,900) and the initial Roth IRA conversion value ($1,000,000) will be recognized as taxable income ($611,100) on Nick's 2009 income tax return.

Based on the recalculation, Nick will have to recognize an additional $111,100 ($611,100–$500,000) of taxable income as a result of the anti-cherry-picking rules.

Although the anti-cherry-picking rules can be quite harsh, these rules can generally be avoided by employing the Roth Segregation Conversion Strategy. When employing the Roth Segregation Conversion Strategy, it is best to separate the investments within your single traditional IRA into several smaller traditional IRAs prior to executing a Roth IRA conversion. In a typical situation, a separate IRA is created for a particular type of investment (for example, corporate bonds, international stocks, "blue-chip" stocks, government securities, and mutual funds). Returns for different stocks, bonds, mutual funds, or market sectors could vary significantly. Some investments may decrease in value and others increase. Thus, if the investment performance of a particular Roth IRA is poor, you may recharacterize this particular Roth IRA back to a traditional IRA to eliminate the taxable income associated with that conversion and allow the other Roth IRAs to remain unchanged. The primary objective of this strategy is to put different types of investments in separate traditional IRAs, convert each traditional IRA to a Roth IRA, and thereafter recharacterize only those Roth IRAs that underperformed.

Example

Assume the preceding example, but instead of creating a single Roth IRA, Nick decides to create separate Roth IRAs, one with the ABC Fund and a second IRA with the XYZ Fund. In this case, Nick would recharacterize the first Roth IRA containing the ABC Fund. Because Nick recharacterized the entire Roth IRA, he will owe no income tax on the IRA containing the ABC Fund. Rather, Nick will only recognize ordinary income on the IRA containing the XYZ Fund ($500,000).

The Roth Segregation Conversion Strategy can be shown pictorially as follows:

STEP 1: Identify separate holdings and convert separate holdings to Roth IRAs.

January 2, 2009

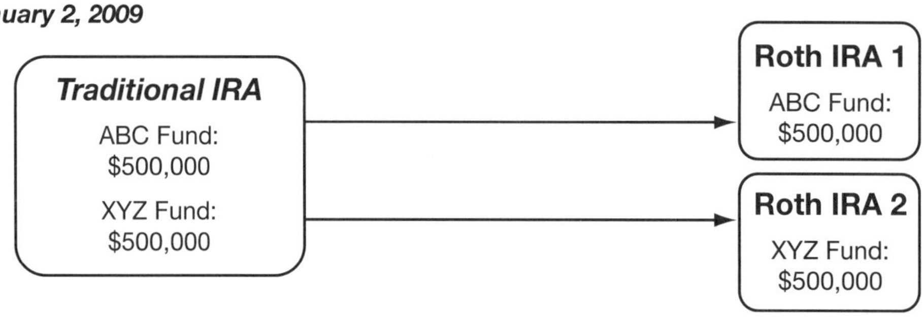

STEP 2: Pay tax on Roth IRA conversion.

April 15, 2010

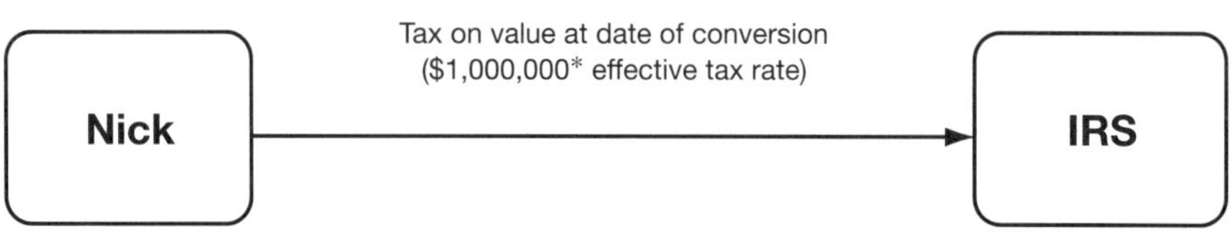

*This amount reflects a change in market value. However, for purposes of determining the tax liability due, the original conversion value of $500,000 would be used to reduce the reportable taxable income.

STEP 3: Recharacterize specific Roth IRA.

September 15, 2010

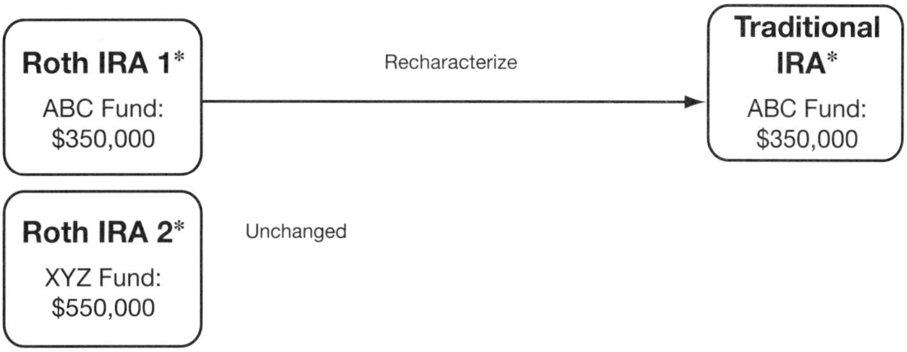

*These amounts reflect a change in market value. However, for purposes of determining the tax liability due, the original conversion value of $500,000 would be used to reduce the reportable taxable income.

STEP 4: File amended return for taxes paid on Roth IRA conversion.

October 15, 2010

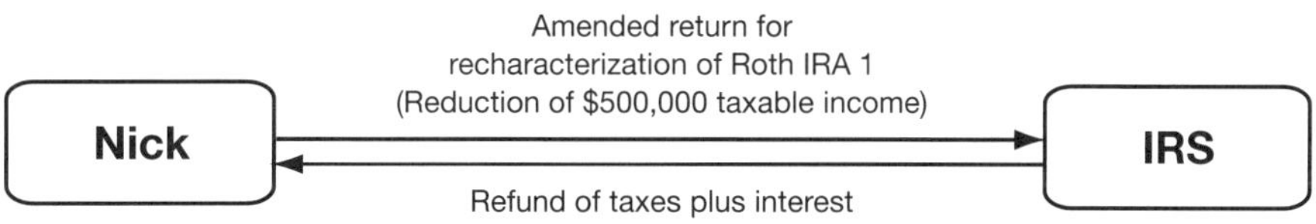

The following table shows the tax savings achieved by employing the Roth Segregation Conversion Strategy.

	Example 1	Example 2	Difference
Value on Date of Conversion	$100,000,000	$1,000,000	$ –
Value of Roth IRA after recharacterization	$ 550,000	$ 550,000	$ –
Value of Traditional IRA after recharacterization	$ 350,000	$ 350,000	$ –
Ordinary Income Recognized	$ 611,100	$ 500,000	$(111,100)
Ordinary Income Tax at 35%	$ 213,885	$ 175,000	$ (38,885)

By segregating the IRA into two separate Roth IRAs, Nick has saved over $38,000 in tax.

As you can see, by using this strategy you can lock in the potential for future growth and simultaneously hedge against market sector fluctuation. In many cases, this strategy poses little downside risk and tremendous upside potential.

Roth Conversion Timetable

The time requirements for making Roth IRA conversions and recharacterizations are explained in the following chart.

January 1, 2009	First date by which a 2009 Roth IRA conversion may take place.
December 31, 2009	Last date by which a 2009 Roth IRA conversion may take place.
April 15, 2010	Roth IRA conversion taxes must be paid for 2009 conversions.
October 15, 2010	Recharacterizations of 2009 Roth IRA conversions must take place no later than this date.

Given this timetable, a taxpayer is able to effectively make a conversion early in the year, wait to determine what effect the market may have on the Roth IRA, and thereafter make a final decision more than nine months after the year in which the conversion took place. If a taxpayer executes a Roth IRA conversion and the value of the IRA assets declines in value, the taxpayer can "undo" (recharacterize) the Roth IRA conversion. Thus, if set up properly, the taxpayer is afforded the opportunity to make a well-informed decision based on the benefit of hindsight.

Conclusion

An understanding of the topics covered in this chapter can give a practitioner a leg up on the competition when it comes to advising clients on Roth conversions or assisting them after unfortunate mistakes have been made.

Appendix A
IRA Creditor Protection Against Claims of Parent's Creditors and Beneficiary's Creditors

	Parent's Exempt IRA → Child	Parent's Exempt IRA → Estate‡	Parent's Exempt IRA → Typical Revocable Trust	Parent's Exempt IRA → Stand Alone Revocable IRA Trust	Parent's Exempt IRA → Subtrusts Under Stand Alone Trust	Parent's Exempt IRA → Irrevocable Trust
Subject to claims of beneficiary's creditors	YES	YES	NO	NO	NO	NO
Subject to claims of parent's creditors	NO	YES	YES*	YES*	Possibly NO†	NO

* Depends upon state law, however, see *Commerce Bank v. Bolander*, 2007 WL 1041760 (Kan. App. 2007) unpublished.

† By naming a Subtrust that is irrevocable you may avid the reach of the Commerce Bank Doctrine.

‡ If the estate is the beneficiary and an outright distribution follows, then the IRA is subject to the claims of both sets of creditors.

Client Considerations

Introduction

Every client situation is, of course, different and requires an analysis of the specific facts to determine the best course of action for that particular client. This chapter will address taxpayers at varying points in their lives and the unique planning opportunities at each stage.

The Roth IRA and the Younger Taxpayer

Younger clients may ask, "Why should I contribute to a Roth IRA?" The Roth individual retirement account (IRA) is superior to the traditional IRA in the following two respects:

1. Once contributed, 100 percent of the growth on the Roth IRA is tax free.
2. It is easier to access funds in a Roth IRA before age 59½ than a regular IRA.

Internal Revenue Code (IRC) Section 408A(d)(l)(B) provides that distributions from a Roth IRA are first treated as made from contributions. Because distributed contributions are a nontaxable return of principal, they are not subject to either income tax or the excise tax imposed under IRC Section 72(t).

Why Would a Younger Taxpayer Contribute to a Roth IRA?

Although contributions are not deductible, the Roth IRA allows a taxpayer to maximize his or her distribution stretch because distributions are not required at age 70½. This feature is further enhanced because there is no prohibition on making contributions after attaining age 70½.

Additionally, qualified distributions from the IRA are not taxable, and earnings on the account are taxable only when nonqualified distributions are made. These features maximize a taxpayer's ability to achieve the deferral of tax and accumulate significant retirement wealth on a tax-free basis for the benefit of future generations.

Income Limitations on Contributions

Annual contribution limitations to Roth IRAs were increased under the Economic Growth and Reconciliation Act of 2001 (the act). The act is reproduced as appendix 4 "Economic Growth and Tax Relief Reconciliation Act of 2001: Text" at the end of this book. For years 2002–2004, the deductible limit was $3,000; for years 2005–2007, the limit was $4,000; and for years 2008 and beyond, the limit is $5,000. For tax years beginning after 2008, the $5,000 contribution limit is adjusted to reflect cost-of-living increases.

Contributions are reduced by any other traditional IRA contributions (except for educational IRA contributions). The contribution limit is phased out as the taxpayer's adjusted gross income (AGI) increases from $166,000 to $176,000[1] for joint filers and $105,000 to $120,000[2] for a single taxpayer in 2009.

Individuals who are 50 years or older before the end of the tax year are allowed a catch-up contribution amount. For years 2002–2005, this amount was $500, and for years 2006 and beyond, the amount is $1,000. The additional amount is added to the regular deductible limit to make limits for those 50 and older as follows in table 7-1, "Catch-Up Contribution Amounts."

Table 7-1: *Catch-Up Contribution Amounts*

Taxable Years	Deductible Amount
2002–2004	$3,500
2005	$4,500
2006–2007	$5,000
2008–2009	$6,000
2010 and beyond	$6,000 (indexed to inflation)

In 2009, married taxpayers with AGI over $176,000 and single taxpayers with AGI over $120,000 cannot contribute to a Roth IRA. The deduction amount is phased out for a married taxpayer whose income is between $166,000 and $176,000 (and between $105,000 and $120,000 for single taxpayers). These taxpayers, however, may still contribute to a nondeductible IRA. Furthermore, in certain instances, proper tax planning may allow a taxpayer to reduce his or her income below $166,000 in a particular year to qualify for the Roth IRA.

---

1 Internal Revenue Code (IRC) Section 408A(c)(3)(C)(ii)(I).
2 IRC Section 408A(c)(3)(C)(ii)(II).

Example

In 2009, John and Betty each earn $60,000. In addition, they have interest and dividend income of about $30,000–$40,000 per year. With proper planning, John and Betty may be able to reduce their AGI to under $166,000, thereby allowing $10,000 of contributions to Roth IRAs.

Withdrawals From the Roth IRA

Any qualified distribution from a Roth IRA is not includible in gross income. Qualified distributions include the following:

- Distributions made after the taxpayer attains age 59½
- Distributions to a beneficiary after the taxpayer's death
- Distributions attributable to disability of the taxpayer
- A qualified special-purpose distribution (a distribution for first time home buyers)

However, no payment can be a qualified distribution unless it is made after the five-year taxable period beginning with the first taxable year in which a contribution was made to a Roth IRA.[3]

Early withdrawals from the Roth IRA (before age 59½) are permitted, on a tax-free basis, as long as the taxpayer is withdrawing contributions, not accumulated earnings. Thus, taxpayers can first withdraw their original contributions to the Roth IRA. Unlike the traditional IRA with nondeductible contributions that follow the annuity rules, the Roth IRA has a special set of rules providing that all distributions first come from nondeductible contributions. Therefore, with a contributory Roth IRA, a taxpayer can get the basis out even within the first five years.

Example

For the last 15 years, Bob, age 45, has been contributing $5,000 annually to his Roth IRA. His basis in the IRA is $75,000, and it has a current market value of $105,000. If Bob makes a $75,000 withdrawal from his Roth IRA, it would be a nontaxable withdrawal that avoids the imposition of the 10 percent excise tax.

Example

Assume the preceding example, except that Bob withdraws $80,000 from his Roth IRA. Although $75,000 is still treated as a tax-free return of the original contribution, the remaining $5,000 is a nonqualified distribution that is subject to both income and excise tax.

3 IRC Section 408A(d)(2)(B)(I).

The Benefit of Creating a Roth IRA Compared With a Traditional IRA or Nonqualified Account

Example

Jessica, who is in the 28 percent tax bracket, has the option of creating a Roth IRA, a traditional IRA, or a nonqualified retirement account. She will contribute $5,000 annually for 36 years to the Roth IRA or a taxable account, or $3,400 (reflecting the $1,400 tax savings) to a traditional IRA. The investments are projected to grow at an annual 10 percent rate. If any capital gains are realized in the nonqualified account, they will be taxed at a 15 percent rate. The required minimum distributions (RMDs) from the traditional IRA start when Jessica is age 70 (in 2059). Table 7-2, "Comparison of Roth IRA, Traditional IRA, and Nonqualified Account—Net to Family, No Estate Tax," shows the comparison.

Table 7-2: *Comparison of Roth IRA, Traditional IRA, and Nonqualified Account—Net to Family, No Estate Tax*

Year	Roth IRA	Traditional IRA	Taxable Account
2009	$ 5,500	$ 5,479	$ 5,425
2014	$ 42,436	$ 41,839	$ 40,603
2019	$ 101,921	$ 99,352	$ 92,746
2024	$ 197,724	$ 190,410	$ 171,604
2029	$ 352,014	$ 334,700	$ 290,178
2034	$ 600,500	$ 563,532	$ 468,473
2039	$1,000,689	$ 926,735	$ 736,568
2044	$1,645,197	$1,503,656	$1,139,691
2049	$2,649,607	$2,387,554	$1,713,704
2054	$4,267,218	$3,793,908	$2,576,823
2059	$6,872,398	$6,033,030	$3,874,657

The Benefit of a Roth IRA Compared to a 401(k) Plan

If a client's funds are limited so that he or she cannot participate in both a Roth IRA and a 401(k) plan, a decision must be made about which savings plan is more advantageous. In general, during a taxpayer's earning years, it may be more feasible to contribute to a 401(k) plan than to a Roth IRA. Remember, mathematically, a Roth IRA has no significant benefit over a 401(k) plan in that the benefit is derived from tax deferral, not from the tax-free treatment of the withdrawals. Whether the tax is paid at the front end (in the case of a Roth IRA) or later, on withdrawals (in the case of a 401(k)), the result is the same as it would be if the rates of return on investment and the tax rates remain the same. If a taxpayer expects his or her tax bracket to increase over time, the Roth IRA may provide a significant benefit. Alternatively, if a taxpayer is currently taking a 401(k) deduction in a high-tax year (in the years before retirement), the 401(k) plan is more attractive than the Roth IRA.

In addition, many 401(k) plans also provide for employer provided matching benefits. Obviously, when a taxpayer receives a matching benefit, the 401(k) plan (at least to the extent of the match) is a more attractive vehicle than the Roth IRA. One possible advantage of the Roth IRA compared with the 401(k) plan is that early withdrawals may be taken from the Roth IRA to the extent they do not exceed the taxpayer's basis. Another advantage of a 401(k) plan is the creditor protection provided under the rule of the Employment Retirement Income Security Act of 1974 rules. See Chapter 6, "Tax Planning Strategy," for a more complete discussion on asset protection.

Many taxpayers accumulate substantial wealth within 401(k) plans. The Roth IRA provides them with the advantage of no RMD at their required beginning date, allowing them to reduce future taxes.

The Roth IRA and Your Client's Retirement

At retirement, your clients will ask you a number of questions about the Roth IRA, including the following:

- I am 56 years old. When can I take distributions from the Roth IRA?
- Should I convert my existing traditional IRA to a Roth IRA?
- Should I pay the taxes on the Roth IRA conversion from my Roth IRA or other assets?
- Should I borrow to pay taxes on the Roth IRA conversion?
- Should I transfer my current qualified plan to a traditional IRA and subsequently make a Roth IRA election?
- Should I roll out employer stock (qualified employer securities) while rolling out a portion of the plan to a regular IRA and subsequently to a Roth IRA?

Retirement Before Age 59½

At retirement, before age 59½, clients often ask, "From which portfolio should I take my retirement income?" One step is to develop a cash flow plan that is designed to avoid the IRC Section 72(t) 10 percent penalty. The exceptions to the 10 percent penalty tax, which apply to both traditional and Roth IRAs, are as follows:

- Payments on account of the participant's death
- Payments on account of the participant's disability
- One of a series of substantially equal periodic payments (SEPP)
- Payments on account of a separation from service after age 55, which do not apply to early distributions from IRAs
- Dividends with respect to qualifying employer securities
- Distributions to an alternate payee pursuant to a qualified domestic relations order, which do not apply to early distributions from Roth IRAs or traditional IRAs
- Amounts not in excess of allowable medical expense deduction

- Specified insurance premium payments (this exception cannot apply to early distributions from IRAs because IRAs cannot hold life insurance, nor can they receive a rollover of the insurance premium payments from a qualified plan)
- Excess deferrals, excess contributions, and excess aggregate contributions
- Amounts rolled over into an IRA because the amounts are not included in income
- Nontaxable portion equal to return of participant's investment (employee contributions or insurance premium payments)
- Distributions to unemployed individuals for health insurance premiums
- Qualified higher education expenses
- Qualified first time home buyer expenses
- Roth IRA conversions

When a taxpayer desires to take funds from a Roth IRA for a nonqualified purpose before age 59½, he or she is subject to regular income tax. However, to the extent the distribution represents a return of original contribution (or income realized upon conversion) the distribution is not taxable and not subject to the special 10 percent penalty tax.[4]

Example

Rich, age 30, saves $2,000 annually for 25 years in a Roth IRA. At age 55, Rich has a balance of $250,000. If Rich began taking SEPP, the results shown in table 7-3, "Tax Consequences of Substantially Equal Periodic Payments," occur.

Table 7-3: *Tax Consequences of Substantially Equal Periodic Payments*

Early Age	SEPP*	Cumulative Basis	Recovery of Basis	Nontaxable Qualified Distribution	Taxable Nonqualified Distribution†	10% Early Distribution Penalty
55	$11,227	$50,000	$11,227	$0	$ 0	$0
56	$11,227	$38,773	$11,227	$0	$ 0	$0
57	$11,227	$27,546	$11,227	$0	$ 0	$0
58	$11,227	$16,319	$11,227	$0	$ 0	$0
59	$11,227	$ 5,092	$11,227	$0	$ 0	$0
60	$11,227	$ 0	$ 5,092	$0	$6,135	$0

*Assumes use of the Uniform Table for Amortization when calculating the substantially equal periodic payment under the amortization method. Also, the reasonable interest rate for the period (January 2009) is 3.57%.

†The amount of the nonqualified distribution is subject to both income tax and the 10 percent excise tax for early withdrawals.

4 IRC Section 408A(d)(l)(B) provides that distributions shall be treated as coming first from basis and second from earnings.

Example

Lee, age 45, saves $2,000 annually in a Roth IRA. At age 55, the balance is $50,000. If Lee began taking SEPP, the results shown in table 7-4, "Tax Consequences of Substantially Equal Periodic Payments," occur.

Early Age	SEPP*	Cumulative Basis	Recovery of Basis	Nontaxable Qualified Distribution	Taxable Nonqualified Distribution	10% Early Distribution Penalty
55	$2,245	$20,000	$2,245	$0	$0	$0
56	$2,245	$17,755	$2,245	$0	$0	$0
57	$2,245	$15,510	$2,245	$0	$0	$0
58	$2,245	$13,265	$2,245	$0	$0	$0
59	$2,245	$11,020	$2,245	$0	$0	$0
60	$2,245	$ 8,775	$2,245	$0	$0	$0

*Assumes use of the Uniform Table for Amortization when calculating the substantially equal periodic payment under the amortization method. Also, the reasonable interest rate for the period (January 2009) is 3.57%.

Taxation of Social Security Benefits

Many clients need to take into account how the Roth IRA conversion election affects the taxation of their Social Security benefits. Below a combined income threshold, up to 50 percent of Social Security benefits are subject to federal income tax. Above the threshold, up to 85 percent of the benefits are taxed. Combined income is the sum of AGI, plus nontaxable interest, plus half of Social Security benefits. If a taxpayer's combined income is between $25,000 and $34,000 for an individual, or between $32,000 and $44,000 for a joint filer, up to 50 percent of the Social Security benefits may be subject to federal income taxation. If the combined income is greater than $34,000 for an individual or greater than $44,000 for a joint filer, then up to 85 percent of the Social Security benefits may be subject to federal income taxation.

If a married couple makes a Roth IRA election, they will have "phantom" income. This phantom income, when added to their regular income, may increase total AGI over $44,000. When this occurs, their Social Security income becomes subject to income tax.

As a practical matter, when you provide advice to clients whose Social Security income is not currently subject to tax, you should try to make sure that income associated with the Roth IRA conversion does not inadvertently subject Social Security benefits to income tax. There may be instances in which this is acceptable. However, for most clients, if $10,000 to $15,000 of Social Security income suddenly becomes subject to income tax, the cost of the Roth IRA conversion may be too high.

Example

Julie is age 70 and has taken her IRA distributions since retirement. Her IRA is valued at $250,000. In 2010, her RMD will make 85 percent of her Social Security benefits subject to income tax. By converting her IRA to a Roth IRA, her Social Security income continues to be taxed for the first year and is not subject to tax after that. Thus, by converting what would be ordinary IRA income into Roth IRA income, it may be possible to avoid taxation of Social Security benefits.

Because Roth IRA income is not part of the Social Security inclusion formula, many taxpayers planning retirement may desire to convert to a Roth IRA.

Rollover of Qualified Plan Balance

In the past, if taxpayers wanted to do a Roth IRA conversion, they would have to first roll the funds from the qualified retirement plan to a traditional IRA and then convert the traditional IRA to a Roth IRA. Under the Pension Protection Act of 2006, taxpayers are now eligible to directly roll funds from *eligible retirement plans*[5] to Roth IRAs starting in the 2008 tax year. For reference, selected portions of the PPA can be found reprinted in appendix 6: "Select Text of Pension Protection Act of 2006" in the back of this book.

Contributions After Retirement

A retired client with wage income or other self-employment income is able to make a contribution to a Roth IRA equal to the lesser of $5,000 (in 2009) or 100 percent of the client's annual compensation less any amounts contributed to a traditional IRA during the year. The income limitation of $166,000 for married couples and $105,000 for individual taxpayers continues to exist.[6] If a client, after formal retirement, continues to earn compensation, the client has tremendous incentive to continue to make contributions to a Roth IRA. In fact, there may be instances in which the client is withdrawing funds from a regular IRA and still contributing to a Roth IRA.

IRA Distributions

At retirement, many clients ask their planners, "Should I take funds from my regular IRA or my Roth IRA first?" This is apparently both an annual income tax planning question and an estate planning question. General rules for the taxpayer are the following:

- Retain funds in the Roth IRA while taking distributions from the traditional IRA.
- Avoid nonqualified (taxable) Roth IRA distributions.
- Monitor taxation of Social Security benefits.
- "Rebalance" one's portfolio to properly position assets in the Roth and traditional IRAs.

5 As defined under IRC Section 402(c)(8)(B).
6 IRC Section 408A(c)(3)(C).

When taxpayers are preparing for retirement, they will benefit by converting their accumulation portfolios into and structuring a reasonably balanced *distribution portfolio*. Fundamentally, this means that the taxpayer's financial advisor will assist the taxpayer in establishing three "baskets" of retirement assets from which to withdraw funds prior to and during retirement. The three baskets consist of (1) tax free assets in a Roth IRA, (2) tax deferred assets in an IRA, and (3) taxable assets outside a retirement account. By structuring his or her retirement assets in such a way, the taxpayer will not only be able to avail themselves of tax planning opportunities before and during their retirement, but they will also afford themselves the ability to employ tax-sensitive withdrawal strategies and extend the duration of their withdrawals and the life of their retirement assets.

Although the optimum distribution of retirement assets between the three baskets is investor specific and is driven by each taxpayer's unique set of income and wealth characteristics in light of individual financial needs, most taxpayers will benefit by structuring their retirement assets this way. As such, the prudent CPA should work collaboratively with the taxpayer's financial advisor to determine the optimum asset distribution for the individual.

Tax-Sensitive Withdrawals

The establishment of a distribution portfolio and the corresponding positioning of assets into the three baskets will afford the individual the ability to employ a tax-sensitive withdrawal strategy. At the foundation of this withdrawal strategy is the determination of the optimal order and mix in which retirement assets should be withdrawn to produce the most favorable overall income tax result. As a result, this strategy may enable the taxpayer to markedly increase the duration of his or her withdrawals and stretch out the longevity of his or her retirement assets.

Although the long term goals and income and wealth attributes of each taxpayer are unique, most professionals will generally benefit by employing a tax-sensitive withdrawal strategy that adheres to the following order:

- Withdraw funds first from taxable accounts (outside taxable investment accounts).
- Withdraw funds next from tax-deferred accounts (traditional IRAs).
- Withdraw funds last from tax-free accounts (Roth IRAs).

Although it will not always be advantageous for the taxpayer to adhere to this withdrawal order, generally speaking, employing this withdrawal strategy may extend the duration of withdrawals and increase the longevity of the taxpayer's retirement assets. This result occurs primarily due to the power of tax-deferred growth and the encumbering effect of tax drag.

By withdrawing funds from taxable accounts first, the funds in the tax-deferred and tax-free accounts are allowed to experience continued tax-deferred and tax-free compounded growth, respectively, which increases the size of the account.

The following example demonstrates the effectiveness of this strategy by comparing the withdrawal of funds from a taxable account first with the withdrawal of funds from a tax-deferred (traditional IRA) account first. As is illustrated by the graph in the example, withdrawing funds first from a taxable account lengthens the period of the overall withdrawals by increasing the overall account balance.

Example of the Effectiveness of Withdrawing Funds From an Outside Taxable Account Before Withdrawing Funds From a Tax-Deferred Account

William, age 60, has a traditional IRA with a balance of $500,000 and a nonqualified, outside taxable investment account with a balance of $500,000. William would like to begin withdrawing funds from his accounts, and he is seeking advice as to which retirement account he should withdraw funds from. Currently, William's only other source of income is Social Security benefits in the amount of $10,000 per year. He would like to withdraw $50,000 a year on an after-tax basis to supplement his Social Security income.[7] As the following graph illustrates, by employing the tax-efficient withdrawal strategy described in the preceding paragraphs and withdrawing funds from his taxable account first, he would increase the duration of his withdrawals and extend the longevity of his retirement assets.

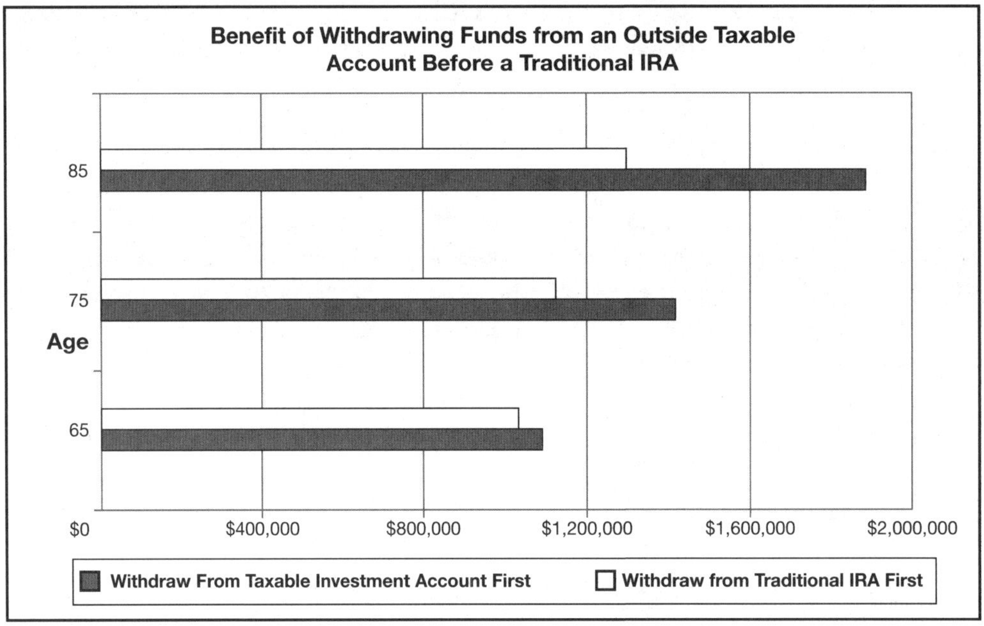

The preceding bar graph represents the total balance William would have in both his retirement accounts if he withdrew funds first from his taxable account compared to the balance he would have in his retirement accounts if he withdrew funds first from his traditional IRA.

As is illustrated by the chart, William will benefit substantially by withdrawing funds from his outside taxable account first instead of withdrawing funds from his tax-deferred (traditional IRA) account first. If William were to continue to follow this tax-efficient

7 For purposes of this example, the following assumptions apply:

- The annual return for both the outside taxable account and the Traditional IRA is 7 percent (3 percent ordinary income and 4 percent growth.
- Of the $10,000 Social Security benefits William receives, 85 percent are taxable.
- William is in the 25 percent federal income tax bracket (15 percent capital gains) and for the purposes of this example, the rates are static.

withdrawal strategy and withdraw funds from his taxable account before his tax-deferred account, by the time he attained the age of 85, he would have accumulated approximately $530,300 in additional assets.

Notwithstanding, there are situations in which the taxpayer may benefit by withdrawing funds from a tax-deferred account prior to withdrawing funds from a taxable account. Generally, there are two main instances in which the taxpayer may benefit by applying this strategy:

- To manage income tax brackets and minimize income tax
- To prevent the RMD "time bomb"

Utilizing Tax-Deferred Funds to Prevent "Bracket Creep" and the RMD "Time Bomb"

Another instance in which a taxpayer may benefit by withdrawing funds first from a tax-deferred account before a taxable account is to prevent what has been referred to as "bracket creep" and the resultant RMD "time bomb." When a taxpayer refrains from taking any distributions from his or her traditional IRA before the required beginning date, the retirement account is allowed to experience uninterrupted growth. This uninterrupted growth equates to a large IRA balance, which produces correspondingly larger distributions that, when received, may push the taxpayer into a higher marginal income tax bracket (bracket creep) and increase the taxpayer's overall income tax liability (the resultant RMD time bomb). In order to prevent this from occurring, the taxpayer may benefit by occasionally making small withdrawals from his or her traditional IRA to manage not only the size of the account but also the size of the future RMDs. Furthermore, if these withdrawals are taken before or early in retirement, when the taxpayer may be in a lower income tax bracket, the withdrawals will be taxed at a lower marginal income tax rate, which may provide tax savings.

Taxpayers at Their Required Beginning Date

RMDs from a traditional IRA must begin on or before April 1 of the year following the year in which a client turns age 70½ (generally known as one's required beginning date).[8] The Roth IRA, however, is not subject to these rules. It seems logical that a taxpayer, to the extent he or she does not need the cash flow, would want to retain funds within the Roth IRA, allowing the funds to continue to grow tax free.

Lifetime Distributions: Traditional IRAs

Lifetime distributions are calculated by reference to the Uniform Lifetime Table in Treasury Regulation Section 1.401(a)(9)-9, Q&A 2, as reproduced in table 7-5, "Determining Factor Lifetime Distributions." A full copy of the 2002 final rules and regulations from the Department of the Treasury, including Treasury Regulation Section 1.401(a)(9)-9, can be found on the accompanying CD-ROM.

8 IRC Section 401(a)(9)(A).

Table 7-5: *Determining Factor Lifetime Distributions*

Attained Age in Year of Distribution	Applicable Divisor Under Final Regulations	Attained Age in Year of Distribution	Applicable Divisor Under Final Regulations
70	27.4	93	9.6
71	26.5	94	9.1
72	25.6	95	8.6
73	24.7	96	8.1
74	23.8	97	7.6
75	22.8	98	7.1
76	22.0	99	6.7
77	21.2	100	6.3
78	20.3	101	5.9
79	19.5	102	5.5
80	18.7	103	5.2
81	17.9	104	4.9
82	17.1	105	4.5
83	16.3	106	4.2
84	15.5	107	3.9
85	14.8	108	3.9
86	14.1	109	3.4
87	13.4	110	3.1
88	12.7	111	2.9
89	12.0	112	2.6
90	11.4	113	2.4
91	10.8	114	2.1
92	10.2	115 and older	1.9

The only time that the Uniform Lifetime Table is not used to calculate RMDs during the owner's life is if the employee's sole beneficiary is the employee's spouse and the spouse is more than ten years younger than the employee. In that case, the longer distribution period measured by the joint life and last survivor life expectancy of the employee and spouse is permitted to be used. This table can be found in Treasury Regulation Section 1.401(a)(9)-9, Q&A 3.

The determination of the beneficiary for purposes of determining post-death distributions is not made until September 30 of the year following the year of death.

The majority of post-death distributions are based on the Single Life Table of Treasury Regulation Section 1.401(a)(9)-9, Q&A 1, and reduced by 1 for each year after the year of death, which is reproduced in table 7-6, "Treasury Regulation Section 1.272-9—Ordinary Life Annuities On Life Expected Return Multiples."[9]

9 There are exceptions to this rule for spousal beneficiaries.

Table 7-6: *Treasury Regulation Section 1.272-9—Ordinary Life Annuities On Life Expected Return Multiples*

A-1 of Treas. Reg. Sec. 1.401(a)(9)-9— Single Life Table					
Age	Multiple	Age	Multiple	Age	Multiple
0	82.4	37	46.5	74	14.1
1	81.6	38	45.6	75	13.4
2	80.6	39	44.6	76	12.7
3	79.7	40	43.6	77	12.1
4	78.7	41	42.7	78	11.4
5	77.7	42	41.7	79	10.8
6	76.7	43	40.7	80	10.2
7	75.8	44	39.8	81	9.7
8	74.8	45	38.8	82	9.1
9	73.8	46	37.9	83	8.6
10	72.8	47	37.0	84	8.1
11	71.8	48	36.0	85	7.6
12	70.8	49	35.1	86	7.1
13	69.9	50	34.2	87	6.7
14	68.9	51	33.3	88	6.3
15	67.9	52	32.3	89	5.9
16	66.9	53	31.4	90	5.5
17	66.0	54	30.5	91	5.2
18	65.0	55	29.6	92	4.9
19	64.0	56	28.7	93	4.6
20	63.0	57	27.9	94	4.3
21	62.1	58	27.0	95	4.1
22	61.1	59	26.1	96	3.8
23	60.1	60	25.2	97	3.6
24	59.1	61	24.4	98	3.4
25	58.2	62	23.5	99	3.1
26	57.2	63	22.7	100	2.9
27	56.2	64	21.8	101	2.7
28	55.3	65	21.0	102	2.5
29	54.3	66	20.2	103	2.3
30	53.3	67	19.4	104	2.1
31	52.4	68	18.6	105	1.9
32	51.4	69	17.8	106	1.7
33	50.4	70	17.0	107	1.5
34	49.4	71	16.3	108	1.4

(continued)

Table 7-6: *Treasury Regulation Section 1.272-9—Ordinary LifeAnnuities On Life Expected Return Multiples (continued)*

A-1 of Treas. Reg. Sec. 1.401(a)(9)-9— Single Life Table					
Age	Multiple	Age	Multiple	Age	Multiple
35	48.5	72	15.5	109	1.2
36	47.5	73	14.8	110	1.1
				111	1.0

By forestalling the post-death determination of the designated beneficiary until September 30 of the year following the year of death, the named primary beneficiary may execute a disclaimer or partial disclaimer and thereby change the beneficiary and, most importantly, the measuring life expectancy.

Example

At age 71, Dr. Jones names Mrs. Jones as the beneficiary of his traditional IRA. At age 73, Mrs. Jones predeceases her husband. At that time, Dr. Jones names his children as beneficiaries. Three years later, Dr. Jones dies. Because Dr. Jones's children were the beneficiaries as of September 30 of the year following the year Dr. Jones died, RMDs are calculated based on the oldest child's life expectancy.

Example

At age 71, Dr. Jones names Mrs. Jones as the primary beneficiary of his traditional IRA and his children as contingent beneficiaries. At age 73, Mrs. Jones predeceases her husband. Three years later, Dr. Jones dies. Despite the fact that Dr. Jones did not execute a new beneficiary designation form before his death, his children, as contingent beneficiaries, can be established as the beneficiaries as of September 30 of the year following the year Dr. Jones died. RMDs, therefore, are calculated based on the oldest child's life expectancy.

Example

At age 71, Dr. Jones names Mrs. Jones as his primary beneficiary of his traditional IRA and his children as contingent beneficiaries. Three years later, at age 74, Dr. Jones dies. Mrs. Jones then disclaims the IRA. His children, as contingent beneficiaries, are the beneficiaries as of September 30 of the year following the year Dr. Jones died. RMDs, therefore, are calculated based on the oldest child's life expectancy.

> **Example**
>
> Assume the preceding example, except that the children create separate shares by December 31 of the year following the year of Dr. Jones's death. Each child can now use his or her individual life expectancy to calculate RMDs.

A client will need to ask the question, "Who is the best beneficiary of my IRA from both an income tax and an estate planning perspective?" From an estate planning perspective, one of the key goals is to fund the applicable exclusion amount (either outright or in a trust); whereas, from the income tax perspective, the goal is to maximize tax deferral. Generally, the maximum deferral is obtained when the client names his or her spouse as the beneficiary and the spouse subsequently rolls over the funds into an IRA in his or her own name and subsequently names the children as the designated beneficiaries.

As shown in table 7-7, "Client Leaves $1 Million IRA to Child," distributions over a child's life expectancy can have a dramatic effect on the wealth transfer to children beneficiaries. If the taxpayer has enough wealth, he or she should consider naming a grandchild, directly, as the beneficiary of a traditional or Roth IRA.

Table 7-7: *Client Leaves $1 Million IRA to Child**

Pension Fund Year	Beginning Value	Life Expectancy	Annual Distribution
2001	$1,000,000	43.6	$22,936
2002	$1,074,771	42.6	$25,229
2003	$1,154,495	41.6	$27,752
2004	$1,239,417	40.6	$30,529
2005	$1,329,779	39.6	$33,580
2006	$1,425,818	38.6	$36,938
2007	$1,527,768	37.6	$40,632
2008	$1,635,850	36.6	$44,695
2009	$1,750,270	35.6	$49,165
2010	$1,871,215	34.6	$54,081
2011	$1,998,847	33.6	$59,490
2012	$2,133,294	32.6	$65,438
2013	$2,274,641	31.6	$71,982
2014	$2,422,924	30.6	$79,181
2015	$2,578,118	29.6	$87,099
2016	$2,740,112	28.6	$95,808

*Assumes a beginning balance of $1 million with 10 percent growth, that estate taxes are paid from probate estate, and that the child is age 40 with a life expectancy of 43.6 years.

Example

Dan names his ten-year old grandson, Dan III, as the beneficiary of his Roth IRA. At age 69, Dan dies. Distributions of the $1 million Roth IRA to his grandchild are shown in table 7-8, "Client Leaves $1 Million IRA to Grand-child."

Table 7-8: *Client Leaves $1 Million IRA to Grandhild**

Pension Fund Year	Beginning Value	Life Expectancy	Annual Distribu-tion
2009	$1,000,000	72.8	$13,736
2010	$1,084,890	71.8	$15,110
2011	$1,176,758	70.8	$16,621
2012	$1,276,151	69.8	$18,283
2013	$1,383,655	68.8	$20,111
2014	$1,499,898	67.8	$22,122
2015	$1,625,553	66.8	$24,335
2016	$1,761,340	65.8	$26,768
2017	$1,908,030	64.8	$29,445
2018	$2,066,443	63.8	$32,389
2019	$2,237,459	62.8	$35,628
2020	$2,422,014	61.8	$39,191
2021	$2,621,105	60.8	$43,110
2022	$2,835,794	59.8	$47,421
2023	$3,067,210	58.8	$52,163

*Assumes a beginning balance of $1 million with 10 percent growth, that estate taxes are paid from probate estate, and that the child is age 10 with a life expectancy of 72.8 years.

When the Roth IRA has been completely liquidated in 73 years, Dan III has received almost $142,000,000 of tax-free distributions.[10]

Conclusion

Once the CPA has assisted the client with IRA tax planning during his or her life, focus can be shifted on planning for disposition of the Roth IRA at the client's death. The remaining chapters address estate planning issues and how to best structure a client's overall estate plan to take full advantage of the tax deferred nature of a Roth IRA.

10 A percent growth rate is assumed.

Beneficiary Considerations

Introduction

One of the most complicated areas of the tax law is the set of rules that address naming a trust as a designated beneficiary of an individual retirement account (IRA). In the typical situation, if an IRA owner does not have enough non-IRA assets to fund his or her credit shelter trust, he or she may need to name the credit shelter trust as the beneficiary of their IRA. In these instances, the owner must follow specific guidelines with regard to naming a trust the designated beneficiary, and the trust must meet specific requirements to be a qualified designated beneficiary trust. This chapter discusses the distribution rules and the qualification rules of trusts that are named the beneficiary of an IRA along with how to prepare a beneficiary designation form. Appendix A: "Roth IRA Distribution Flowchart" and appendix B: "Distributions to Beneficiary Under IRC Section 401(a)(9) Roth IRAs" graphically show the process and rules for different kinds of beneficiary designations.

The Importance of Having a Designated Beneficiary

To maximize the tax deferral of any IRA, it is important to choose the proper designated beneficiary. This choice will significantly affect the calculation of the required minimum distributions (RMDs) and will therefore determine the amount of tax deferral that will ultimately be available. In making this choice, it is very important that the tax regulations are closely followed. The regulations under Internal Revenue Code (IRC) Section 401(a)(9) allow taxpayers certain advantages in their planning, including greater flexibility as to when they can name a beneficiary.

Distributions After the Death of the Owner Without a Designated Beneficiary

If the owner of a qualified plan or traditional IRA does not have a designated beneficiary and the owner dies before the required beginning date, the IRC dictates that the qualified plan or IRA must be distributed by December 31 of the year of the fifth anniversary of the death of the owner. A Roth IRA owner is always deemed to die before the required beginning date. The distribution can be made in any fashion the beneficiary chooses. It may be made ratably over this five-year period of time or in a lump sum on December 31 of the year of the fifth anniversary of the death of the IRA owner. This relatively rapid withdrawal will cause the beneficiaries of the IRA to lose many years of deferral.

If the owner of a qualified plan or traditional IRA dies after his or her required beginning date and does not have a designated beneficiary by September 30 of the year following the year of death, distributions are taken out by referencing the owner's age in the year of death in the Single Life Table in Treasury Regulation Section 1.401(a)(9)-9, Q&A 7, and reducing the factor by one for any year thereafter.[1] A full copy of the 2002 final rules and regulations from the Department of the Treasury, including Treasury Regulation Section 1.401(a)(9)-9, can be found on the accompanying CD-ROM.

Distributions After the Death of the Owner With a Designated Beneficiary

The IRC allows a designated beneficiary to receive distributions over his or her single life expectancy.[2] This is usually far more advantageous than the five year rule discussed in the preceding paragraphs for death before the required beginning date if there is no designated beneficiary. Therefore, having a designated beneficiary is critical to preserve the deferral that can be achieved with proper planning.

If the participant has a designated beneficiary and dies after the required beginning date, the IRC states that the remaining portion of the IRA must be distributed at least as rapidly as it would have been had the participant not died.[3]

For individuals who die after their required beginning date and have a qualified beneficiary as of September 30 of the year following the year of death, distributions are determined based upon the beneficiary's life expectancy as referenced in the Single Life Table of Treasury Regulation Section 1.401(a)(9)-9, Q&A 7. For each succeeding year, this factor is reduced by one.[4]

1 Treasury Regulation Section 1.401(a)(9)-5 Q&A 5(c)(3).
2 Internal Revenue Code (IRC) Section 401(a)(9)(B)(iii).
3 IRC Section 401(a)(9)(B)(i).
4 Special rules apply when the spouse is the beneficiary.

Trusts as Designated Beneficiary of an IRA

It is clearly very important that IRAs have proper designated beneficiaries to allow the most favorable tax deferral.

A *designated beneficiary* is defined as any individual who is designated by the owner of the qualified plan or IRA. However, trusts can qualify as a designated beneficiary if the trusts meet certain criteria found in the regulations.

A trust can qualify as a designated beneficiary if it is revocable while the individual is alive, provided that it becomes irrevocable upon the individual's death.[5] Therefore, a person can name a revocable living trust as a designated beneficiary of the person's IRA if, by its terms, the trust could become irrevocable at the person's death.

Treasury Regulation Section 1.401(a)(9)-4 Q&A 5(6) states that in order for a trust to be a designated beneficiary, the following requirements must be met:

1. The trust is a valid trust under state law, or would be but for the fact that there is no corpus.
2. The trust is irrevocable or will, by its terms, become irrevocable upon the death of the participant.
3. The beneficiaries of the trust, who are beneficiaries with respect to the trust's interest in the participant's benefit, are identifiable from the trust instrument.
4. The documentation required has been provided to the plan administrator.

In addition, the regulations create deadlines as to when documentation must be provided to the plan administrator when a trust is named as the designated beneficiary. The following is an outline of what must be submitted to the plan administrator.[6]

When the participant reaches his or her required beginning date, if the participant designates a trust as the beneficiary of his or her entire benefit and the employee's spouse is the sole beneficiary of the trust, the participant must do either of the following:

1. Provide the plan administrator with a copy of the trust instrument and agree that if the trust instrument is amended at any time in the future, the participant will, within a reasonable time, provide a copy of the amendment to the plan administrator.
2. Provide the plan administrator with a list of all the beneficiaries (including contingent and remainderman beneficiaries with a description of the conditions on their entitlement sufficient to establish that the spouse is the sole beneficiary) of the trust, certify to the best of the participant's knowledge that this list is correct and complete and that the specific requirements for a trust to qualify as a designated beneficiary are met, agree to provide corrected certifications to the extent that there are any amendments or changes to the information previously submitted, and agree to provide a copy of the trust instrument to the plan administrator upon demand.

---

5 Special care should be taken when naming a revocable trust as the beneficiary of an individual retirement account (IRA) that splits the estate into 2 trusts. The funding clause of this type of trust should fund family and marital trusts with a fractional funding clause. A *pecuniary clause* would accelerate recognition of income because the IRA is income in respect of a decedent. See IRC Section 691(a). In addition, naming a revocable trust as beneficiary could cause asset protection problems depending on state law. See *Commerce Bank v. Bolander*, 2007 WL 1041760 (Kan. App. 2007), unpublished.

6 Treasury Regulation Section 1.401(a)(9)-4 Q&A 6(a) and (b).

In order to satisfy the documentation requirement after the death of the participant, the trustee must do the following by October 31 of the year after the year of the death of the participant:

1. Provide the plan administrator with a final list of all beneficiaries (including contingent and remainderman beneficiaries with a description of the conditions on their entitlement) of the trust as of September 30 of the year following the year of the participant's death, certify that to the best of the trustee's knowledge this list is correct and complete, certify that the specific requirements of a trust qualifying as a designated beneficiary are met, and agree to provide a copy of the trust instrument to the plan administrator upon demand.
2. Provide the plan administrator with a copy of the actual trust document for the trust that was named as a beneficiary as of the participant's date of death.

A qualified designated beneficiary cannot be an estate, a charity, a trust with a charity as a beneficiary of the trust, or a trust that does not meet the requirements described in the preceding paragraphs.[7] However, if that is the situation, there may be an outside opportunity to assign or cash-out of the nonqualified beneficiary's interest from the trust. If this is accomplished prior to September 30 of the year following death, it is allowable to disregard such cashed-out beneficiary and use the remaining qualified beneficiary's life expectancies.

Unless there is an estate planning reason (for example, the credit shelter needs to be funded with IRA assets), naming a credit shelter trust may not be advisable. In the typical situation, the taxpayer's spouse will be the oldest beneficiary, and, therefore, distributions will have to be calculated based on his or her life expectancy. The better choice of beneficiaries may be a trust for the benefit of the children made either through a spousal disclaimer or by naming the trust directly. The additional deferral that can be achieved is illustrated in table 8-1, "Traditional IRA Designated Beneficiaries."

Table 8-1: *Traditional IRA Designated Beneficiaries*

	Credit Shelter Trust as Designated Beneficiary			Child as Designated Beneficiary		
Year	Beginning Balance	Life Expectancy	Required Minimum Distribution	Beginning Balance	Life Expectancy	Required Minimum Distribution
1	$500,000	11.0	$ 45,455	$500,000	33.1	$15,106
2	$500,000	10.0	$ 50,000	$533,384	32.1	$16,616
3	$495,000	9.0	$ 55,000	$568,444	31.1	$18,278
4	$484,000	8.0	$ 60,500	$605,183	30.1	$20,106
5	$465,850	7.0	$ 66,550	$643,585	29.1	$22,116

7 Certain exceptions apply, such as when a trust is structured as a "conduit trust," requiring all IRA distributions to be distributed to the trust beneficiaries. A full explanation of the structure and uses of a conduit trust, however, is beyond the scope of this book.

Table 8-1: *Traditional IRA Designated Beneficiaries (continued)*

	Credit Shelter Trust as Designated Beneficiary			Child as Designated Beneficiary		
Year	Beginning Balance	Life Expectancy	Required Minimum Distribution	Beginning Balance	Life Expectancy	Required Minimum Distribution
6	$439,230	6.0	$ 73,205	$683,615	28.1	$24,328
7	$402,628	5.0	$ 80,526	$725,216	27.1	$26,761
8	$354,312	4.0	$ 88,578	$768,301	26.1	$29,437
9	$292,307	3.0	$ 97,436	$812,750	25.1	$32,380
10	$214,358	2.0	$107,179	$858,407	24.1	$35,619

Although the requirements listed in the preceding paragraphs may seem simple to meet, designating a trust that qualifies as a designated beneficiary is no easy task and is filled with numerous traps for the unwary. CPAs should work with their clients to retain an attorney who is experienced in drafting trusts designated to qualify as designated beneficiaries.

Figure 8-1, "Trust as the Designated Beneficiary of an IRA," illustrates the typical operation of naming a credit shelter trust the designated beneficiary of an IRA.

Figure 8-1: *Trust as the Designated Beneficiary of an IRA*

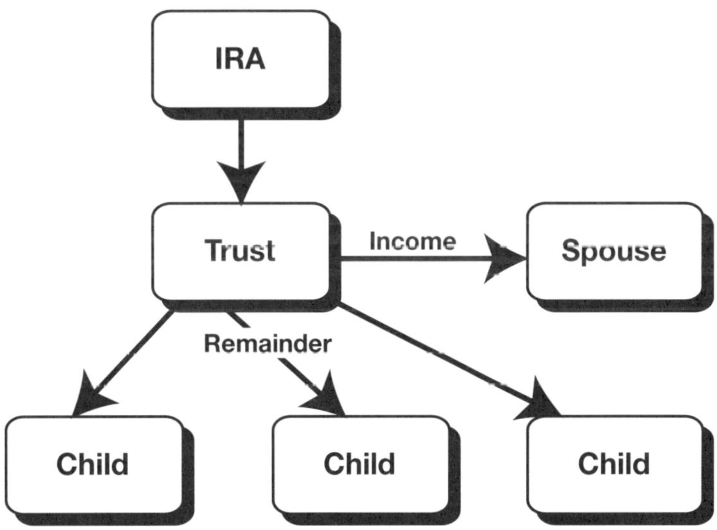

Distributions will be made over the oldest beneficiary's life expectancy (i.e. spouse).

Nontax Benefits of Utilizing a Trust

Oftentimes, the discussion on the benefits of trusts centers primarily on the estate and income tax benefits with the funding of the unified credit amount. There are, however, numerous nontax benefits of using a trust. This memorandum outlines the sometimes overlooked nonestate tax benefits that come from naming a trust as beneficiary of a retirement account.

Creditor Protection

Creditor protection is an important reason for using a trust. Although qualified plans are generally protected under the Employee Retirement Income Security Act of 1974 (ERISA), a beneficiary's interest in an IRA may not be protected from creditors, depending on state law. If the IRA is left outright to a child or grandchild, creditors may, under state law, have a right to the asset to settle outstanding debts or tort liabilities (for example, an automobile accident). With the use of a trust, many of these concerns are alleviated. In almost every state, the assets held in a trust created by another person (for example, a parent or a grandparent) are not subject to the claims of creditors. The trust also is an especially important tool for malpractice purposes if the beneficiary is a successful professional (for example, a doctor, nurse, lawyer, or engineer). A trust can help protect the beneficiary from losing the asset altogether in a creditor claim.

Example

Alex inherited an IRA from his father. Alex, a surgeon, lives in a state that does not exempt inherited IRAs from creditor claims. A former patient's family brings, and subsequently wins, a large tort action against Alex for an unsuccessful surgery. Because Alex's IRA is not exempt from creditors, the family can go after the IRA to recover the damages. Had the IRA been payable to an asset protection trust for the benefit of Alex, the IRA could have been protected from such claim.

Divorce Protection

If assets are payable directly to a child or grandchild, the divorcing spouse of the child or grandchild may have a right to a portion of these assets (this depends upon state law). If the parent had instead put these assets in a trust for the benefit of the child, the beneficiary would have an additional layer of protection because he or she would be entitled to 100 percent of the trust assets that were designated for the beneficiary's benefit. In this case, trust assets should not be part of a divorce settlement payable to the nonbeneficiary spouse.

Spendthrift Protection

Inheriting a retirement account in a multigenerational trust can also protect the beneficiary from poor financial decisions. Having the retirement account in a trust protects children and grandchildren from wealth foolishly spent. When a retirement account is payable to a child outright, the child has the option of withdrawing any amount from the account as he or she wishes. The temptation to withdraw the entire account may be particularly strong for young beneficiaries. This, of course, results in the loss of many years of tax deferred growth.

Example

Linda, a single mother, dies unexpectedly at age 45. Linda left her entire estate, including her $50,000 IRA, to her only son, James, age 19. James decides to withdraw the entire IRA to buy an expensive sports car. Had the IRA been payable to a trust, the trust could have still been used for James's benefit but James could not have controlled the speed of the distributions.

Investment Management

The trust is a good tool to facilitate professional investment advice. Naming a trust as beneficiary of a retirement account allows the account owner the ability to select a trustee who is financially wise in order to preserve and create wealth for future generations. This helps prevent a beneficiary from making uneducated investment decisions or being influenced by others, thereby losing a major benefit of the retirement account.

Keeping Wealth in the Family

By using a trust, the retirement account owner can ensure that the account will continue down his or her family line after the primary beneficiary passes away. If a retirement account is left outright to a child, upon that child's death, he or she can leave the assets to whomever he or she chooses, such as a spouse or charity.

Example

Keith leaves his $500,000 IRA outright to his daughter, Melissa, and other assets to his other two children. Melissa dies only two years after her father. She dies with no children but with a husband, Joe. Melissa leaves the inherited IRA to Joe. Keith would have preferred that the IRA go to his other two children upon Melissa's death if she died with no children. Using a trust with Keith's desired dispositive provisions could have accomplished this goal.

Disabled Beneficiaries

In the event that a beneficiary becomes disabled or incapacitated and cannot manage his or her affairs, the trustee of a trust can continue to manage the assets of the trust. Therefore, a trust would be beneficial in situations in which, because of sickness or injury, the beneficiary is no longer physically able to attend to his or her affairs. The trust would also be beneficial in the event he or she should become *incapacitated* or *incompetent*, as defined under state law, in which case, without a trust, a guardian or conservator may have to be appointed by the local probate court to manage his or her property. The expenses, delays, and restrictions of a court-supervised conservatorship over one's assets could be avoided if the assets were held and managed in a trust.

Special Needs Trust

Estate planning for a client who has a disabled beneficiary needs to be structured to provide maximum care and financial support for that beneficiary without jeopardizing the beneficiary's eligibility for government benefits. Instead of having a retirement account payable outright to such a beneficiary, a special needs trust should be created to supplement government benefits or assistance rather than diminishing such benefits.

By naming a special needs trust as beneficiary of the retirement account, the beneficiary will still be able to qualify for Medicaid and other government benefits. The objective of using a trust in this case is to maintain the beneficiary's eligibility for public benefits and to preserve adequate funds to provide special items needed by the beneficiary that are not otherwise provided. This is extremely important to the beneficiary because it promotes stability for the beneficiary and avoids the disruption and anxiety that could be caused by the discontinuance of these benefits.

Preparing IRA Beneficiary Designation Forms

Planners helping their clients with beneficiary forms are always advised to approach a beneficiary designation form with the same care used to approach a will. It is prudent to have the client's legal counsel review the beneficiary designation form, and it may often be more practical to have legal counsel draft the form because the contingent and secondary beneficiary designations may become extremely complex from a drafting perspective. Secondary and contingent beneficiaries are commonly trusts for the benefit of minor children, a family trust, or other nominee necessitating integration with the client's overall estate plan.[8]

Generally, customized drafting will be required for any beneficiary designation form. The standardized forms provided by the brokerage or similar firms simply do not provide enough flexibility (and in many cases, simply not enough space) for proper drafting.

Community Property Issues

Community property has special issues that affect beneficiary designation forms. In many states, notwithstanding the fact that the IRA is in the name of one spouse, if the IRA is a community property asset, up to 50 percent of the IRA may be owned by each spouse. Thus, the overall estate plan must take into account the death of either spouse.[9]

8 Whether the preparation of a beneficiary form without the guidance of an attorney is the unauthorized practice of law is a matter better left to other studies.

9 The tax court case *Bunney v. Commissioner*, 114 TC 259 (2000), has cast some doubt on the ability to rely on community property laws in order to establish ownership of an IRA in the nontitled spouse.

Example

Rick has a $500,000 IRA that is community property under state law at the time of his death. Because of the community property law, Rick is not able to leave 100 percent of the IRA to a bypass trust for his family but only his community property interest of 50 percent. The other 50 percent interest, under state law, is his spouse's property.

This provides the nine community or marital property states (Arizona, California, Idaho, Louisiana, Nevada, New Mexico, Texas, Washington, and Wisconsin) with a tremendous planning strategy. The following is a typical situation.

Several Private Letter Rulings (PLRs), including PLR 9439020, allowed the classification of a person's community property IRA into separate components in conformity with applicable state law. The inclusion in the taxable estate is fairly well established, and, in the event that the nontitled owner spouse dies first, it is possible that the nontitled spouse will be able to direct the payment of his or her community property interest to someone other than the retirement asset owner. This issue often arises when one spouse has substantial retirement assets but there are few other assets in the remainder of the estate. If the nontitled spouse predeceases the retirement asset owner spouse, her unified credit could be substantially underutilized, resulting in a larger estate tax bill upon the death of the surviving spouse. This could be avoided if the nontitled spouse could direct a community property interest to a person other than the retirement asset owner spouse in the event that the nontitled spouse dies first. Although IRAs may be divided between spouses according to local community property laws, and after such division the nontitled spouse will have ownership of his or her half interest in that account included in his or her taxable estate, it is yet unclear whether or not that spouse can transfer his or her interest in the account to someone other than his or her spouse. Therefore, the use of this technique for funding a unified credit gift is uncertain. However, it should be used when no other technique is available and the clients have a full understanding of the risk involved.

Example

Brent and Amy come to you for some estate planning advice. Their total estate consists of $1,600,000, of which $1,200,000 is in Brent's IRA. In a separate property state, the practitioner can only reclassify $400,000 of property in Amy's name, thereby losing $600,000 of Amy's estate tax exemption ($1,000,000 less $400,000). On the other hand, the practitioner in a community property state can break off a section of the $1,200,000 IRA, say $500,000, and classify that IRA as community property. Now, if Amy dies first, she has $400,000 of other assets and a $250,000 claim in Brent's IRA because it is classified as community property. She will have enough assets to fund her unified credit trust. This planning results in substantial estate tax savings. At Brent's death, his estate would be $950,000 ($1,600,000 less $650,000).

Reviewing the Plan or IRA Document

Although tax law is a critical consideration when preparing a beneficiary designation form, the IRA or plan document is equally important. In many instances, the plan document may be more restrictive than the tax law. For example, many older plans may still provide that after a participant's death, distributions must be taken over a five year period. In contrast, a more recent plan might provide that distributions may be taken over a beneficiary's life expectancy. If the plan document provides for a faster payout than the IRC Section 401(a)(9) regulations, the plan document will govern distributions.

Drafting in Anticipation of Disclaimer

When preparing beneficiary designation forms, the client should generally consider designating his or her spouse as the primary beneficiary with the contingent beneficiary being a bypass trust (assuming the trust is drafted to qualify as a designated beneficiary. See the previous sections). This allows rollover flexibility while having a contingency provision to fund a bypass trust. (See chapter 9, "Estate Planning for the Roth IRA," regarding estate planning.)

Creating Separate Shares at Death

The creation of separate IRAs can be done after death but before December 31 of the year following the year of death. For example, if Tony, a widower, has two children who are ages 40 and 50, the beneficiaries may be well advised to create separate traditional or Roth IRAs upon Tony's death. Each child is then able to use his or her own life expectancy to determine distributions from the IRA (see table 8-2, "Distributions Over Life Expectancy for Adult Children"). A provision should be added to the beneficiary designation form giving the beneficiaries the power to create these separate shares. Keeping a single IRA during life simplifies the administration of an IRA.

Table 8-2: *Distributions Over Life Expectancy for Adult Children*

40-Year-Old Child			50-Year-Old Child		
Beginning Balance	Life Expectancy	Required Distribution*	Beginning Balance	Life Expectancy	Required Distribution*
$ 500,000	43.6	$11,468	$ 500,000	34.2	$14,620
$ 537,385	42.6	$12,615	$ 533,918	33.2	$16,082
$ 577,248	41.6	$13,876	$ 569,620	32.2	$17,690
$ 619,709	40.6	$15,264	$ 607,123	31.2	$19,459
$ 664,889	39.6	$16,790	$ 646,430	30.2	$21,405
$ 712,909	38.6	$18,469	$ 687,528	29.4	$23,545
$ 763,884	37.6	$20,316	$ 730,380	28.4	$25,900
$ 817,925	36.6	$22,348	$ 774,928	27.4	$28,490
$ 875,135	35.6	$24,582	$ 821,082	26.4	$31,339
$ 935,608	34.6	$27,041	$ 868,718	25.4	$34,473
$ 999,424	33.6	$29,745	$ 917,669	24.4	$37,920
$1,066,647	32.6	$32,719	$ 967,724	23.4	$41,712
$1,137,320	31.6	$35,991	$1,018,613	22.4	$45,883
$1,211,462	30.6	$39,590	$1,070,002	21.4	$50,472
$1,289,059	29.6	$43,549	$1,121,483	20.4	$55,519
$1,370,061	28.6	$47,904	$1,172,561	19.4	$61,071
$1,454,372	27.6	$52,695	$1,222,639	18.4	$67,178
$1,541,845	26.6	$57,964	$1,271,007	17.4	$73,896
$1,632,269	25.6	$63,761	$1,316,823	16.4	$81,285
$1,725,360	24.6	$70,137	$1,359,091	15.4	$89,414

*If Tony dies after his required beginning date, the year of death RMD must be calculated based on Tony's age the year of death, using the Uniform Lifetime Table of Treasury Regulation Section 1.401(a)(9)-9, Q&A 2.

Coordination With Revocable Trust

When a trust allows for payments of debts, expenses, and taxes, there is a strong possibility that the IRS will take the position that a nonindividual is a beneficiary of the trust and thus the trust will not qualify as a designation beneficiary.

This issue first began to take shape with the issuance of PLR 9820021 and PLR 9809059. In PLR 9820021, the IRS ruled that a trust was not a qualified designated beneficiary. In PLR 9809059, the IRS ruled that a trust was a qualified designated beneficiary. Neither of these rulings specifically stated that payment of debts, expenses, and taxes would disqualify the trust. They did, however, specifically point out that the trust either did or did not allow for such payments.

The IRS has argued that where IRA or qualified plan proceeds can be used for such expenses, the estate is in effect the beneficiary of the IRA or qualified plan. Where this is the case, a significant loss of income tax deferral occurs.

With the issuance of the final IRC Section 401(a)(9) regulations, taxpayers are now provided the opportunity to correct this error by September 30 of the year following the year of death (that is, the date the designated beneficiary must be determined). Beneficiaries that were previously locked in can now be eliminate or "cashed out" by the September 30 date. If all debts, expenses, and taxes are paid by such date, the estate and creditors are, in essence, eliminated as beneficiaries.

Funding the Credit Shelter Trust

An important question for estate planning clients is, "Should my traditional IRA or my Roth IRA be payable to my credit shelter trust?" Initial analysis shows that paying the Roth IRA to the credit shelter trust is more beneficial. This is true because income tax has already been paid on the Roth IRA. Thus, 100 percent of the funds passing to the bypass trust eventually pass to the taxpayer's family, compared with a traditional IRA used to fund the bypass trust. In the latter case, income taxes may absorb up to 35 percent of a traditional IRA.

Example

At the time of Harold's death, $600,000 passes from his Roth IRA into an irrevocable IRA trust. The entire $600,000 continues working for Harold's family. Minimum distributions are required over the oldest beneficiary's life expectancy, which at age 47 is 37 years. Once the distributions start, 100 percent of the distribution may be invested for the benefit of the taxpayer's family. There will be no income tax due on the RMD because of the Roth IRA. See table 8-3, "Roth IRA Analysis—Post-Death Situation."

Table 8-3: *Roth IRA Analysis—Post-Death Situation*

Year	Required Minimum Distribution	Taxes at 0%	Beginning Outside Balance	Growth at 10%	Taxes at 15%	Ending Outside Balance
2009	$16,216	$0	$ 16,216	$ 1,622	($ 243)	$ 17,595
2010	$17,838	$0	$ 35,432	$ 3,543	($ 531)	$ 38,444
2011	$19,622	$0	$ 58,066	$ 5,807	($ 871)	$ 63,001
2012	$21,584	$0	$ 84,585	$ 8,459	($ 1,269)	$ 91,775
2013	$23,742	$0	$115,517	$11,552	($ 1,733)	$125,336
2014	$26,116	$0	$151,452	$15,145	($ 2,272)	$164,326
2015	$28,728	$0	$193,054	$19,305	($ 2,896)	$209,463
2016	$31,601	$0	$241,064	$24,106	($ 3,616)	$261,555
2017	$34,761	$0	$296,316	$29,632	($ 4,445)	$321,502
2018	$38,237	$0	$359,739	$35,974	($ 5,396)	$390,317
2019	$42,061	$0	$432,378	$43,238	($ 6,486)	$469,130
2020	$46,267	$0	$515,397	$51,540	($ 7,731)	$559,206
2021	$50,893	$0	$610,099	$61,010	($ 9,151)	$661,958
2022	$55,983	$0	$717,940	$71,794	($10,769)	$778,965
2023	$61,581	$0	$840,546	$84,055	($12,608)	$911,993

Example

Assume the preceding example, but instead a traditional IRA is used to fund the irrevocable IRA trust. See table 8-4, "Traditional IRA Analysis—Post-Death Situation," and figure 8-2, "Traditional IRA Versus Roth IRA."

Table 8-4: *Traditional IRA Analysis—Post-Death Situation*

Year	Required Minimum Distribution	Taxes at 35%	Beginning Outside Balance	Growth at 10%	Taxes at 15%	Ending Outside Balance
2009	$16,216	($ 5,676)	$ 10,541	$ 1,054	($ 158)	$ 11,436
2010	$17,838	($ 6,243)	$ 23,031	$ 2,303	($ 345)	$ 24,989
2011	$19,622	($ 6,868)	$ 37,743	$ 3,774	($ 566)	$ 40,951
2012	$21,584	($ 7,554)	$ 54,980	$ 5,498	($ 825)	$ 59,654
2013	$23,742	($ 8,310)	$ 75,086	$ 7,509	($1,126)	$ 81,468
2014	$26,116	($ 9,141)	$ 98,444	$ 9,844	($1,477)	$106,812
2015	$28,728	($10,055)	$125,485	$12,549	($1,882)	$136,151
2016	$31,601	($11,060)	$156,692	$15,669	($2,350)	$170.01
2017	$34,761	($12,166)	$192,605	$19,261	($2,889)	$208,977
2018	$38,237	($13,383)	$233,831	$23,383	($3,507)	$253,706
2019	$42,061	($14,721)	$281,046	$28,105	($4,216)	$304,935
2020	$46,267	($16,193)	$335,008	$33,501	($5,025)	$363,484
2021	$50,893	($17,813)	$396,564	$39,656	($5,948)	$430,272
2022	$55,983	($19,594)	$466,661	$46,666	($7,000)	$506,327
2023	$61,581	($21,553)	$546,355	$54,636	($8,195)	$592,795

Figure 8-2: *Traditional FRA Versus Roth IRA*

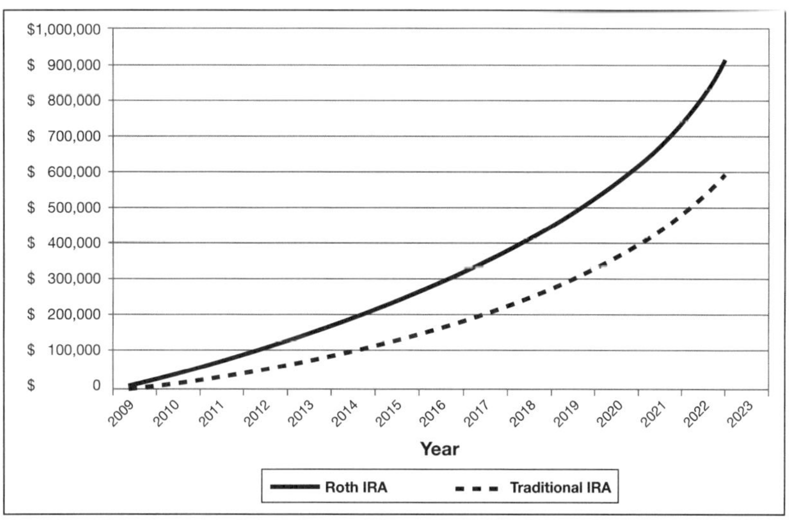

Conclusion

Drafting a trust to qualify as a designated beneficiary of a Roth IRA can be a difficult task and CPAs should direct their clients to an attorney who is experienced in drafting such specialized trusts. The next chapter will delve deeper into the different types of trusts that can be considered when a client wishes to utilize a trust as beneficiary of their Roth IRA.

Appendix A
IRA Creditor Protection Against Claims of Parent's Creditors and Beneficiary's Creditors

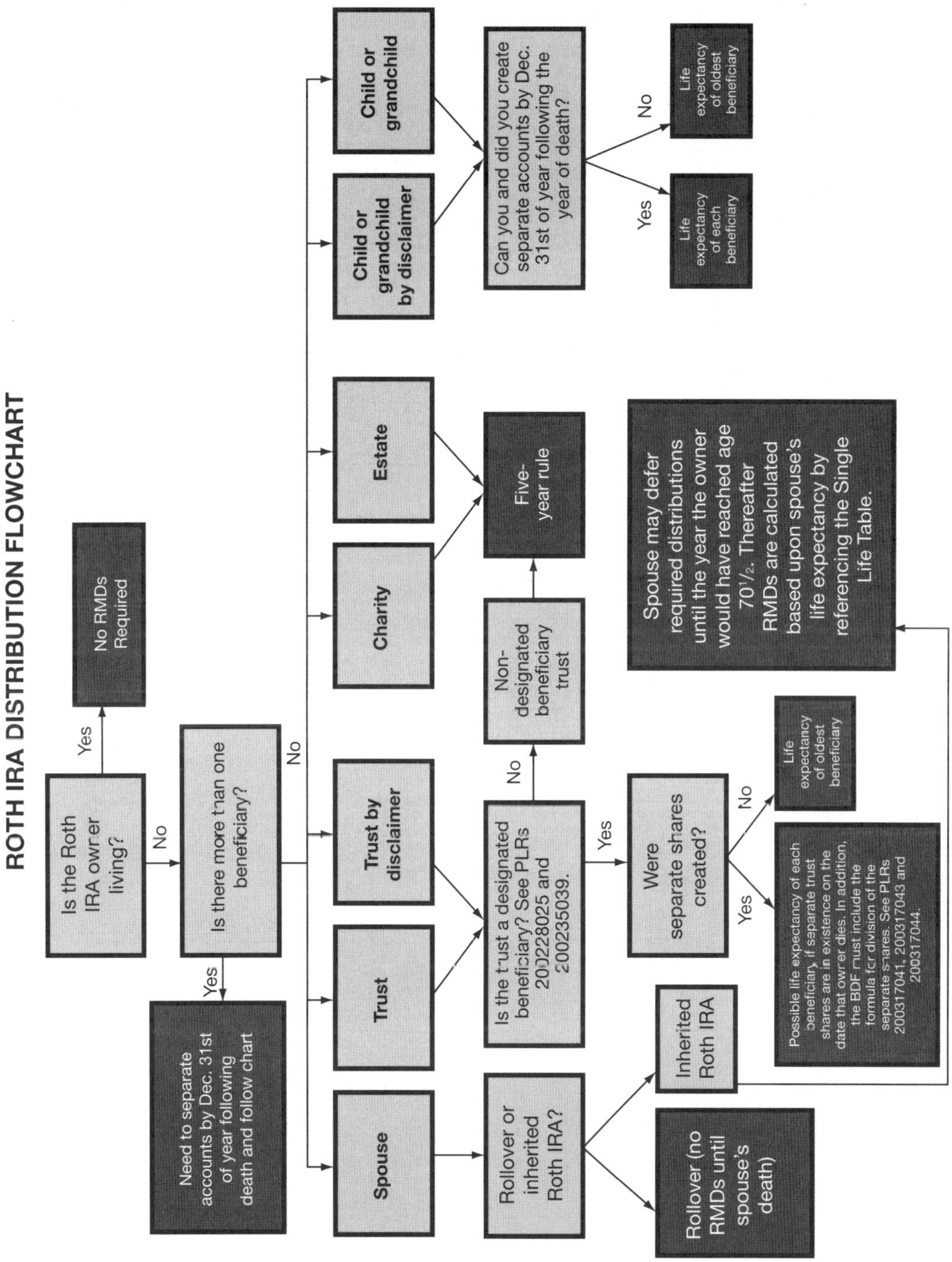

ROTH IRA SUMMARY

	Inherited Spousal Beneficiary
Roth IRA	Spouse may defer required distributions until the year the owner would have reached age $70^{1}/_{2}$. Thereafter, RMDs are calculated based upon spouse's life expectancy by referencing her attained age for the year of distribution based on the Single Life Table in A-1 of Treas. Reg. § 1.401(a)(9)-9. For each succeeding year, this process is repeated. (RECALC'D)

	Non-Designated Beneficiary
Death Before RBD	Entire balance must be distributed no later than December 31st of the fifth anniversary year of the decedent's death. However, consider (if possible) the potential to cash out non-individual beneficiaries, or segregate interests. PLR required.

A-1 of Treas. Reg § 1.40(a)(9)-9 Single Life Table					
Age	Multiple	Age	Multiple	Age	Multiple
0	82.4	37	46.5	74	14.1
1	81.6	38	45.6	75	13.4
2	80.6	39	44.6	76	12.7
3	79.7	40	43.6	77	12.1
4	78.7	41	42.7	78	11.4
5	77.7	42	41.7	79	10.8
6	76.7	43	40.7	80	10.2
7	75.8	44	39.8	81	9.7
8	74.8	45	38.8	82	9.1
9	73.8	46	37.9	83	8.6
10	72.8	47	37.0	84	8.1
11	71.8	48	36.0	85	7.6
12	70.8	49	35.1	86	7.1
13	69.9	50	34.2	87	6.7
14	68.9	51	33.3	88	6.3
15	67.9	52	32.3	89	5.9
16	66.9	53	31.4	90	5.5
17	66.0	54	30.5	91	5.2
18	65.0	55	29.6	92	4.9
19	64.0	56	28.7	93	4.6
20	63.0	57	27.9	94	4.3
21	62.1	58	27.0	95	4.1
22	61.1	59	26.1	96	3.8
23	60.1	60	25.2	97	3.6
24	59.1	61	24.4	98	3.4
25	58.2	62	23.5	99	3.1
26	57.2	63	22.7	100	2.9
27	56.2	64	21.8	101	2.7
28	55.3	65	21.0	102	2.5
29	54.3	66	20.2	103	2.3
30	53.3	67	19.4	104	2.1
31	52.4	68	18.6	105	1.9
32	51.4	69	17.8	106	1.7
33	50.4	70	17.0	107	1.5
34	49.4	71	16.3	108	1.4
35	48.5	72	15.5	109	1.2
36	47.5	73	14.8	110	1.1
				111	1.0

Appendix B
Distributions to Beneficiary Under IRC Section 401(a)(9): Roth IRAs

Beneficiary	Owner Died Prior to Required Beginning Date
Spouse—Inherited IRA (No rollover)	Spouse may defer required distributions until the year the owner would have reached age 70½. In this year, the RMD is calculated based upon spouse's life expectancy by referencing her attained age for the year of distribution based on the Single Life Table of Treas. Reg. § 1.401(a)(9)-9. For each succeeding year, the surviving spouse references his or her age under the Single Life Table.
	Upon the death of the surviving spouse: (1) If the surviving spouse dies **prior** to the year in which the owner would have been age 70½, the spouse is deemed to be the owner/participant and a beneficiary is determined as of September 30th of the year following death. In this following year, such beneficiary must begin to receive RMDs based upon his or her corresponding life expectancy under the Single Life Table. For each succeeding year, the factor is reduced by one. (2) If the surviving spouse dies **on or after** the date in which the owner would have reached age 70½, an RMD for the current year must be taken. Thereafter, RMDs are calculated based upon the now deceased spouse's life expectancy by reference to his or her attained age in the year of death by reference to the Single Life Table. For each succeeding year, the factor is reduced by one.
Spouse—Rollover	RMDs begin the year the spouse reaches age 70½ (subject to deferral to 4/1 of year following). If the spouse is already age 70½, RMDs begin by December 31st of the year following the rollover. For such years, RMDs based upon spouse's life expectancy factor determined under the Uniform Lifetime Table. **(RECALC'D)**
Child or Grandchild	The first year distribution (year after the year of death) is determined based upon corresponding life expectancy factor for the child/grandchild's age in the year of the first distribution by reference to the Single Life Table. For succeeding years, this factor is reduced by one.
Child or Grandchild by Qualified Disclaimer	The first year distribution (year after the year of death) is determined based upon corresponding life expectancy factor for the child/grandchild's age in the year of the first distribution by reference to the Single Life Table. For succeeding years, this factor is reduced by one.
Other Non-Spouse Individual Designated Beneficiary	The first year distribution (year after the year of death) is determined based upon corresponding life expectancy factor for the designated beneficiary's age in the year of the first distribution by reference to the Single Life Table. For succeeding years, this factor is reduced by one.
Multiple Individual Beneficiaries: See PLRs 200317041, 200317043 and 200317044 for separate shares in relation to a trust.	As long as the account is segregated prior to December 31st of the year following death, each beneficiary may independently calculate RMDs. Thus, with respect to each beneficiary, the first year distribution (year after the year of death) is determined based upon corresponding life expectancy factor for the beneficiary's age in the year of the first distribution by reference to the Single Life Table. For succeeding years, this factor is reduced by one.
Designated Beneficiary Trust See PLRs 200317041, 200317043 and 200317044 for separate shares in relation to a trust. See also PLRs 200228025 and 200235039.	The first year distribution (year after the year of death) is determined based upon corresponding life expectancy factor for the oldest beneficiary's age in the year of the first distribution by reference to the Single Life Table. For succeeding years, this factor is reduced by one. If the trust is designed to create "one pot" for the benefit of multiple beneficiaries, RMDs are based upon the oldest beneficiary's life expectancy. However, if the Beneficiary Designation is payable to separate sub-trusts, each separate sub-trust beneficiary **may** be able to use their respective life expectancies to calculate RMDs. Note however, multiple shares must be established prior to death. *A PLR should be requested if separate share treatment is desired.*

(continued)

Beneficiary	Owner Died Prior to Required Beginning Date
Non Designated Beneficiary Trust: See PLRs 200228025 and 200235039.	Entire balance must be distributed no later than December 31st of the fifth anniversary year of the decedent's death. ***However, consider the potential to cash out non-individual beneficiaries where and if possible.***
Charity	Entire balance must be distributed no later than December 31st of the fifth anniversary year of the decedent's death. ***However, consider the potential to cash out the charity or segregate interests where multiple beneficiaries exist.***
Estate	Entire balance must be distributed no later than December 31st of the fifth anniversary year of the decedent's death.
Conduit Trust for the Benefit of Spouse	**During the life of the surviving spouse:** Spouse may defer required distributions until the year the owner would have reached age 70½. In this year, the RMD is calculated based upon spouse's life expectancy by referencing her attained age for the year of distribution based on the Single Life Table. For each succeeding year, the surviving spouse references his or her age under the Single Life Table.
	Upon the death of the surviving spouse: (1) If the surviving spouse dies prior to the year in which the owner would have been age 70½, the spouse is deemed to be the owner/participant and a beneficiary is determined as of September 30th of the year following death. In this following year, such beneficiary must begin to receive RMDs based upon his or her corresponding life expectancy under the Single Life Table. For each succeeding year, the factor is reduced by one. If the surviving spouse has no designated beneficiary, the five year rule applies. In PLR 200644022, the IRS held that the spouse did not have a designated beneficiary even though the trust for her benefit had contingent beneficiaries. (2) If the surviving spouse dies on or after the date in which the owner would have reached age 70½, an RMD for the current year must be taken. Thereafter, RMDs are calculated based upon the now deceased spouse's life expectancy by reference to his or her attained age in the year of death by reference to the Single Life Table. For each succeeding year, the factor is reduced by one.

Distributions to Conduit Trust for the Benefit of Spouse

Owner Died Prior to Required Beginning Date	Owner Died After Required Beginning Date
During the life of the surviving spouse: Spouse may defer required distributions until the year the owner would have reached age 70½. In this year, the RMD is calculated based upon spouse's life expectancy by referencing her attained age for the year of distribution based on the Single Life Table. For each succeeding year, the surviving spouse references his or her age under the Single Life Table.	**During the life of the surviving spouse:** RMD for year of death must be taken based upon decedent's life expectancy factor under the Uniform Lifetime Table (if not already taken by the decedent during his/her lifetime). Thereafter, the applicable distribution period is longer of: (1) the surviving spouse's life expectancy based on the Single Life Table using the surviving spouse's birthday for each distribution calendar year after the calendar year of the employee's death up through the calendar year of the spouse's death. For each succeeding year, this process is repeated; or (2) the life expectancy of the deceased spouse under the Single Life Table using the age of the deceased spouse as of his or her birthday in the year of death, whereby in subsequent years, this factor is reduced by one.

Distributions to Conduit Trust for the Benefit of Spouse *(continued)*	
Owner Died Prior to Required Beginning Date	Owner Died After Required Beginning Date
Upon the death of the surviving spouse: (1) If the surviving spouse dies prior to the year in which the owner would have been age 70½, the spouse is deemed to be the owner/participant and a beneficiary is determined as of September 30th of the year following death. In this following year, such beneficiary must begin to receive RMDs based upon his or her corresponding life expectancy under the Single Life Table. For each succeeding year, the factor is reduced by one. If the surviving spouse has no designated beneficiary, the five year rule applies. In PLR 200644022, the IRS held that the spouse did not have a designated beneficiary even though the trust for her benefit had contingent beneficiaries. (2) If the surviving spouse dies on or after the date in which the owner would have reached age 70½, an RMD for the current year must be taken. Thereafter, RMDs are calculated based upon the now deceased spouse's life expectancy by reference to his or her attained age in the year of death by reference to the Single Life Table. For each succeeding year, the factor is reduced by one.	**Upon death of the surviving spouse:** the RMD determined above must be withdrawn for the year of death (if not already taken by the decedent during his/her lifetime). For subsequent years, the RMD factor is fixed based upon the method employed above, note, if surviving spouse's life expectancy is being used, his or her life expectancy is now fixed based upon the age of this spouse in the year of death by reference to the Single Life Table. For each succeeding year, the factor is reduced by one.

Estate Planning for the Roth IRA

Introduction

For estate planning purposes, the Roth IRA provides a wide range of opportunities. This is particularly true because of the tax-free nature of Roth IRA distributions. This chapter outlines the important options available to clients when executing their estate plans as well as post-mortem planning options available to the Roth IRA beneficiaries.

In years to come, many clients will strategically name a unified credit trust as the beneficiary of their Roth IRAs. By using the Roth IRA (compared to a traditional IRA) to fund the bypass trust, these clients will be able to use assets that will not be subject to income tax in the future.

Under the Economic Growth and Tax Relief Act of 2001 (the act), the amount that can be used to fund a credit shelter trust is annually increased, as shown in table 9-1, "Growth in Credit Shelter Trust by Year." The act is reproduced as appendix 4 "Economic Growth and Tax Relief Reconciliation Act of 2001: Text" at the end of this book.

Table 9-1: *Growth in Credit Shelter Trust by Year*

Year	Unified Credit Amount
2002	$1,000,000
2003	$1,000,000
2004	$1,500,000
2005	$1,500,000
2006	$2,000,000
2007	$2,000,000
2008	$2,000,000
2009	$3,500,000
2010	Estate tax eliminated
2011	Estate tax reinstated unless Congress acts

The Effect on Estate Tax Liability

For many taxpayers with substantial wealth in their qualified plans or IRAs, the analysis of whether to convert a traditional IRA to a Roth IRA should include the effect of estate taxes. Estate planning affects this decision in the following three ways:

1. If an IRA is converted to a Roth IRA, the overall estate is reduced by the amount of the income taxes paid. This results in a lower overall estate tax base.

> **Example**
>
> Tom and Sue have an IRA valued at $1 million. If they elect to convert the IRA to a Roth IRA, their estate is decreased by $350,000 assuming a 35 percent income tax rate.

2. From a wealth-transfer perspective, it is often better to pay income tax before paying estate tax. See table 9-2, "Benefit of Paying Income Tax Before the Estate Tax."
3. It will generally be advantageous to fund the bypass trust with Roth IRA assets rather than with a traditional IRA. See table 9-3, "The Value of Assets Passing to the Bypass Trust."

Table 9-2: *Benefit of Paying Income Tax Before the Estate Tax*

	Estate Tax First Traditional IRA	Income Tax First Roth IRA
IRA balance	$ 2,500,000	$ 2,500,000
Less federal and state income tax at 40%	0	(1,000,000)
Less federal estate tax at 45%	(1,125,000)	(675,000)
Less state estate tax at 10%*	(250,000)	(150,000)
Total taxes	(1,375,000)	(1,825,000)
Net to family	$ 1,125,000	$ 675,000
IRA balance subject to income tax	$ 2,500,000	
Less IRC Section 691(c) deduction	(1,125,000)	
Balance subject to income tax	1,375,000	
Less federal and state income tax at 40%	(550,000)	
Net to family	$ 575,000	$ 675,000

*Assumed a weighted average rate of 10 percent. The lower the effective state soak up tax is, the less advantageous it will be to pay income tax first.

Table 9-3: *The Value of Assets Passing to the Bypass Trust*

	Traditional IRA	Roth IRA
Exemption amount in 2009	$ 3,500,000	$3,500,000
Less income taxes at 35 percent	(1,225,000)	0
Net to family	$ 2,275,000	$3,500,000
Additional wealth transfer		$1,225,000

Analyzing the Interrelationship of Income Tax and Estate Tax

At the time of a client's death, the traditional IRA is subject to both income tax and estate tax. In contrast, the Roth IRA is subject only to the estate tax because the income tax has already been paid. It is generally better to pay income tax before paying the estate tax. If, at the time of a client's death, he or she holds a traditional IRA, it will be subject to estate tax based on the fair market value at the date of death.

Example

Tom owns an IRA valued at $5 million at his date of death. In this case, $5 million is included in his estate. On the other hand, if Tom had already made a Roth IRA election and the IRA was valued at $3.5 million, only $3.5 million would be included in his estate. Table 9-3 in the previous section shows the impact of making the Roth IRA conversion election and unified credit funding versus the traditional IRA.

The same logic also applies to a generation-skipping transfer (GST) tax-exempt trust. The increased exemptions discussed in the preceding example also affect the importance of this type of planning.

The IRC Section 691(c) Deduction Compared to Paying Income Tax First

Is it really better to pay income taxes first?

Example

Tony has a $3 million stock portfolio in addition to his $2.5 million IRA. At his death, his IRA will be exposed to a 45 percent estate tax. Table 9-2 in the previous section illustrates the computation. (For ease of reference, death is assumed to occur on January 1, 2009.)

The wealth transfer is enhanced by $100,000 by paying the income tax before paying the estate tax. This occurs because the Internal Revenue Code (IRC) Section 691(c) deduction allows only for the deduction of federal estate tax. (The state estate tax is not deductible in determining federal taxable income.)

The IRC Section 691(c) income tax deduction for estate tax paid is not subject to the 2 percent adjustment to itemized deductions.[1]

The Estate Tax Marital Deduction

Outright IRA distributions to a participant's surviving spouse generally qualify for the marital deduction under IRC Section 2056(b). IRA beneficiary designations payable to a marital deduction trust also qualify for the marital deduction.

1 Internal Revenue Code (IRC) Section 67(b)(7).

Example

Joe dies and leaves his entire $6,000,000 estate to his spouse. This transfer qualifies for the marital deduction and will not be subject to estate tax.

Example

Assume the preceding example except that instead of leaving his entire estate to his spouse outright, Joe leaves it in trust for her. If the trust qualifies as a qualified terminable interest property (QTIP) trust under IRC Section 2056(b), the assets left in trust for Joe's spouse will qualify for the marital deduction.

The Estate Charitable Deduction

Assets that are included in a decedent's gross estate and pass to qualified charities qualify for the charitable deduction.[2] Qualified plan benefits and IRAs can be ideal assets to satisfy charitable gifts because the amounts passing from the plan to the charity can escape both estate and income tax if properly structured. Charities do not qualify as designated beneficiaries and so do not qualify for the exception to the accelerated minimum distribution rules.[3]

Under the prior distribution regulations, if less than all of the account is to be paid to a charity, it was advised that a separate account be established for the charity's share to avoid tainting the entire account and so avoid the accelerated minimum distribution requirements applying to the entire account.[4]

The current distribution rules, however, provide opportunities for postmortem planning. The final determination date for beneficiaries is September 30 of the year following the year of death.[5] If the beneficiary designation includes a beneficiary that does not qualify under the law as a designated beneficiary (charity), that beneficiary could be "cashed out." Only the beneficiaries remaining on September 30 of the year following the year of the owner's death must be taken into consideration in determining distributions.

2 IRC Section 2055.
3 Treasury Regulation Section 1.401(a)(9)-4, Q&A 3.
4 See Proposed Treasury Regulation Section 1.401(a)(9)-l, Q&A E-5(a)(2).
5 Treasury Regulation Section 1.401(a)(9)-4, A-4(a).

> **Example**
>
> Dr. Jones named his spouse, Mrs. Jones; a church; and an adult child, Bill, as equal primary beneficiaries of his IRA. The church, not a designated beneficiary, taints the individual beneficiaries. However, if the church receives its bequest between the date of the owner's death and September 30 of the year following the year of Dr. Jones' death, it is no longer considered a beneficiary. Under this scenario, when the identity of the beneficiary is finalized (on September 30 of the year following the year of death), there are only two beneficiaries: Mrs. Jones and Bill.

However, because a Roth IRA should never be subject to income tax, it should generally pass to one's family and not to a charitable beneficiary.

Revocable Trust

IRC Section 401(a)(9) regulations allow a revocable trust to qualify for designated beneficiary status as long as it meets certain requirements. See chapter 8, "Beneficiary Considerations," for a detailed discussion of the requirements for naming a trust as the beneficiary of retirement assets.

If used, the revocable living trust should contain a fractional funding clause. This tax effect is important in creating and funding marital deduction estate plans. If a plan benefit or IRA is used to fund a marital or credit shelter bequest, it should be used to fund a *fractional* rather than a *pecuniary* formula bequest. Using the plan or IRA even to make a partial funding of a pecuniary bequest accelerates taxable income and should, therefore, ordinarily be avoided.[6]

Source of Payment of Estate Tax

When designing an estate plan for large traditional or Roth IRAs, one should understand how estate taxes are apportioned among probate and nonprobate assets. In a number of states, the estate tax is apportioned among each and every asset, whereas in other states the estate tax is borne by the probate estate. No federal statute apportions the estate tax against plan assets or IRAs, unlike the rules that require apportionment for life insurance,[7] power-of-appointment assets,[8] QTIP assets,[9] or retained-interest assets.[10] The following examples, absent specific guidance under state law, illustrate the federal apportionment treatment.

6 See Private Letter Rulings (PLR) 9507008 and 9315016 and CCA 200644020.
7 IRC Section 2206.
8 IRC Section 2207.
9 IRC Section 2207A.
10 IRC Section 2207B.

Example

John's $4,000,000 IRA is paid to his children, and his will leaves the residue of his estate, $600,000, to his wife, Sue. The entire estate tax is paid from the spouse's residual bequest. Further, to the extent that a tax is paid, the marital deduction is reduced, causing additional estate taxes to be paid.

Example

John's $2,000,000 IRA is paid to his son, and John's will leaves the residue of his probate estate (a $2,000,000 business) to his daughter. John's will does not allocate the estate tax liability. His daughter pays estate taxes of $225,000 on a taxable estate of $4,000,000 (minus $3,500,000 applicable credit so $500,000 is subject to estate tax at 45 percent). The son can take an in respect of a decedent (IRD) deduction under IRC Section 691(c), even though he did not pay an estate tax. The bottom line is that the daughter nets $1,775,000 ($2,000,000 IRA – estate tax of $225,000 = $1,775,000), and the son nets $1,378,750 ($2,000,000 IRA – $225,000 IRD deduction = $1,775,000) ($1,775,000 taxable income × 35% = income tax of $621,500).

A critical part of every plan is to work with legal counsel to determine exactly how estate taxes are apportioned among probate and nonprobate assets. Generally, it should be possible to override state law and for the estate planning documents to specify how estate taxes are apportioned. In these instances, it is often critical that estate taxes not be apportioned against IRAs or Roth IRAs but against regular probate assets. This allows for the maximum deferral of both the traditional and Roth IRA.

The Generation-Skipping Transfer Tax

Generally, transfers of property from a donor or decedent to a person who is, or who is deemed to be, two or more generations younger than the donor or decedent, are subject to the GST tax.[11]

To the extent that it is likely that a client's IRA or Roth IRA bequest to a grandchild will exceed the client's remaining GST tax exemption, care should be taken to limit transfers to the grandchildren or, at a minimum, advise the client that the transfers will be subject to the GST tax. Under the Economic Growth and Tax Relief Act of 2001 (appendix 4 "Economic Growth and Tax Relief Reconciliation Act of 2001: Text"), the GST tax exemption equals the exemption equivalent of the unified credit against estate tax, with a temporary repeal in 2010. In 2009, the exemption amount is $3.5 million. The exemption amount in 2011 will depend on what legislature is passed.

11 IRC Section 2601.

If plan or IRA proceeds are distributed after the participant's death to the participant's grandchild, or to a trust of which the participant's grandchildren are the only beneficiaries, a *direct skip* occurs, and the proceeds are subject to GST tax.[12]

Utilizing a properly designed trust for the benefit of children and grandchildren is an important planning opportunity for many individuals. By utilizing this type of trust, a taxpayer can pass greater wealth to his or her grandchildren. Table 9-4, "Growth Resulting From Generation-Skipping Transfer Tax Exemption," shows the additional wealth that the grandchildren receive by using a GST exemption and a properly designed trust for the benefit of children and grandchildren versus giving the assets outright to the children.

Table 9-4: *Growth Resulting From Generation-Skipping Transfer Tax Exemption*

	Distributions To Children Outright	Distributions in Trust for Children and Grandchildren
Gross estate above unified credit amount	$4,000,000	$4,000,000
Estate tax at child's death	1,800,000	0
Net to estate grandchildren	2,200,000	$4,000,000

Creating Wealth With the Roth IRA

For the larger estate, the Roth IRA provides even more dynamic opportunities to create wealth for a client's family. Because minimum distributions are not required until the client's death, it may be possible for a couple to build substantial wealth in their Roth IRAs. The key to protecting this wealth is to ensure adequate estate liquidity to allow for the Roth IRA to continue and to be distributed over the life expectancies of the beneficiaries. Table 9-5, "Client Leaves $500,000 IRA to Child," and table 9-6, "Client Leaves $500,000 to Grandchild," show distributions over the life expectancy of both a child's life expectancy (age 40) and grandchild's life expectancy (age 10) assuming growth in the Roth IRA of ten percent.

12 IRC Section 2612(c).

Table 9-5: *Client Leaves $500,000 IRA to Child*

Year	Roth IRA Beginning Value	Life Expectancy	Annual Distribution
1	$ 500,000	43.6	$11,468
2	$ 537,385	42.6	$12,615
3	$ 577,248	41.6	$13,876
4	$ 619,709	40.6	$15,264
5	$ 664,889	39.6	$16,790
6	$ 712,909	38.6	$18,469
7	$ 763,884	37.6	$20,316
8	$ 817,925	36.6	$22,348
9	$ 875,135	35.6	$24,582
10	$ 935,608	34.6	$27,041
11	$ 999,424	33.6	$29,745
12	$1,066,647	32.6	$32,719
13	$1,137,320	31.6	$35,991
14	$1,211,462	30.6	$39,590
15	$1,289,059	29.6	$43,549

Table 9-6: *Client Leaves $500,000 IRA to Grandchild*

Year	Roth IRA Beginning Value	Life Expectancy	Annual Distribution
1	$ 500,000	72.8	$ 6,868
2	$ 542,445	71.8	$ 7,555
3	$ 588,379	70.8	$ 8,310
4	$ 638,076	69.8	$ 9,141
5	$ 691,827	68.8	$10,056
6	$ 749,949	67.8	$11,061
7	$ 812,777	66.8	$12,167
8	$ 880,670	65.8	$13,384
9	$ 954,015	64.8	$14,722
10	$1,033,222	63.8	$16,195
11	$1,118,730	62.8	$17,814
12	$1,211,007	61.8	$19,596
13	$1,310,553	60.8	$21,555
14	$1,417,897	59.8	$23,711
15	$1,533,605	58.8	$26,082

Figure 9-1, "Leaving $500,000 Roth IRA to Child Versus Grandchild," illustrates the wealth that is created by a Roth IRA owner naming his or her grandchild as the beneficiary as opposed to his or her child as beneficiary. Lower required minimum distributions (RMDs) allow for substantially more tax-free growth in the Roth IRA over time for the grandchild.

Figure 9-1: *Leaving $500,000 Roth IRA to Child Versus Grandchild*

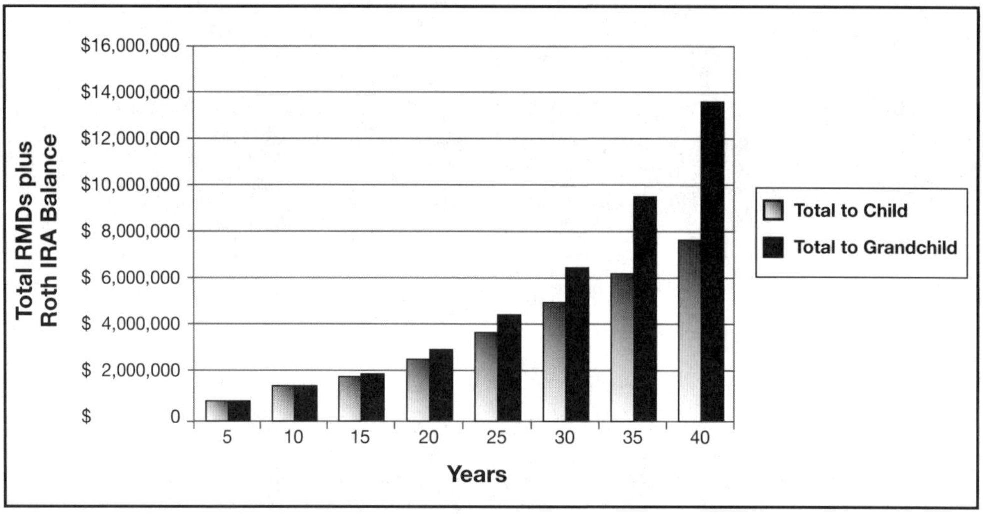

Taxation of Traditional IRAs at Death

At a participant's death, a traditional IRA does not receive a step-up in basis. Distributions received after the participant's death are IRD and eventually will be taxed to the beneficiary.[13] In designing an estate plan, care must be taken that income is not immediately recognized upon the death of the IRA holder. This can be done by proper beneficiary designation planning.

IRC Section 691(c) Deduction (IRD)

The person receiving income (the IRD) from an IRA can deduct the federal estate tax paid with respect to the IRA benefits.[14] This is shown in the table 9-7, "Federal Estate Tax Deduction Resulting From an IRA."

13 IRC Section 691, GCM 39858.
14 IRC Section 691(c)(1).

Table 9-7: *Federal Estate Tax Deduction Resulting From an IRA*

	Total Estate	Federal Estate Tax
With IRA	$4,500,000	$450,000
Without IRA	$3,500,000	$ 0
IRC Section 691(c) deduction		$450,000

In determining the value of this deduction, it is important to remember the following:

- The deduction is a miscellaneous itemized deduction but is not subject to the 2 percent floor.[15]
- The deduction is likely, however, to be restricted by limitations on the amount of itemized deductions.
- The benefit of the IRD deduction is lost if no federal estate tax is paid on the taxable income (for example, in an optimal marital deduction plan).
- In a typical marital deduction estate plan, qualified plan and IRA proceeds should not be payable to credit shelter beneficiaries but rather should be paid to the marital deduction beneficiary, if possible. When the spouse or a marital trust receives the IRD and pays the income tax, the tax paid is effectively deducted from the spouse's estate at the spouse's death.

Example

John and Sue each have taxable estates and have used their applicable exclusion amounts. John leaves his $300,000 IRA to Sue and $1 million of other (non-IRD) assets to a credit shelter trust. Over Sue's lifetime, she draws out the full $300,000 and pays federal and state income taxes of $100,000. At her death, only $200,000 remains ($300,000 IRA – $100,000 tax = $200,000) to be taxed in her estate, and the credit shelter trust remains $1 million. Conversely, if the $300,000 IRA had been paid to the credit shelter trust, the credit shelter trust would be reduced by the $100,000 of income taxes and Sue's estate would have the full value of $300,000 of the other assets received from John's estate.

Additional Planning Points

1. The IRD deduction under IRC Section 691(c) only applies to federal estate tax paid and does not give any benefit for state death taxes paid. On the other hand, if the surviving spouse pays both state and federal income tax on distributions received from the plan or IRA, the spouse's estate effectively receives an estate tax deduction for the full amount of both income taxes and so benefits from payment of both taxes.
2. The IRD deduction under IRC Section 691(c) applies only when a federal estate tax is incurred. This is why it is important to ensure that IRD passes at the second death when the optimal marital deduction is used, rather than at the first death.

15 IRC Section 67(b)(8).

Example

Assume Brad and Stacey have $8,000,000, of which $1,000,000 is an IRA. The $1,000,000 IRA and $2,500,000 of cash passes to a family trust for the benefit of their children at the first death. The entire $3,500,000 exclusion is used, so no federal estate tax is incurred. Correspondingly, at the second death, $4,500,000 of cash passes to the children from Stacey's estate with a $450,000 federal estate tax being incurred ($4,500,000 – $3,500,000 = $1,000,000 × 45% = $450,000). However, the $4,500,000 passing to the children at the second death would not contain the IRD associated with the qualified plan or IRA distribution.

In the alternative, if $3,500,000 of cash is passed to the family trust at the first death, with the IRA balance passing at the second death, the IRD income tax deduction is available for the $1,000,000 of IRA proceeds (based on the assumption that both deaths occur in 2009). This computation is shown in table 9-8, "Computation of Tax Benefit of Deduction."

Table 9-8: *Computation of Tax Benefit of Deduction*

Taxable estate	$ 4,500,000
Less exclusion	(3,500,000)
Taxable estate (net of exclusion)	1,000,000
Income tax deduction equals Federal estate tax attributable to IRD	450,000
Tax benefit of deduction (at combined federal and state rate of 40 percent)	$ 180,000

A lifetime transfer of one spouse's IRA to the other spouse's IRA is a taxable distribution to the spouse from whose IRA the transfer was made and is not excludible from income as an interspousal transfer.[16]

Prior Estate Tax Exemptions

Retirement benefits, IRAs, and Roth IRAs are subject to estate tax in the participant's estate.[17] Prior law allowed a complete, and then a partial, estate tax exclusion for qualified plan assets if favorable income tax treatment was waived. Transition rules allow for the continuation of the exclusion in specified circumstances.[18]

16 IRC Section 1041. See PLR 9422060 (March 14, 1994).

17 IRC Section 2039(a).

18 See Tax Equity and Fiscal Responsibility Act of 1982 (TEFRA) Section 456(c), Deficit Reduction Act of 1984 (DEFRA) Sec. 525(b), and the Taxpayer Relief Act (TRA) of 1986 Section 1852(e)(3). See also PLR 9211041 and Rev. Rul. 92-22, 1992-1 C.B. 313 for a discussion of the transition rules as they relate to qualified plans. The transition rules do not apply to the traditional or Roth IRAs (Rev. Rul. 92-22).

Disclaimer and Beneficiary Designations

If a person makes a qualified disclaimer with respect to any interest in property, the interest is treated as never having been transferred to that person.[19] For a qualified disclaimer to be effective, it must meet several requirements. The term *qualified disclaimer* is defined as an irrevocable and unqualified refusal by a person to accept an interest in property, but only if

- the refusal is in writing.
- the writing is received by the transferor of the interest, a legal representative, or the holder of legal title to the property to which the interest relates within a specified time frame.
- the person has not accepted the interest or any of its benefits.
- as a result of the refusal, the interest passes without any direction on the part of the person making the disclaimer and passes either to the spouse of the decedent or to a person other than the person making the disclaimer.[20]

If all of the preceding requirements are met, the disclaimer is a qualified disclaimer within IRC Section 2518.

A few other issues need to be addressed when reviewing qualified disclaimers under IRC Section 2518. The first is whether a disclaimer of benefits under a qualified plan constitutes either an assignment or alienation of plan benefits contrary to IRC Section 401(a)(13) and Employee Retirement Income Security Act of 1974 Section 206(d) or an assignment of income. General Counsel Memorandum (GCM) 39858 states that a disclaimer of qualified plan benefits that satisfies the requirements of state law and IRC Section 2518(b) is neither a prohibited assignment or alienation nor an assignment of income.

Another issue is whether a disclaimer of benefits from either an IRA or an individual retirement annuity constitutes an assignment of income and whether a disclaimer is contrary to IRC Section 408(a)(4) or IRC Section 408(b)(1). IRC Section 408(a)(4) and IRC Section 408(b)(1) address the nonforfeitability and nontransferability of IRAs or individual retirement annuities. GCM 39858 concludes that a disclaimer of benefits from an IRA that satisfies the requirements of state law and IRC Section 2518(b) is not an assignment of income. Also, the disclaimer is not contrary to IRC Section 408(a)(4) and IRC Section 408(b)(1).[21] The IRS has also ruled that a beneficiary's disclaimer of an IRA was a qualified disclaimer even though, prior to making the disclaimer, the beneficiary received an RMD from the IRA for the year of the decedent's death. The IRS stated that the beneficiary could make a qualified disclaimer with respect to all or a portion of the balance of the account (other than the income attributable to the RMD that the beneficiary received) provided that at the time the disclaimer is made, the disclaimed amount and the income attributable to the disclaimed amount are paid to the beneficiary entitled to receive the disclaimed amount, or are segregated in a separate account.[22]

---

19 IRC Section 2518(a).
20 IRC Section 2518(b).
21 General Counsel Memorandum (GCM) 39858, September 9, 1991.
22 Rev. Rul. 2005-36, 2005-26 IRB 1368.

The Importance of Having a Designated Beneficiary

To maximize the tax deferral of any IRA, it is important to choose the proper designated beneficiary. This choice will significantly affect the calculation of the RMDs and will therefore determine the amount of tax deferral that will ultimately be available. In making this choice, it is very important that the tax regulations are closely followed.

Distributions After the Death of the Owner Without a Designated Beneficiary

If the owner of a qualified plan or traditional IRA does not have a designated beneficiary and the owner dies before his or her required beginning date, the IRC dictates that the qualified plan or IRA must be distributed by December 31 of the year of the fifth anniversary of the death of the owner.[23] The distribution can be made in any fashion the beneficiary chooses. It may be made ratably over this period of time or in a lump sum on December 31 of the year containing the fifth anniversary of the death of the IRA owner. This relatively rapid withdrawal may cause the beneficiaries of the IRA to lose many years of deferral. A Roth IRA owner is always treated as dying before the required beginning date.

If the owner of a qualified plan or traditional IRA dies after his or her required beginning date and does not have a designated beneficiary, distributions are taken out by referencing the decedent's age in the year of death in the Single Life Table in Treasury Regulation Section 1.401(a)(9)-9, Q&A 7 and reducing the distribution factor by one for any year thereafter.[24] A full copy of the 2002 final rules and regulations from the Department of the Treasury, including Treasury Regulation Section 1.401(a)(9)-9, can be found on the accompanying CD-ROM.

Death Before Required Beginning Date

The IRC allows a designated beneficiary to receive distributions over his or her single-life expectancy.[25] This is usually far more advantageous than the five year rule discussed in the preceding paragraphs for death before the required beginning date if there is no designated beneficiary. Therefore, having a designated beneficiary is critical to preserve the deferral that can be achieved with proper planning.

If a qualified disclaimer under IRC Section 2518 and relevant state law is executed by a beneficiary, that beneficiary is assumed to have predeceased the participant. When a disclaimer by the primary beneficiary results in transfer to a trust, the oldest beneficiary of the trust is treated as the designated beneficiary for purposes of determining distributions assuming the family trust meets the requirements of a designated beneficiary (see chapter 4, "Tax Planning Basics").

Death After the Required Beginning Date

If the participant has a designated beneficiary and dies after the required beginning date, the IRC states that the remaining portion of the IRA must be distributed at least as rapidly as before.[26]

---

23 IRC Section 401(a)(9)(B)(ii).
24 Treasury Regulation Section 1.401(a)(9)-5 Q&A 5(c)(3).
25 IRC Section 401(a)(9)(B)(iii). Special rules apply when the spouse is the beneficiary.
26 IRC Section 401(a)(9)(B)(I).

For individuals who die after their required beginning date and have a qualified beneficiary as of September 30 of the year following the year of death, distributions are determined based upon the beneficiary's life expectancy as referenced in the Single Life Table of Treasury Regulation Section 1.401(a)(9)-9, Q&A 7, Table V. For each succeeding year, this factor is reduced by one.[27]

Similar provisions apply if the participant dies after the required beginning date and the primary beneficiary disclaims a portion resulting in transfer to a trust. Because the trust will be a beneficiary as of September 30 of the year following the year of death, the distributions after the death of the participant are determined based on the oldest trust beneficiary's life expectancy. If separate shares are created for each trust beneficiary by December 31 of the year following the year of death and the separate trust shares are specifically named as separate beneficiaries in the beneficiary designation form, each beneficiary can use his or her own individual life expectancy to determine RMDs. Again, for this trust to be a designated beneficiary, certain requirements must be met. If the trust is not a qualified trust for purposes of Treasury Regulation Section 1.401 (a)(9)-4, Q&A 5 and 6, and the owner dies after his required beginning date, the IRA must be distributed based upon the owner's life expectancy in the year of death.

In summary, if a qualified disclaimer is exercised, the disclaiming party is treated as having predeceased the participant. Therefore, if the trust is named as the contingent beneficiary, the family trust is treated as a designated beneficiary if the trust meets all of the requirements set forth in the preceding paragraph and distributions from the IRA are determined based on the oldest trust beneficiary's life expectancy. If the trust is not a qualified trust under IRC Section 401(a)(9), the distribution is determined depending on when the participant died (before or after the required beginning date).

Drafting the Disclaimer

Care must be taken when drafting a disclaimer. It is a legal document and should be drafted in collaboration with the client's attorney. A disclaimer should not refer to a pecuniary amount that passes to the trust (that is, the amount that results in no federal estate tax). If a pecuniary amount is used to fund the trust, the income IRD is accelerated and income tax is due on the entire amount disclaimed (or pecuniary amount).[28] Furthermore, the disclaimer must be coordinated with the funding clause in the revocable trust or will.

Distributions After Death

Postmortem distributions from both the traditional and the Roth IRA are driven by the IRC Section 401(a)(9) rules. For a traditional IRA, if your client names his or her spouse as the primary beneficiary, at your client's death (when survived by the spouse), distributions from the traditional IRA are shown in table 9-9, "Naming Spouse as the Designated Beneficiary—Inherited Treatment After the Death of a Participant," which assumes the spouse (age 74) does not roll over the IRA.

27 Treasury Regulation Section 1.401(a)(9)-5 Q&A 5(c)(1).

28 See IRC Section 691(a).

Table 9-9: *Naming Spouse as the Designated Beneficiary—Inherited Treatment After the Death of a Participant**

Year	Begin Pension Fund Balance	Life Expectancy†	Annual Distribution
2009	$1,000,000	14.1	$ 70,922
2010	$1,021,986	13.4	$ 76,268
2011	$1,040,290	12.7	$ 81,913
2012	$1,054,215	12.1	$ 87,125
2013	$1,063,799	11.4	$ 93,316
2014	$1,067,532	10.8	$ 98,846
2015	$1,065,555	10.2	$104,466
2016	$1,057,197	9.7	$108,989
2017	$1,043,029	9.1	$114,619
2018	$1,021,251	8.6	$118,750
2019	$ 992,751	8.1	$122,562

*At the surviving spouse's death, the first distribution is determined based upon the spouse's attained age in the year of death by reference to Table V of Treasury Regulation Section 1.72-9. For each succeeding year, this process is repeated.

†The life expectancy of the surviving spouse is the surviving spouse's life expectancy at age 74.

Postmortem Distributions From a Roth IRA

IRC Section 408A(c)(4) provides that the distribution rules of IRC Section 401(a)(9)(A) do not apply before death for Roth IRAs. In the event of a nonspousal beneficiary (or a spouse who does not perform a rollover), distributions can be made over the beneficiary's life expectancy by referencing the Single Life Table of Treasury Regulation Section 1.401(a)(9)-9, Q&A 7. These distributions provide the potential for deferral.

Spousal Distributions

At the death of a Roth IRA holder, his or her spouse has two distinct choices. The surviving spouse can

1. roll over the Roth IRA into his or her own name.
2. receive the Roth IRA as an inherited Roth IRA with distributions beginning no later than the year in which the deceased spouse would have turned age 70½.

The spouse, of course, may also disclaim the Roth IRA in favor of a stand-alone IRA Legacy Trust. This has the advantage of saving estate tax when used to fully fund the unified credit amount while allowing the spouse to continue as a beneficiary of the trust. See chapter 4, "Tax Planning Basics" for an expanded discussion of tax planning and spousal designations.

Spousal Rollovers

At the death of a Roth IRA holder, the surviving spouse is allowed to roll over the Roth IRA into his or her own Roth IRA. Furthermore, the surviving spouse is allowed to roll over the decedent spouse's traditional IRA into the surviving spouse's traditional IRA and subsequently make a Roth IRA conversion election.

Traditional IRA-to-Roth IRA Rollover

Similar to the traditional IRA-to-traditional IRA rollover, IRC Section 408 governs Roth IRA-to-Roth IRA rollovers. There is no time limit to when a spousal beneficiary can perform a spousal rollover. It can be done before or after age 70½. The only applicable deadline is the 60 day rollover deadline.

In the context of both the traditional and, presumably, the Roth IRA, spousal rollovers from estates and revocable trusts may be allowed in limited circumstances. Generally, if a decedent's IRA proceeds pass through a third party (such as a trust or estate) and then are distributed to the decedent's surviving spouse, said spouse will be treated as acquiring them from the third party and not from the decedent (and therefore is not eligible to perform a rollover). However, if the trustee or executor of a trust or estate that distributes IRA proceeds to a surviving spouse has no discretion with respect to the payment of the IRA proceeds to the surviving spouse, then the IRS has frequently treated the surviving spouse as having acquired the IRA proceeds from the decedent and not from the trust or estate and allowed a spousal rollover. See, for example, Private Letter Rulings (PLRs) 200720024, 200707159, and 200705032.

In addition, numerous nonbinding private letter rulings have allowed a spousal rollover in situations in which the IRA was payable to a trust or estate where the surviving spouse had the authority to distribute the IRA funds to him- or herself. For example, under PLR 200615032, the decedent's IRA was payable to his or her trust. The surviving spouse was the sole trustee of the trust and the sole beneficiary of the trust. As sole trustee, the surviving spouse causes the IRA proceeds to be allocated to the marital trust. The surviving spouse would then subsequently demand payment of the IRA assets from the trust, after which he or she would transfer the IRA proceeds into an IRA set up and maintained in his or her name. The IRS allowed him or her to rollover the proceeds of the IRA into an IRA set up and maintained in his or her name. See also PLRs 200707159, 200703047, 200646026, 200644028, and 200621020.

The Inherited IRA Concept

Perhaps the most powerful planning strategy involving both the traditional and the Roth IRA is the inherited IRA concept. For many families whose assets are substantial, the inherited IRA concept represents the best chance of transferring retirement wealth to their children through the following steps:

- The IRA is payable to one's spouse.
- Plan distributions are used to fund a life insurance policy.
- A second-to-die life insurance policy is purchased and held in an irrevocable life insurance trust.

- At the first death, a spousal rollover is performed.
- The spouse names children (or a trust for the benefit of children) as the IRA beneficiaries.
- The spouse has proper tax-apportionment clauses.
- The children use life insurance to pay any estate tax liability.
- The children enjoy distributions over their life expectancies.

When 100 percent of the IRAs needs to be used to fund the bypass trust, the IRA being paid to the spouse as primary beneficiary may not be desirable. When this occurs, a surviving spouse should consider disclaiming any interest in the bypass trust to utilize the younger trust beneficiary's life expectancy.

Conversion to Roth From Qualified Plan

In the past, if taxpayers wanted to do a Roth IRA conversion, they would have to first roll the funds from the qualified plan to a traditional IRA and then convert the traditional IRA to a Roth IRA. However, under the Pension Protection Act of 2006, taxpayers are eligible to directly roll funds from *eligible retirement plans*[29] to Roth IRAs starting in 2008.

Nonspousal Beneficiary Roth Conversion

Previously, only spousal beneficiaries, because of their ability to perform spousal rollovers into an account in their own names, had the option of converting to a Roth IRA. Nonspousal beneficiaries, however, did not have this option. In Notice 2008-30[30] (which provides guidance regarding certain distribution related provisions of the Pension Protection Act of 2006), however, the IRS seems to have expanded the conversion power to nonspousal beneficiaries. The notice states that beneficiaries can make qualified rollover contributions to Roth IRAs. In the case of a distribution from an eligible retirement plan other than a Roth IRA, the modified adjusted gross income and filing status of the beneficiary are used to determine eligibility to make a qualified rollover contribution to a Roth IRA.

State-of-the-Art Recommendations for the Traditional IRA

For many years, the traditional IRA has represented the most complex portion of the modern estate plan. Planners throughout the country struggle with how to best integrate the IRA into planning for a surviving spouse and planning to fund the unified credit trust.

Transfers to the surviving spouse are relatively easy. In many estate plans, the surviving spouse simply is the primary beneficiary, with the intention that the surviving spouse rolls over the funds into his or her own name. Transfers to the surviving spouse generally qualify

29 As defined under IRC Section 402(c)(8)(B).
30 2008-12 IRB 638.

for the estate tax marital deduction, and no estate tax will be due until the surviving spouse's death. Transfers to a nonspousal beneficiary or to a trust require more involved planning. At the death of the first spouse, the second spouse has the right to roll over the decedent spouse's IRA into his or her own IRA.[31]

> **Example**
>
> Jim dies at age 65, naming his wife, Margaret, the beneficiary of his IRA. Subsequent to Jim's death, Margaret has the option of rolling Jim's IRA into an IRA in her own name. Once the IRA is rolled into Margaret's name, Margaret will have the ability to name new beneficiaries. Later, at Margaret's death, distributions are made over the beneficiaries' life expectancies.

Basically, the following nine planning strategies are useful to fund the bypass trust:

1. A direct payment to a testamentary trust
2. Direct payment to both a testamentary trust and spouse using a fractional funding clause
3. Disclaimer to a testamentary trust
4. Direct payment to a revocable trust
5. Disclaimer to a revocable trust
6. Direct payment to an irrevocable IRA trust
7. Disclaimer to an irrevocable IRA bypass trust
8. Direct payment to a QTIP trust later followed by a partial QTIP election
9. Disclaimer to a QTIP trust later followed by a partial QTIP election

As if the preceding list were not complex enough, you should remember that fractional funding clauses must be used when passing the IRA to a bypass trust. Many wills and estate plans use a pecuniary funding clause, and when a pecuniary clause is used to transfer IRD, the income will be accelerated.[32]

Funding the Bypass Trust With the Roth IRA

Clients will now ask, "Should I use my traditional IRA or my Roth IRA to fund my bypass trust?" At first, this may seem like a difficult question; however, it may be relatively straightforward. Income tax has already been paid on the Roth IRA. If $3.5 million of Roth IRA assets[33] are used to fund a bypass trust, this may actually result in a greater wealth transfer than $3.5 million of traditional IRA assets. This is shown in table 9-10, "Value of Assets Passing to the Bypass Trust."

31 Treasury Regulation Section 1.408-8, A-5(a).
32 IRC Section 691(a)(1). An example of a pecuniary funding clause is the amount that results in no federal estate tax.
33 2009 unified credit exemption amount.

Table 9-10: *Value of Assets Passing to the Bypass Trust*

	Traditional IRA	Roth IRA
Exemption amount	$3,500,000	$3,500,000
Less income taxes at 31 percent	1,225,000	0
Net to family	$2,275,000	$3,500,000
Additional wealth transfer		$1,225,000

Income taxes severely affect the amount of wealth that actually transfers to the bypass trust. In the preceding instance, only $2,275,000 out of the original $3.5 million survives the income tax system to pass to the family. In the alternative, if the Roth IRA is used, greater distributions occur.

Naming the Children Beneficiaries

In the context of a traditional IRA, it may be advisable in certain circumstances to name a child or children the beneficiaries of a taxpayer's IRA. By naming the children the direct beneficiaries of the IRA, a taxpayer guarantees deferral over a child's life expectancy. The taxpayer could achieve the same result by naming his or her spouse as the designated beneficiary of his or her IRA. If the taxpayer were to die first, his or her spouse could roll over the IRA and subsequently name the children as the beneficiaries. In situations in which a taxpayer and his or her spouse do not need the money from a rollover IRA, consideration should be given to naming the children the direct beneficiaries of his or her IRA. Naming the spouse as beneficiary, however, allows for greater post-death planning flexibility (which means a disclaimer by spouse). With both a traditional and Roth IRA, a taxpayer can change his or her beneficiary up until his or her death.

Creditor Protection

Before converting to a Roth IRA, the practitioner would be well advised to look at the state statutes for creditor protection. By now, most states have the same protection for a Roth IRA as a traditional IRA; however, there may be some states that do not allow the same creditor protection for Roth IRAs. In circumstances in which a state does not have the same creditor protection for Roth IRAs as for traditional IRAs, the client should be notified of this adverse consequence. If this consequence is significant, a Roth IRA conversion should not be made.

Conclusion

Hopefully the above illustrates that estate planning for an IRA does not stop at simply filling out a beneficiary designation form. The planning opportunities for IRAs are tremendous and should be incorporated fully into the client's estate plan involving their non-retirement account assets. The next chapter will walk the advisor through the many beneficiary choices available to a client.

The Roth Legacy Trust

Introduction

The Roth Legacy Trust[1] is an exciting wealth transfer planning vehicle available to many individual retirement account (IRA) holders. Since the Taxpayer Relief Act of 1997 (reproduced in part as appendix 1: "Taxpayer Relief Act of 1997" at the back of this book), much has been written about the advantages of the Roth IRA. Included in these advantages is the ability to defer distributions after age 70½. This chapter will discuss the advantages of the Roth IRA before discussing the potential available through a Roth Legacy Trust to stretch the required distributions over a longer time frame.

Required Beginning Date Planning

At age 70½, one does not need to take distributions from his or her Roth IRA.[2] Rather than taking funds from the Roth IRA and reinvesting them in an investment account, one can simply continue the deferral within the Roth IRA. The following chart shows the value of this deferral beyond the required beginning date. If the IRA is a traditional IRA, the owner must begin taking minimum distributions. This is illustrated in the three columns under the heading "Traditional IRA." The required minimum distribution (RMD) is invested, after tax (30 percent tax rate), in an outside account that earns 10 percent. It is also assumed that the outside account growth is taxed at 30 percent. In contrast, the Roth IRA is not subject to minimum distributions during the IRA owner's lifetime. Therefore, the $500,000

1 The Roth Legacy Trust is a Service Mark of Baker Tilly Virchow Krause, LLP.
2 Internal Revenue Code Section 408A(c)(5).

beginning balance will continue to grow tax free until the account owner's death. This is shown in table 10-1, "Comparison of Traditional and Roth IRA Distributions," in the three columns under the heading "Roth IRA."

Table 10-1: *Comparison of Traditional and Roth IRA Distributions*

	Traditional IRA			Roth IRA		
Year	Beginning Balance	Required Minimum Distribution	Ending IRA and Outside Balance	Beginning Balance	Required Minimum Distribution	Ending Roth IRA Balance
1	$500,000	$23,041	$ 541,912	$ 500,000	$0	$ 550,000
2	$524,654	$25,346	$ 586,690	$ 550,000	$0	$ 605,000
3	$549,240	$27,880	$ 634,449	$ 605,000	$0	$ 665,500
4	$573,495	$30,668	$ 685,301	$ 665,500	$0	$ 732,050
5	$597,110	$33,735	$ 739,344	$ 732,050	$0	$ 805,255
6	$619,712	$37,109	$ 796,665	$ 805,255	$0	$ 885,781
7	$640,864	$40,819	$ 857,330	$ 885,781	$0	$ 974,359
8	$660,049	$44,901	$ 921,384	$ 974,359	$0	$1,071,794
9	$676,663	$49,391	$ 988,844	$1,071,794	$0	$1,178,974
10	$689,999	$54,331	$1,059,693	$1,178,974	$0	$1,296,871

One of the key advantages of both ordinary IRAs and Roth IRAs is the ability to stretch an IRA over the life expectancy of the designated beneficiary. The greatest wealth transfer will generally coincide with the longest deferral period.

Example

Mr. Jones dies at age 69, with his only child, age 47, as the primary beneficiary of his IRA. The tax law provides that the designated beneficiary shall have the right to take distributions over his life expectancy rather than an immediate lump-sum distribution. This is shown in table 10-2, "Traditional IRA Analysis—Post-Death Situation."

Table 10-2: *Traditional IRA Analysis—Post-Death Situation**

Year	Beginning IRA Balance	Required Minimum Distribution	Taxes at 36%	Beginning Outside Balance	Growth at 10%	Taxes at 20%	Ending Outside Balance
1	$ 600,000	$16,216	($ 5,838)	$ 10,378	$ 1,038	($ 208)	$ 11,209
2	$ 642,162	$17,838	($ 6,422)	$ 22,625	$ 2,262	($ 452)	$ 24,435
3	$ 686,757	$19,622	($ 7,064)	$ 36,993	$ 3,699	($ 740)	$ 39,952
4	$ 733,849	$21,584	($ 7,770)	$ 53,766	$ 5,377	($ 1,075)	$ 58,067
5	$ 783,491	$23,742	($ 8,547)	$ 73,262	$ 7,326	($ 1,465)	$ 79,123
6	$ 835,724	$26,116	($ 9,402)	$ 95,837	$ 9,584	($ 1,917)	$103,504
7	$ 890,569	$28,728	($10,342)	$121,890	$12,189	($ 2,438)	$131,642
8	$ 948,025	$31,601	($11,376)	$151,866	$15,187	($ 3,037)	$164,015
9	$1,008,066	$34,761	($12,514)	$186,262	$18,626	($ 3,725)	$201,163
10	$1,070,636	$38,237	($13,765)	$225,635	$22,564	($ 4,513)	$243,686
11	$1,135,639	$42,061	($15,142)	$270,605	$27,060	($ 5,412)	$292,253
12	$1,202,936	$46,267	($16,656)	$321,864	$32,186	($ 6,437)	$347,613
13	$1,272,336	$50,893	($18,322)	$380,185	$38,018	($ 7,604)	$410,599
14	$1,343,587	$55,983	($20,154)	$446,428	$44,643	($ 8,929)	$482,143
15	$1,416,364	$61,581	($22,169)	$521,555	$52,155	($10,431)	$563,277

*Assumes a $600,000 beginning IRA balance. The beneficiary has a 37 year single-life expectancy because he is age 47.

Example

Assume the preceding example, except now the IRA is a Roth IRA. This is shown in table 10-3, "Roth IRA Analysis—Post-Death Situation."

Table 10-3: *Roth IRA Analysis—Post-Death Situation**

Year	Beginning Roth IRA Balance	Required Minimum Distribution	Taxes at 0%	Beginning Outside Balance	Growth at 10%	Taxes at 20%	Ending Outside Balance
1	$ 600,000	$16,216	$0	$ 16,216	$ 1,622	($ 324)	$ 17,514
2	$ 642,162	$17,838	$0	$ 35,351	$ 3,535	($ 707)	$ 38,179
3	$ 686,757	$19,622	$0	$ 57,801	$ 5,780	($ 1,156)	$ 62,425
4	$ 733,849	$21,584	$0	$ 84,009	$ 8,401	($ 1,680)	$ 90,730
5	$ 783,491	$23,742	$0	$114,472	$11,447	($ 2,289)	$123,630
6	$ 835,724	$26,116	$0	$149,746	$14,975	($ 2,995)	$161,726
7	$ 890,569	$28,728	$0	$190,454	$19,045	($ 3,809)	$205,690
8	$ 948,025	$31,601	$0	$237,291	$23,729	($ 4,746)	$256,274
9	$1,008,066	$34,761	$0	$291,035	$29,103	($ 5,821)	$314,318
10	$1,070,636	$38,237	$0	$352,555	$35,255	($ 7,051)	$380,759
11	$1,135,639	$42,061	$0	$422,820	$42,282	($ 8,456)	$456,645
12	$1,202,936	$46,267	$0	$502,912	$50,291	($10,058)	$543,145
13	$1,272,336	$50,893	$0	$594,039	$59,404	($11,881)	$641,562
14	$1,343,587	$55,983	$0	$697,544	$69,754	($13,951)	$753,348
15	$1,416,364	$61,581	$0	$814,929	$81,493	$16,299	$880,123

*Assumes a $600,000 beginning IRA balance. The beneficiary has a 37 year single-life expectancy, because he is age 47. No income tax is due on the RMD because of the Roth IRA.

The key difference between these scenarios is that the Roth IRA is tax exempt. In both of these scenarios, the child is the direct beneficiary of the traditional or Roth IRA.

There are at least the following four disadvantages of having a child as a direct IRA beneficiary:

1. The child may accelerate IRA distributions, thus negating the benefit of deferral. The advantage of deferral is shown in table 10-4, "Comparison of Roth IRA Withdrawals."
2. A financially unsophisticated child may not obtain proper investment counsel. Table 10-5, "Comparisons of Returns of Roth IRAs," illustrates the benefit of higher returns in a Roth IRA.
3. The inherited or Roth IRA may (in some states) be subject to the claims of creditors or, in a less common situation, the claims of one's spouse.

4. A direct payment generally provides the beneficiary with a general power of appointment. This will also result in 100 percent of the postmortem growth being included in the estate of the decedent.

Table 10-4: *Comparison of Roth IRA Withdrawals*

	Immediate Withdrawal			Distributions Over Life Expectancy		
Year	Beginning Roth IRA Balance	Distribution	Ending Roth IRA and Outside Balance	Beginning Roth IRA Balance	Required Minimum Distribution	Ending Roth IRA and Outside Balance
1	$500,000	$500,000	$ 535,000	$ 500,000	$ 11,468	$ 549,656
2	$ 0	$ 0	$ 572,450	$ 537,385	$ 12,615	$ 603,875
3	$ 0	$ 0	$ 612,522	$ 577,248	$ 13,876	$ 663,047
4	$ 0	$ 0	$ 655,398	$ 619,709	$ 15,264	$ 727,594
5	$ 0	$ 0	$ 701,276	$ 664,889	$ 16,790	$ 797,969
6	$ 0	$ 0	$ 750,365	$ 712,909	$ 18,469	$ 874,660
7	$ 0	$ 0	$ 802,891	$ 763,884	$ 20,316	$ 958,193
8	$ 0	$ 0	$ 859,093	$ 817,925	$ 22,348	$1,049,134
9	$ 0	$ 0	$ 919,230	$ 875,135	$ 24,582	$1,148,090
10	$ 0	$ 0	$ 983,576	$ 935,608	$ 27,041	$1,255,713
11	$ 0	$ 0	$1,052,426	$ 999,424	$ 29,745	$1,372,703
12	$ 0	$ 0	$1,126,096	$1,066,647	$ 32,719	$1,499,810
13	$ 0	$ 0	$1,204,923	$1,137,320	$ 35,991	$1,637,837
14	$ 0	$ 0	$1,289,267	$1,211,462	$ 39,590	$1,787,642
15	$ 0	$ 0	$1,379,516	$1,289,059	$ 43,549	$1,950,142
16	$ 0	$ 0	$1,476,082	$1,370,061	$ 47,904	$2,126,316
17	$ 0	$ 0	$1,579,408	$1,454,372	$ 52,695	$2,317,209
18	$ 0	$ 0	$1,689,966	$1,541,845	$ 57,964	$2,523,930
19	$ 0	$ 0	$1,808,264	$1,632,269	$ 63,761	$2,747,660
20	$ 0	$ 0	$1,934,842	$1,725,360	$ 70,137	$2,989,653
21	$ 0	$ 0	$2,070,281	$1,820,745	$ 77,150	$3,251,237
22	$ 0	$ 0	$2,215,201	$1,917,955	$ 84,865	$3,533,816
23	$ 0	$ 0	$2,370,265	$2,016,398	$ 93,352	$3,838,874
24	$ 0	$ 0	$2,536,183	$2,115,351	$102,687	$4,167,976
25	$ 0	$ 0	$2,713,716	$2,213,931	$112,956	$4,522,763

Table 10-5: *Comparison of Returns of Roth IRAs*

Year	5% Growth	10% Growth	15% Growth
Today	$250,000	$ 250,000	$ 250,000
5	$319,070	$ 402,628	$ 502,839
10	$407,224	$ 648,436	$1,011,389
15	$519,732	$1,044,312	$2,034,265
20	$663,324	$1,681,875	$4,091,634
25	$846,589	$2,708,676	$8,229,738

The Roth Legacy Trust allows for multigenerational planning. The use of this trust will allow longer control of funds within the family, thus guaranteeing its availability to grandchildren.

A Technical Perspective

The Internal Revenue Code (IRC) Section 401(a)(9) regulations allows a Roth IRA holder to name either a revocable or an irrevocable trust as the beneficiary of a Roth IRA. When the proper procedures are followed, distributions from the Roth IRA will be paid over the life expectancy of the oldest trust beneficiary.[3] Qualified distributions from the Roth IRA to a trust will not be subject to income taxes. If the distributions from a traditional IRA are not paid by the trustee to the beneficiary, the trust income will be subject to income tax at trust tax rates. If the IRA distributions are paid to the beneficiary, a distributable net income deduction should be available to the trust to the extent of the trust's taxable income. The use of a Roth IRA overcomes the issue of a "trapping distribution."

Designing the Roth Legacy Trust Plan

Single-Generation Trust

The single-generation trust will typically be termed the *Roth Legacy Trust*. In the Roth Legacy Trust, the grantor (for example, surviving spouse) creates trust for the benefit of a particular child (or in some instances several children). In concept, this trust is very similar to a standard testamentary trust for the benefit of a child. Under the IRC Section 401(a)(9) regulations, distributions will be made over the life expectancy of the oldest trust beneficiary.[4] Key provisions of such a trust would be as follows:

- The trustee should generally be an independent trustee.
- The trust should have adequate provisions for distributions for the health, education, and future retirement of a beneficiary.

3 If separate shares are created in the trust and each separate share is specifically named as a beneficiary, each subtrust containing a separate share will be entitled to distributions based upon the individual beneficiary's life expectancy. See Private Letter Ruling (PLR) 200537044.

4 Treasury Regulation Section 1.401(a)(9)-4 Q&A 5. A full copy of the 2002 final rules and regulations from the Department of the Treasury, including Treasury Regulation Section 1.401(a)(9)-4, can be found on the accompanying CD-ROM.

- The trust should generally contain specific instructions to the trustee to take the smallest distribution under the RMD rules, unless such distributions would be distributed to a beneficiary under the education, health, and retirement scenario discussed in the preceding bullet point.
- From an estate tax perspective, the planner will need to review whether the trust should contain a general power of appointment, vesting the trust in the beneficiary's estate, or contain a limited power of appointment. It will be important that the general power of appointment be structured so as not to run afoul of the requirements of a trust being a qualified designated beneficiary. This can be accomplished by limiting the general power of appointment so that it may only be exercised in favor of individual creditors no older than the oldest trust beneficiary. Because the trust will be long term, this will be a critical tax and practical question. When evaluating this decision, the grantor must determine whether the beneficiary would follow a distribution plan that would be acceptable to the grantor or whether the grantor should simply provide that at the death of the primary beneficiary the trust will pass to specified individuals. If this occurs, it would typically be classified as a multiple-generation trust. The trustee should
  - be prohibited from using IRA funds for payment of a decedent's debts, taxes, and expenses of administration after September 30 of the year following the year of the IRA owner's death.
  - have the power to make in-kind distributions.
  - have the authority to continue the trust at the death of a child.
  - have the power to cash out nonindividual beneficiaries.
  - be specific that distributions from the Roth IRA to the trustee will be based upon the life expectancy of the oldest trust beneficiary. Further, if that beneficiary dies, distributions will continue over the remaining life expectancy of the (now deceased) oldest trust beneficiary.

Distributions over a child's life expectancy to a Roth Legacy Trust are shown in table 10-6, "Client Leaves $500,000 IRA to Child."[5]

5 Assumes the child is age 40 and the growth rate on the individual retirement account (IRA) is 10 percent.

Table 10-6: *Client Leaves $500,000 IRA to Child*

Year	Pension Fund Beginning Value	Life Expectancy	Annual Distribution
1	$ 500,000	43.6	$ 11,468
2	$ 537,385	42.6	$ 12,615
3	$ 577,248	41.6	$ 13,876
4	$ 619,709	40.6	$ 15,264
5	$ 664,889	39.6	$ 16,790
6	$ 712,909	38.6	$ 18,469
7	$ 763,884	37.6	$ 20,316
8	$ 817,925	36.6	$ 22,348
9	$ 875,135	35.6	$ 24,582
10	$ 935,608	34.6	$ 27,041
11	$ 999,424	33.6	$ 29,745
12	$1,066,647	32.6	$ 32,719
13	$1,137,320	31.6	$ 35,991
14	$1,211,462	30.6	$ 39,590
15	$1,289,059	29.6	$ 43,549
16	$1,370,061	28.6	$ 47,904
17	$1,454,372	27.6	$ 52,695
18	$1,541,845	26.6	$ 57,964
19	$1,632,269	25.6	$ 63,761
20	$1,725,360	24.6	$ 70,137
21	$1,820,745	23.6	$ 77,150
22	$1,917,955	22.6	$ 84,865
23	$2,016,398	21.6	$ 93,352
24	$2,115,351	20.6	$102,687
25	$2,213,931	19.6	$112,956
26	$2,311,073	18.6	$124,251
27	$2,405,504	17.6	$136,676
28	$2,495,710	16.6	$150,344
29	$2,579,903	15.6	$165,378
30	$2,655,977	14.6	$181,916

Multiple-Generation Trust

In the multiple-generation trust, the grantor is designing the trust for the benefit of several generations (typically, either children and grandchildren or both). This trust will be termed the *Roth Dynasty Trust*.

Distributions over a grandchild's life expectancy are shown in table 10-7, "Client Leaves $500,000 to Grandchild."[6]

Table 10-7: ***Client Leaves $500,000 to Grandchild***

Year	Pension Fund Beginning Value	Life Expectancy	Annual Distribution
1	$ 500,000	72.8	$ 6,868
2	$ 542,445	71.8	$ 7,555
3	$ 588,379	70.8	$ 8,310
4	$ 638,076	69.8	$ 9,141
5	$ 691,827	68.8	$ 10,056
6	$ 749,949	67.8	$ 11,061
7	$ 812,777	66.8	$ 12,167
8	$ 880,670	65.8	$ 13,384
9	$ 954,015	64.8	$ 14,722
10	$1,033,222	63.8	$ 16,195
11	$1,118,730	62.8	$ 17,814
12	$1,211,007	61.8	$ 19,596
13	$1,310,553	60.8	$ 21,555
14	$1,417,897	59.8	$ 23,711
15	$1,533,605	58.8	$ 26,082
16	$1,658,276	57.8	$ 28,690
17	$1,792,544	56.8	$ 31,559
18	$1,937,084	55.8	$ 34,715
19	$2,092,606	54.8	$ 38,186
20	$2,259,862	53.8	$ 42,005
21	$2,439,643	52.8	$ 46,205
22	$2,632,781	51.8	$ 50,826
23	$2,840,151	50.8	$ 55,908
24	$3,062,667	49.8	$ 61,499
25	$3,301,284	48.8	$ 67,649
26	$3,556,998	47.8	$ 74,414
27	$3,830,842	46.8	$ 81,856
28	$4,123,886	45.8	$ 90,041
29	$4,437,229	44.8	$ 99,045
30	$4,772,002	43.8	$108,950

6 Assumes the grandchild is age 10 and the growth rate on the IRA is 10 percent.

Generation-Skipping Transfer Tax Aspects

Whether one is designing a single-generation trust or a multiple-generation trust, special care must be taken to allocate generation-skipping transfer (GST) tax exemption when appropriate. Generally, if a trust is for a child and that child has a general power of appointment,[7] it will not be necessary to allocate GST exemption. This occurs because the trust is vested in the estate of the child. However, in instances in which a trust is for the benefit of a particular child, and in the event that the child dies before reaching a particular age, the trust shall pass to his or her issue, and it may be necessary to allocate GST exemption. Lastly, in those situations in which a trust is strictly for the benefit of a grandchild, it will be necessary to allocate GST exemption to this trust. Furthermore, in those instances in which a trust is for the benefit of a child and, subsequently, grandchildren (with no intervening general power of appointment), GST tax exemption should also be allocated.

Flow Charts of Roth Legacy Trusts

Figure 10-1, "Operation of Roth Legacy Trust—Lifetime Beneficiaries," depicts the operation of a Roth Legacy Trust of which spouse and children are the beneficiaries during their lifetimes. RMDs are made to the trust based upon the spouse's life expectancy. The spouse has a limited power of appointment, exercisable at his or her death, to appoint which children are to be the ultimate beneficiaries upon termination of the trust.

Figure 10-1: *Operation of Roth Legacy Trust Lifetime—Beneficiaries*

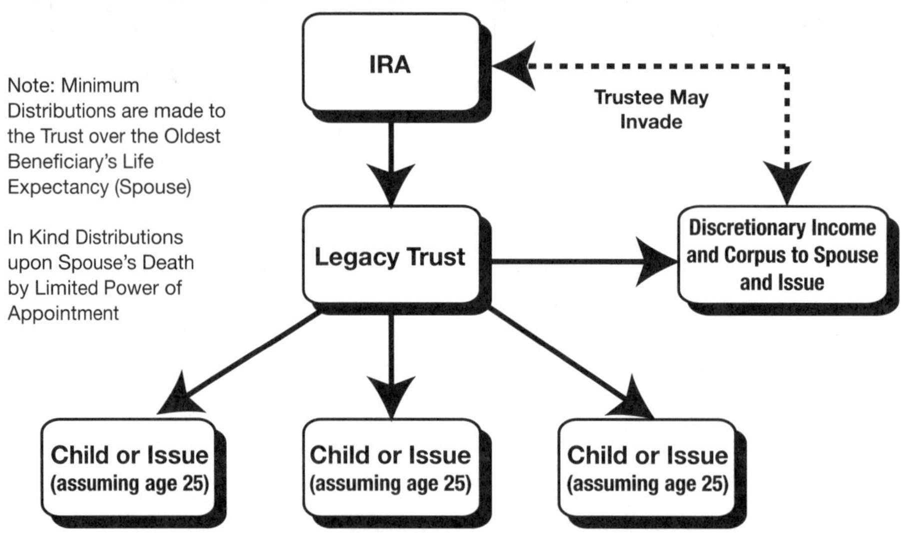

Figure 10-2, "Operation of a Roth Legacy Trust—Discretionary Distributions," depicts the use of a Roth Legacy Trust if the trustee has authority to make discretionary distributions to children and or issue of deceased children. RMDs are made to the trust over the oldest child's life expectancy. Upon the death of the trustor and, further, when the youngest beneficiary has reached age 25, the trust assets are distributed.

7 Care must be taken in drafting a general power of appointment so as to ensure that the oldest trust beneficiary is an identifiable individual.

Figure 10-2: *Operation of Roth Legacy Trust—Discretionary Distributions*

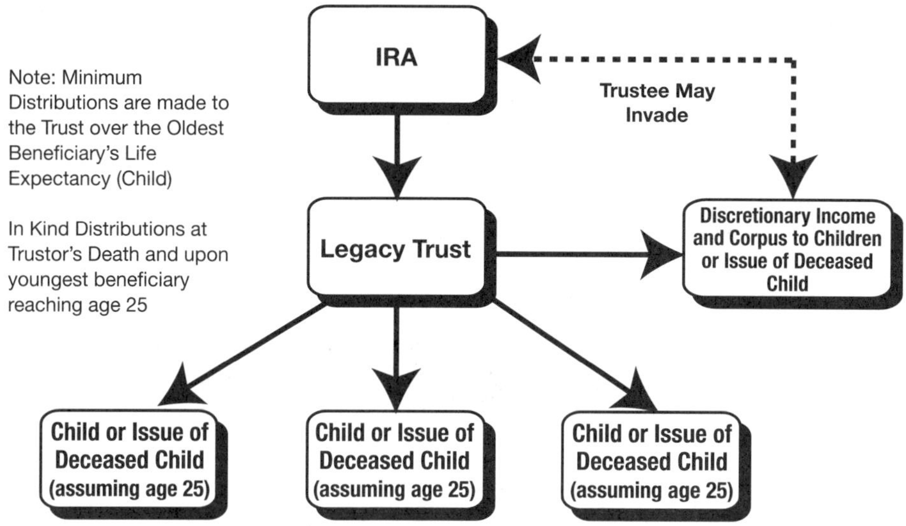

Figure 10-3, "Operation of Roth Legacy Trust—Discretionary Payments to Beneficiaries," illustrates the use of a Roth Legacy Trust of which children and grandchildren are beneficiaries of discretionary payments. RMDs are made to the trust over the life expectancy of the oldest child. Upon the death of the last living child, the trust is disbursed to those grandchildren who have attained 25 years of age. If any grandchild has not yet attained this age, his or her share will be held in trust until he or she reaches age 25.

Figure 10-3: *Operation of Roth Legacy Trust—Discretionary Payments to Beneficiaries*

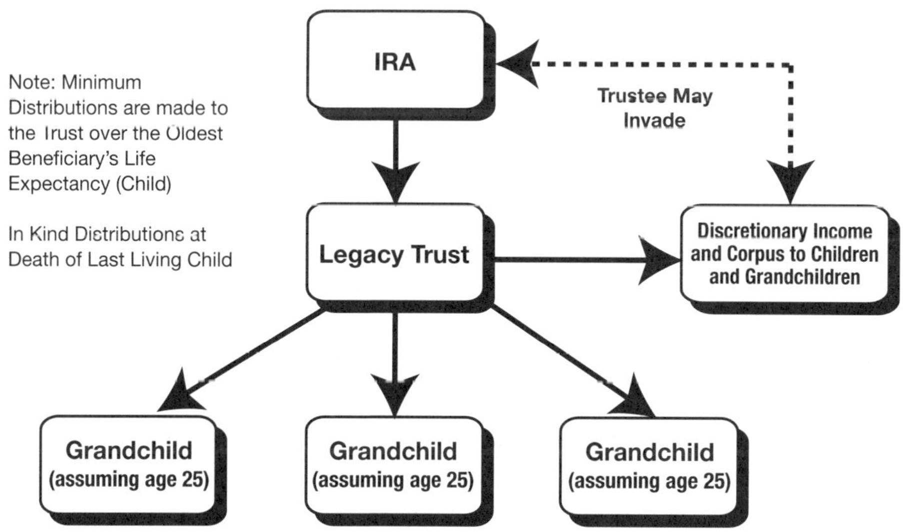

Finally, Figure 10-4, "Operation of a Roth Legacy Trust—Discretionary Payments to Grandchildren," outlines the use of a Roth Legacy Trust of which only the grandchildren are beneficiaries of discretionary payments. RMDs are made to the trust over the life expectancy of the oldest grandchild. Upon the death of the trustor and the youngest grandchild reaching age 65, the trust is terminated and the proceeds are disbursed to the grandchildren.

Figure 10-4: *Operation of Roth Legacy Trust—Discretionary Payments to Grandchildren*

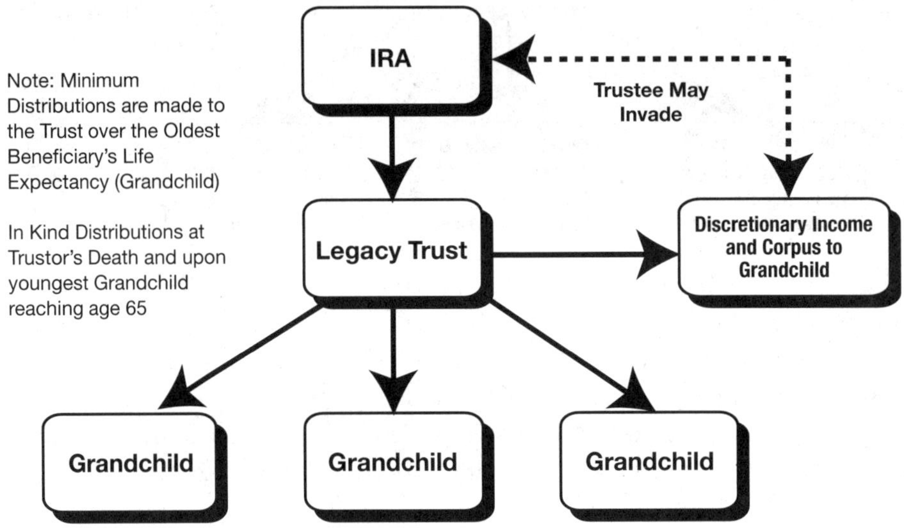

Conclusion

The Roth Legacy Trust continues to be an exciting planning technique that will be used by both wealthy and middle-class families. The Roth Legacy Trust and the Roth Dynasty Trust both provide substantial income tax, estate tax, and GST tax advantages. These advantages will be critical in designing estate plans in the years to come. Prior to any client making a decision not to convert at least a portion of his or her IRA to a Roth IRA, he or she may wish to become familiar with the advantages and disadvantages of the Roth Legacy Trust and Roth Dynasty Trust. If the client decides to utilize a Roth Legacy Trust, it is critical that the trust be drafted by an attorney who is familiar with the regulations necessary to qualify the trust as a qualified designated beneficiary.

With retirement assets making up such a large portion of clients' estates, paying retirement assets to trusts is becoming more and more prevalent. But a trust should not be named beneficiary of an IRA without first carefully considering the provisions of the trust and the requirements necessary to obtain designated beneficiary status discussed in this and the preceding chapter.

Appendix 1

Taxpayer Relief Act of 1997

TITLE III—SAVINGS AND INVESTMENT INCENTIVES

Subtitle A—Retirement Savings

SEC. 301. RESTORATION OF IRA DEDUCTION FOR CERTAIN TAXPAYERS.

(a) INCREASE IN INCOME LIMITS APPLICABLE TO ACTIVE PARTICIPANTS.—

(1) IN GENERAL.—Subparagraph (B) of section 219(g)(3) (relating to applicable dollar amount) is amended to read as follows:

"(B) APPLICABLE DOLLAR AMOUNT.—The term 'applicable dollar amount' means the following:

"(i) In the case of a taxpayer filing a joint return:

"For taxable years beginning in:	*The applicable dollar amount is:*
1998	*$50,000*
1999	*$51,000*
2000	*$52,000*
2001	*$53,000*
2002	*$54,000*
2003	*$60,000*
2004	*$65,000*
2005	*$70,000*
2006	*$75,000*
2007 and thereafter	*$80,000.*

"(ii) In the case of any other taxpayer (other than a married individual filing a separate return):

"For taxable years beginning in:	*The applicable dollar amount is:*
1998	*$30,000*
1999	*$31,000*
2000	*$32,000*
2001	*$33,000*
2002	*$34,000*
2003	*$40,000*
2004	*$45,000*
2005 and thereafter	*$50,000.*

"(iii) In the case of a married individual filing a separate return, zero.".

(2) INCREASE IN PHASE-OUT RANGE FOR JOINT RETURNS.—Clause (ii) of section 219(g)(2)(A) is amended by inserting "($20,000 in the case of a joint return for a taxable year beginning after December 31, 2006)".

(b) LIMITATIONS FOR ACTIVE PARTICIPATION NOT BASED ON SPOUSE'S PARTICIPATION.—Section 219(g) (relating to limitation on deduction for active participants in certain pension plans) is amended—

(1) by striking "or the individual's spouse" in paragraph (1), and

(2) by adding at the end the following new paragraph:

"(7) SPECIAL RULE FOR CERTAIN SPOUSES.—In the case of an individual who is an active participant at no time during any plan year ending with or within the taxable year but whose spouse is an active participant for any part of any such plan year—

"(A) the applicable dollar amount under paragraph (3)(B)(i) with respect to the taxpayer shall be $150,000, and

"(B) the amount applicable under paragraph (2)(A)(ii) shall be $10,000."

(c) EFFECTIVE DATE.—The amendments made by this section shall apply to taxable years beginning after December 31, 1997.

SEC. 302. ESTABLISHMENT OF NONDEDUCTIBLE TAX-FREE INDIVIDUAL RETIREMENT ACCOUNTS.

(a) IN GENERAL.—Subpart A of part I of subchapter D of chapter 1 (relating to pension, profit-sharing, stock bonus plans, etc.) is amended by inserting after section 408 the following new section:

"SEC. 408A. ROTH IRAS.

"(a) GENERAL RULE.—Except as provided in this section, a Roth IRA shall be treated for purposes of this title in the same manner as an individual retirement plan.

"(b) ROTH IRA.—For purposes of this title, the term 'Roth IRA' means an individual retirement plan (as defined in section 7701(a)(37)) which is designated (in such manner as the Secretary may prescribe) at the time of establishment of the plan as a Roth IRA. Such designation shall be made in such manner as the Secretary may prescribe.

"(c) TREATMENT OF CONTRIBUTIONS.—

"(1) NO DEDUCTION ALLOWED.—No deduction shall be allowed under section 219 for a contribution to a Roth IRA.

"(2) CONTRIBUTION LIMIT.—The aggregate amount of contributions for any taxable year to all Roth IRAs maintained for the benefit of an individual shall not exceed the excess (if any) of—

"(A) the maximum amount allowable as a deduction under section 219 with respect to such individual for such taxable year (computed without regard to subsection (d)(1) or (g) of such section), over

"(B) the aggregate amount of contributions for such taxable year to all other individual retirement plans (other than Roth IRAs) maintained for the benefit of the individual.

"(3) LIMITS BASED ON MODIFIED ADJUSTED GROSS INCOME.—

"(A) DOLLAR LIMIT.—The amount determined under paragraph (2) for any taxable year shall be reduced (but not below zero) by the amount which bears the same ratio to such amount as—

"(i) the excess of—

"(I) the taxpayer's adjusted gross income for such taxable year, over

"(II) the applicable dollar amount, bears to

"(ii) $15,000 ($10,000 in the case of a joint return).

The rules of subparagraphs (B) and (C) of section 219(g)(2) shall apply to any reduction under this subparagraph.

"(B) ROLLOVER FROM IRA.—A taxpayer shall not be allowed to make a qualified rollover contribution to a Roth IRA from an individual retirement plan other than a Roth IRA during any taxable year if—

"(i) the taxpayer's adjusted gross income for such taxable year exceeds $100,000, or

"(ii) the taxpayer is a married individual filing a separate return.

"(C) DEFINITIONS.—For purposes of this paragraph—

"(i) adjusted gross income shall be determined in the same manner as under section 219(g)(3), except that any amount included in gross income under subsection (d)(3) shall not be taken into account and the deduction under section 219 shall be taken into account, and

"(ii) the applicable dollar amount is—

"(I) in the case of a taxpayer filing a joint return, $150,000,

"(II) in the case of any other taxpayer (other than a married individual filing a separate return), $95,000, and

"(III) in the case of a married individual filing a separate return, zero.

"(D) MARITAL STATUS.—Section 219(g)(4) shall apply for purposes of this paragraph.

"(4) CONTRIBUTIONS PERMITTED AFTER AGE 70½.—Contributions to a Roth IRA may be made even after the individual for whom the account is maintained has attained age 70½.

"(5) MANDATORY DISTRIBUTION RULES NOT TO APPLY BEFORE DEATH.—Notwithstanding subsections (a)(6) and (b)(3) of section 408 (relating to required distributions), the following provisions shall not apply to any Roth IRA:

"(A) Section 401(a)(9)(A).

"(B) The incidental death benefit requirements of section 401(a).

"(6) ROLLOVER CONTRIBUTIONS.—

"(A) IN GENERAL.—No rollover contribution may be made to a Roth IRA unless it is a qualified rollover contribution.

"(B) COORDINATION WITH LIMIT.—A qualified rollover contribution shall not be taken into account for purposes of paragraph (2).

"(7) TIME WHEN CONTRIBUTIONS MADE.—For purposes of this section, the rule of section 219(f)(3) shall apply.

"(d) DISTRIBUTION RULES.—For purposes of this title—

"(1) GENERAL RULES.—

"(A) EXCLUSIONS FROM GROSS INCOME.—Any qualified distribution from a Roth IRA shall not be includible in gross income.

"(B) NONQUALIFIED DISTRIBUTIONS.—In applying section 72 to any distribution from a Roth IRA which is not a qualified distribution, such distribution shall be treated as made from contributions to the Roth IRA to the extent that such distribution, when added to all previous distributions from the Roth IRA, does not exceed the aggregate amount of contributions to the Roth IRA.

"(2) QUALIFIED DISTRIBUTION.—For purposes of this subsection—

"(A) IN GENERAL.—The term 'qualified distribution' means any payment or distribution—

"(i) made on or after the date on which the individual attains age 59½,

"(ii) made to a beneficiary (or to the estate of the individual) on or after the death of the individual,

"(iii) attributable to the individual's being disabled (within the meaning of section 72(m)(7)), or

"(iv) which is a qualified special purpose distribution.

"(B) CERTAIN DISTRIBUTIONS WITHIN 5 YEARS.—A payment or distribution shall not be treated as a qualified distribution under subparagraph (A) if—

"(i) it is made within the 5-taxable year period beginning with the 1st taxable year for which the individual made a contribution to a Roth IRA (or such individual's spouse made a contribution to a Roth IRA) established for such individual, or

"(ii) in the case of a payment or distribution properly allocable (as determined in the manner prescribed by the Secretary) to a qualified rollover contribution from an individual retirement plan other than a Roth IRA (or income allocable thereto), it is made within the 5-taxable year period beginning with the taxable year in which the rollover contribution was made.

"(3) ROLLOVERS FROM AN IRA OTHER THAN A ROTH IRA.—

"(A) IN GENERAL.—Notwithstanding section 408(d)(3), in the case of any distribution to which this paragraph applies—

"(i) there shall be included in gross income any amount which would be includible were it not part of a qualified rollover contribution,

"(ii) section 72(t) shall not apply, and

"(iii) in the case of a distribution before January 1, 1999, any amount required to be included in gross income by reason of this paragraph shall be so included ratably over the 4-taxable year period beginning with the taxable year in which the payment or distribution is made.

"(B) DISTRIBUTIONS TO WHICH PARAGRAPH APPLIES.—This paragraph shall apply to a distribution from an individual retirement plan (other than a Roth IRA) maintained for the benefit of an individual which is contributed to a Roth IRA maintained for the benefit of such individual in a qualified rollover contribution.

"(C) CONVERSIONS.—The conversion of an individual retirement plan (other than a Roth IRA) to a Roth IRA shall be treated for purposes of this paragraph as a distribution to which this paragraph applies.

"(D) CONVERSION OF EXCESS CONTRIBUTIONS.—If, no later than the due date for filing the return of tax for any taxable year (without regard to extensions), an individual transfers, from an individual retirement plan (other than a Roth IRA), contributions for such taxable year (and any earnings allocable thereto) to a Roth IRA, no such amount shall be includible in gross income to the extent no deduction was allowed with respect to such amount.

"(E) ADDITIONAL REPORTING REQUIREMENTS.—Trustees of Roth IRAs, trustees of individual retirement plans, or both, whichever is appropriate, shall include such additional information in reports required under section 408(i) as the Secretary may require to ensure that amounts re-

quired to be included in gross income under subparagraph (A) are so included.

"(4) COORDINATION WITH INDIVIDUAL RETIREMENT ACCOUNTS.—Section 408(d)(2) shall be applied separately with respect to Roth IRAs and other individual retirement plans.

"(5) QUALIFIED SPECIAL PURPOSE DISTRIBUTION.—For purposes of this section, the term 'qualified special purpose distribution' means any distribution to which subparagraph (F) of section 72(t)(2) applies.

"(e) QUALIFIED ROLLOVER CONTRIBUTION.—For purposes of this section, the term 'qualified rollover contribution' means a rollover contribution to a Roth IRA from another such account, or from an individual retirement plan, but only if such rollover contribution meets the requirements of section 408(d)(3). For purposes of section 408(d)(3)(B), there shall be disregarded any qualified rollover contribution from an individual retirement plan (other than a Roth IRA) to a Roth IRA.".

(b) EXCESS CONTRIBUTIONS.—Section 4973(b), as amended by title II, is amended by adding at the end the following new subsection:

"(f) EXCESS CONTRIBUTIONS TO ROTH IRAS.—For purposes of this section, in the case of contributions to a Roth IRA (within the meaning of section 408A(b)), the term 'excess contributions' means the sum of—

"(1) the excess (if any) of—

"(A) the amount contributed for the taxable year to such accounts (other than a qualified rollover contribution described in section 408A(e)), over

"(B) the amount allowable as a contribution under sections 408A (c)(2) and (c)(3), and

"(2) the amount determined under this subsection for the preceding taxable year, reduced by the sum of—

"(A) the distributions out of the accounts for the taxable year, and

"(B) the excess (if any) of the maximum amount allowable as a contribution under sections 408A (c)(2) and (c)(3) for the taxable year over the amount contributed to the accounts for the taxable year.

For purposes of this subsection, any contribution which is distributed from a Roth IRA in a distribution described in section 408(d)(4) shall be treated as an amount not contributed."

(c) SPOUSAL IRA.—Clause (ii) of section 219(c)(1)(B) is amended to read as follows:

"(ii) the compensation includible in the gross income of such individual's spouse for the taxable year reduced by—

"(I) the amount allowed as a deduction under subsection (a) to such spouse for such taxable year, and

"(II) the amount of any contribution on behalf of such spouse to a Roth IRA under section 408A for such taxable year.".

(d) AUTHORITY TO PRESCRIBE NECESSARY REPORTING.—Section 408(i) is amended—

(1) by striking "under regulations", and

(2) by striking "in such regulations" each place it appears.

(e) CONFORMING AMENDMENT.—The table of sections for subpart A of part I of subchapter D of chapter 1 is amended by inserting after the item relating to section 408 the following new item:

"Sec. 408A. Roth IRAs.".

(f) EFFECTIVE DATE.—The amendments made by this section shall apply to taxable years beginning after December 31, 1997.

SEC. 303. DISTRIBUTIONS FROM CERTAIN PLANS MAY BE USED WITHOUT PENALTY TO PURCHASE FIRST HOMES.

(a) IN GENERAL.—Paragraph (2) of section 72(t) (relating to exceptions to 10-percent additional tax on early distributions from qualified retirement plans), as amended by section 203, is amended by adding at the end the following new subparagraph:

"(F) DISTRIBUTIONS FROM CERTAIN PLANS FOR FIRST HOME PURCHASES.—Distributions to an individual from an individual retirement plan which are qualified first-time homebuyer distributions (as defined in paragraph (8)). Distributions shall not be taken into account under the preceding sentence if such distributions are described in subparagraph (A), (C), (D), or (E) or to the extent paragraph (1) does not apply to such distributions by reason of subparagraph (B).".

(b) DEFINITIONS.—Section 72(t), as amended by section 203, is amended by adding at the end the following new paragraphs:

"(8) QUALIFIED FIRST-TIME HOMEBUYER DISTRIBUTIONS.—For purposes of paragraph (2)(F)—

"(A) IN GENERAL.—The term 'qualified first-time homebuyer distribution' means any payment or distribution received by an individual to the extent such payment or distribution is used by the individual before the close of the 120th day after the day on which such payment or distribution is received to pay qualified acquisition costs with respect to a principal residence of a first-time homebuyer who is such individual, the spouse of such individual, or any child, grandchild, or ancestor of such individual or the individual's spouse.

"(B) LIFETIME DOLLAR LIMITATION.—The aggregate amount of payments or distributions received by an individual which may be treated as qualified first-time homebuyer distributions for any taxable year shall not exceed the excess (if any) of—

"(i) $10,000, over

"(ii) the aggregate amounts treated as qualified first-time homebuyer distributions with respect to such individual for all prior taxable years.

"(C) QUALIFIED ACQUISITION COSTS.—For purposes of this paragraph, the term 'qualified acquisition costs' means the costs of acquiring, constructing, or reconstructing a residence. Such term includes any usual or reasonable settlement, financing, or other closing costs.

"(D) FIRST-TIME HOMEBUYER; OTHER DEFINITIONS.—For purposes of this paragraph—

"(i) FIRST-TIME HOMEBUYER.—The term 'first-time homebuyer' means any individual if—

"(I) such individual (and if married, such individual's spouse) had no present ownership interest in a principal residence during the 2-year period ending on the date of acquisition of the prin-

cipal residence to which this paragraph applies, and

"(II) subsection (h) or (k) of section 1034 (as in effect on the day before the date of the enactment of this paragraph) did not suspend the running of any period of time specified in section 1034 (as so in effect) with respect to such individual on the day before the date the distribution is applied pursuant to subparagraph (A).

"(ii) PRINCIPAL RESIDENCE.—The term 'principal residence' has the same meaning as when used in section 121.

"(iii) DATE OF ACQUISITION.—The term 'date of acquisition' means the date—

"(I) on which a binding contract to acquire the principal residence to which subparagraph (A) applies is entered into, or

"(II) on which construction or reconstruction of such a principal residence is commenced.

"(E) SPECIAL RULE WHERE DELAY IN ACQUISITION.—If any distribution from any individual retirement plan fails to meet the requirements of subparagraph (A) solely by reason of a delay or cancellation of the purchase or construction of the residence, the amount of the distribution may be contributed to an individual retirement plan as provided in section 408(d)(3)(A)(i) (determined by substituting '120 days' for '60 days' in such section), except that—

"(i) section 408(d)(3)(B) shall not be applied to such contribution, and

"(ii) such amount shall not be taken into account in determining whether section 408(d)(3)(B) applies to any other amount.".

(c) EFFECTIVE DATE.—The amendments made by this section shall apply to payments and distributions in taxable years beginning after December 31, 1997.

Appendix 2

Conference Committee Explanation (1997 Act)

2. Tax-free nondeductible IRAs (sec. 301 of the House bill and sec. 302 of the Senate amendment)

Present Law

No provision. However, present law provides that an individual can make nondeductible contributions to an IRA to the extent the individual cannot or does not make deductible contributions. Earnings on nondeductible contributions are includible in income when withdrawn.

House Bill

In general

The House bill replaces present-law nondeductible IRAs with new American Dream IRAs ("AD IRAs") to which individuals may make nondeductible contributions of up to $2,000 annually. No income limits apply to AD IRAs, and contributions to AD IRAs are in addition to other IRA contributions. The $2,000 contribution limit is indexed for inflation in $50 increments.

Taxation of distributions

Qualified distributions from an AD IRA are not includible in income. Qualified distributions are distributions (1) made after the 5-taxable year period beginning with the first taxable year for which a contribution was made to an AD IRA and (2) which are (a) made on or after the date on which the individual attains age 59½, (b) made to a beneficiary on or after the death of the individual, (c) attributable to the individual's being disabled, or (d) for a qualified special purpose distribution. A qualified special purpose distribution is a distribution for first-time homebuyer expenses.

Conversions of IRAs to AD IRAs

An IRA may be converted to an AD IRA before January 1, 1999. Amounts that would have been includible in income had the amounts converted been withdrawn are includible in income ratably over 4 years. The additional tax on early withdrawals does not apply to conversions of IRAs to AD IRAs.

Effective date

Taxable years beginning after December 31, 1997.

Senate Amendment

In general

Same as the House bill, except that: (1) the new IRAs are called IRA Plus accounts and (2) no more than $2,000 of annual contributions can be made to all an individual's IRAs.

Taxation of distributions

Same as the House bill, except that special purpose distributions also include distributions to long-term unemployed individuals.

Conversions of IRAs to AD IRAs

Same as the House bill, except that conversions of an IRA to an IRA Plus can be made at any time. If the conversion is made before January 1, 1999, the amounts that would have been includible in income had the amounts converted been withdrawn are includible in income ratably over 4 years. In any case, the 10-percent tax on early withdrawals does not apply.

Effective date

Same as the House bill.

Conference Agreement

The conference agreement follows the Senate amendment, with modifications. Under the conference agreement, the new IRA is called the "Roth IRA" rather than the IRA Plus. The maximum contribution that can be made to a Roth IRA is phased out for individuals with AGI between $95,000 and $110,000 and for joint filers with AGI between $150,000 and $160,000. Under the conference agreement, distributions to long-term unemployed individuals do not qualify as special purpose distributions. Thus, only first-time homebuyer expenses (as defined under the Senate amendment) qualify as special purpose distributions.

Under the conference agreement, only taxpayers with AGI of less than $100,000[51] are eligible to roll over or convert an IRA into a Roth IRA.

The conference agreement retains present-law nondeductible IRAs. Thus, an individual who cannot (or does not) make contributions to a deductible IRA or a Roth IRA can make contributions to a nondeductible IRA. In no case can contributions to all an individual's IRAs for a taxable year exceed $2,000.

3. Modifications to early withdrawal tax (sec. 301 of the House bill and sec. 303 of the Senate amendment)

Present Law

Under present law, a 10-percent additional tax applies to distributions from an IRA prior to age 59½, unless an exception applies.

House Bill

The House bill adds an additional exception to the early withdrawal tax for AD IRAs only. The early withdrawal tax does not apply to distributions from an AD IRA for first-time homebuyer expenses, subject to a $10,000 life-time cap.

Effective date.—Taxable years beginning after December 31, 1997.

Senate Amendment

The early withdrawal tax does not apply to distributions from any IRA for first-time homebuyer expenses or for long-term unemployed individuals.

Effective date.—Same as the House bill.

[51] For this purpose, AGI is determined before any amount includible in income as a result of the rollover or conversion.

Conference Agreement

The conference agreement follows the Senate amendment but does not include the provision relating to long-term unemployed individuals.[52]

[52] As under the House bill and Senate amendment, the conference agreement includes a penalty-free withdrawal provision for education expenses.

Appendix 3

1998 Roth IRA Amendments: Text

H.R.2676

Internal Revenue Service Restructuring and Reform Act of 1997 (Reported in the Senate)

SEC. 6005. AMENDMENTS RELATED TO TITLE III OF 1997 ACT.

(a) AMENDMENTS RELATED TO SECTION 301 OF 1997 ACT-

(1) Section 219(g) of the 1986 Code is amended--

(A) by inserting `or the individual's spouse' after `individual' in paragraph (1), and

(B) by striking paragraph (7) and inserting:

`(7) SPECIAL RULE FOR SPOUSES WHO ARE NOT ACTIVE PARTICIPANTS- If this subsection applies to an individual for any taxable year solely because their spouse is an active participant, then, in applying this subsection to the individual (but not their spouse)--

`(A) the applicable dollar amount under paragraph (3)(B)(i) shall be $150,000, and

`(B) the amount applicable under paragraph (2)(A)(ii) shall be $10,000.'

(2) Paragraph (2) of section 301(a) of the 1997 Act is amended by inserting `after `$10,000' before the period.

(b) AMENDMENTS RELATED TO SECTION 302 OF 1997 ACT-

(1) Section 408A(c)(3)(A) of the 1986 Code is amended by striking `shall be reduced' and inserting `shall not exceed an amount equal to the amount determined under paragraph (2)(A) for such taxable year, reduced'.

(2) Section 408A(c)(3) of the 1986 Code (relating to limits based on modified adjusted gross income) is amended--

(A) by inserting `or a married individual filing a separate return' after `joint return' in subparagraph (A)(ii),

(B) in subparagraph (B)--

(i) by inserting `, for the taxable year of the distribution to which such contribution relates' after `if', and

(ii) by striking `for such taxable year' in clause (i), and

(C) by striking `and the deduction under section 219 shall be taken into account' in subparagraph (C)(i).

(3)(A) Section 408A(d)(2) of the 1986 Code (defining qualified distribution) is amended by striking subparagraph (B) and inserting the following:

`(B) DISTRIBUTIONS WITHIN NONEXCLUSION PERIOD- A payment or distribution from a Roth IRA shall not be treated as a qualified distribution under subparagraph (A) if such payment or distribution is made within the 5-taxable year period beginning with the 1st taxable year for which the individual made a contribution to a Roth IRA (or such individual's spouse made a contribution to a Roth IRA) established for such individual.'

(B) Section 408A(d)(2) of the 1986 Code is amended by adding at the end the following new subparagraph:

`(C) DISTRIBUTIONS OF EXCESS CONTRIBUTIONS AND EARNINGS- The term `qualified distribution' shall not include any distribution of any contribution described in section 408(d)(4) and any net income allocable to the contribution.'

Appendix 4

Economic Growth and Tax Relief Reconciliation Act of 2001: Text

TITLE VI—PENSION AND INDIVIDUAL RETIREMENT ARRANGEMENT PROVISIONS

Subtitle A—Individual Retirement Accounts

SEC. 601. MODIFICATION OF IRA CONTRIBUTION LIMITS.

(a) INCREASE IN CONTRIBUTION LIMIT.—

26 USC 219. (1) IN GENERAL.—Paragraph (1)(A) of section 219(b) (relating to maximum amount of deduction) is amended by striking "$2,000" and inserting "the deductible amount".

(2) DEDUCTIBLE AMOUNT.—Section 219(b) is amended by adding at the end the following new paragraph:

"(5) DEDUCTIBLE AMOUNT.—For purposes of paragraph (1)(A)—

"(A) IN GENERAL.—The deductible amount shall be determined in accordance with the following table:

"For taxable years beginning in:	The deductible amount is:
2002 through 2004	$3,000
2005 through 2007	$4,000
2008 and thereafter	$5,000.

"(B) CATCH-UP CONTRIBUTIONS FOR INDIVIDUALS 50 OR OLDER.—

"(i) IN GENERAL.—In the case of an individual who has attained the age of 50 before the close of the taxable year, the deductible amount for such taxable year shall be increased by the applicable amount.

"(ii) APPLICABLE AMOUNT.—For purposes of clause (i), the applicable amount shall be the amount determined in accordance with the following table:

"For taxable years beginning in:	The applicable amount is:
2002 through 2005	$500
2006 and thereafter	$1,000.

"(C) COST-OF-LIVING ADJUSTMENT.—

"(i) IN GENERAL.—In the case of any taxable year beginning in a calendar year after 2008, the $5,000 amount under subparagraph (A) shall be increased by an amount equal to—

"(I) such dollar amount, multiplied by

"(II) the cost-of-living adjustment determined under section 1(f)(3) for the calendar year in which the taxable year begins, determined by substituting 'calendar year 2007' for 'calendar year 1992' in subparagraph (B) thereof.

"(ii) ROUNDING RULES.—If any amount after adjustment under clause (i) is not a multiple of $500, such amount shall be rounded to the next lower multiple of $500.".

(b) CONFORMING AMENDMENTS.—

(1) Section 408(a)(1) is amended by striking "in excess of $2,000 on behalf of any individual" and inserting "on behalf of any individual in excess of the amount in effect for such taxable year under section 219(b)(1)(A)". 26 USC 408.

(2) Section 408(b)(2)(B) is amended by striking "$2,000" and inserting "the dollar amount in effect under section 219(b)(1)(A)".

(3) Section 408(b) is amended by striking "$2,000" in the matter following paragraph (4) and inserting "the dollar amount in effect under section 219(b)(1)(A)".

(4) Section 408(j) is amended by striking "$2,000".

(5) Section 408(p)(8) is amended by striking "$2,000" and inserting "the dollar amount in effect under section 219(b)(1)(A)".

(c) EFFECTIVE DATE.—The amendments made by this section shall apply to taxable years beginning after December 31, 2001. Applicability. 26 USC 219 note.

SEC. 602. DEEMED IRAs UNDER EMPLOYER PLANS.

(a) IN GENERAL.—Section 408 (relating to individual retirement accounts) is amended by redesignating subsection (q) as subsection (r) and by inserting after subsection (p) the following new subsection:

"(q) DEEMED IRAS UNDER QUALIFIED EMPLOYER PLANS.—

"(1) GENERAL RULE.—If—

"(A) a qualified employer plan elects to allow employees to make voluntary employee contributions to a separate account or annuity established under the plan, and

"(B) under the terms of the qualified employer plan, such account or annuity meets the applicable requirements of this section or section 408A for an individual retirement account or annuity,

then such account or annuity shall be treated for purposes of this title in the same manner as an individual retirement plan and not as a qualified employer plan (and contributions to such account or annuity as contributions to an individual retirement plan and not to the qualified employer plan). For purposes of subparagraph (B), the requirements of subsection (a)(5) shall not apply.

"(2) SPECIAL RULES FOR QUALIFIED EMPLOYER PLANS.—For purposes of this title, a qualified employer plan shall not fail to meet any requirement of this title solely by reason of establishing and maintaining a program described in paragraph (1).

"(3) DEFINITIONS.—For purposes of this subsection—

"(A) QUALIFIED EMPLOYER PLAN.—The term 'qualified employer plan' has the meaning given such term by section 72(p)(4); except such term shall not include a government plan which is not a qualified plan unless the plan is an eligible deferred compensation plan (as defined in section 457(b)).

"(B) VOLUNTARY EMPLOYEE CONTRIBUTION.—The term 'voluntary employee contribution' means any contribution (other than a mandatory contribution within the meaning of section 411(c)(2)(C))—

"(i) which is made by an individual as an employee under a qualified employer plan which allows employees to elect to make contributions described in paragraph (1), and

"(ii) with respect to which the individual has designated the contribution as a contribution to which this subsection applies.".

(b) AMENDMENT OF ERISA.—

(1) IN GENERAL.—Section 4 of the Employee Retirement Income Security Act of 1974 (29 U.S.C. 1003) is amended by adding at the end the following new subsection:

"(c) If a pension plan allows an employee to elect to make voluntary employee contributions to accounts and annuities as provided in section 408(q) of the Internal Revenue Code of 1986, such accounts and annuities (and contributions thereto) shall not be treated as part of such plan (or as a separate pension plan) for purposes of any provision of this title other than section 403(c), 404, or 405 (relating to exclusive benefit, and fiduciary and co-fiduciary responsibilities).".

(2) CONFORMING AMENDMENT.—Section 4(a) of such Act (29 U.S.C. 1003(a)) is amended by inserting "or (c)" after "subsection (b)".

Applicability. 26 USC 408 note.

(c) EFFECTIVE DATE.—The amendments made by this section shall apply to plan years beginning after December 31, 2002.

Appendix 5

Economic Growth and Tax Relief Reconciliation Act of 2001: Committee Report

VI. PENSION AND INDIVIDUAL RETIREMENT ARRANGEMENT PROVISIONS [55]

A. INDIVIDUAL RETIREMENT ARRANGEMENTS ("IRAS") (SEC. 101 OF THE HOUSE BILL, SECS. 601–603 OF THE SENATE AMENDMENT AND SECS. 219, 408, AND 408A OF THE CODE)

PRESENT LAW

In general

There are two general types of individual retirement arrangements ("IRAs") under present law: traditional IRAs, to which both deductible and nondeductible contributions may be made, and Roth IRAs. The Federal income tax rules regarding each type of IRA (and IRA contribution) differ.

Traditional IRAs

Under present law, an individual may make deductible contributions to an IRA up to the lesser of $2,000 or the individual 's compensation if neither the individual nor the individual 's spouse is an active participant in an employer-sponsored retirement plan. In the case of a married couple, deductible IRA contributions of up to $2,000 can be made for each spouse (including, for example, a homemaker who does not work outside the home), if the combined compensation of both spouses is at least equal to the contributed amount. If the individual (or the individual 's spouse) is an active participant in an employer-sponsored retirement plan, the $2,000

[55] The provisions of the bill as passed by the House did not contain provisions relating to pensions and individual retirement arrangements. Provisions described under the House bill refer to the provisions of H.R. 10, the "Comprehensive Retirement Security and Pension Reform Act of 2001," as passed by the House.

deduction limit is phased out for taxpayers with adjusted gross income ("AGI") over certain levels for the taxable year.

The AGI phase-out limits for taxpayers who are active participants in employer-sponsored plans are as follows.

Single Taxpayers

Taxable years beginning in:	*Phase-out range*
2001	$33,000–43,000
2002	34,000–44,000
2003	40,000–50,000
2004	45,000–55,000
2005 and thereafter	50,000–60,000

Joint Returns

Taxable years beginning in:	*Phase-out range*
2001	$53,000–63,000
2002	54,000–64,000
2003	60,000–70,000
2004	65,000–75,000
2005	70,000–80,000
2006	75,000–85,000
2007 and thereafter	80,000–100,000

The AGI phase-out range for married taxpayers filing a separate return is $0 to $10,000.

If the individual is not an active participant in an employer-sponsored retirement plan, but the individual 's spouse is, the $2,000 deduction limit is phased out for taxpayers with AGI between $150,000 and $160,000.

To the extent an individual cannot or does not make deductible contributions to an IRA or contributions to a Roth IRA, the individual may make nondeductible contributions to a traditional IRA.

Amounts held in a traditional IRA are includible in income when withdrawn (except to the extent the withdrawal is a return of nondeductible contributions). Includible amounts withdrawn prior to attainment of age 59½ are subject to an additional 10-percent early withdrawal tax, unless the withdrawal is due to death or disability, is made in the form of certain periodic payments, is used to pay medical expenses in excess of 7.5 percent of AGI, is used to purchase health insurance of an unemployed individual, is used for education expenses, or is used for first-time homebuyer expenses of up to $10,000.

Roth IRAs

Individuals with AGI below certain levels may make nondeductible contributions to a Roth IRA. The maximum annual contribution that may be made to a Roth IRA is the lesser of $2,000 or the individual's compensation for the year. The contribution limit is reduced to the extent an individual makes contributions to any other IRA for the same taxable year. As under the rules relating to IRAs generally, a contribution of up to $2,000 for each spouse may be made to a Roth IRA provided the combined compensation of the spouses is at least equal to the contributed amount. The maximum annual contribution that can be made to a Roth IRA is phased out for single individuals with AGI between $95,000 and $110,000 and for joint filers with AGI between $150,000 and $160,000.

Taxpayers with modified AGI of $100,000 or less generally may convert a traditional IRA into a Roth IRA. The amount converted is includible in income as if a withdrawal had been made, except that the 10-percent early withdrawal tax does not apply and, if the conversion occurred in 1998, the income inclusion may be spread ratably over four years. Married taxpayers who file separate returns cannot convert a traditional IRA into a Roth IRA.

Amounts held in a Roth IRA that are withdrawn as a qualified distribution are not includible in income, or subject to the additional 10-percent tax on early withdrawals. A qualified distribution is a distribution that (1) is made after the five-taxable year period beginning with the first taxable year for which the individual made a contribution to a Roth IRA, and (2) which is made after attainment of age 59½, on account of death or disability, or is made for first-time homebuyer expenses of up to $10,000.

Distributions from a Roth IRA that are not qualified distributions are includible in income to the extent attributable to earnings, and subject to the 10-percent early withdrawal tax (unless an exception applies).[56] The same exceptions to the early withdrawal tax that apply to IRAs apply to Roth IRAs.

Taxation of charitable contributions

Generally, a taxpayer who itemizes deductions may deduct cash contributions to charity, as well as the fair market value of contributions of property. The amount of the deduction otherwise allowable for the taxable year with respect to a charitable contribution may be reduced, depending on the type of property contributed, the type of charitable organization to which the property is contributed, and the income of the taxpayer.

For donations of cash by individuals, total deductible contributions to public charities may not exceed 50 percent of a taxpayer 's adjusted gross income ("AGI") for a taxable year. To the extent a taxpayer has not exceeded the 50-percent limitation, contributions of cash to private foundations and certain other nonprofit organizations and contributions of capital gain property to public charities generally may be deducted up to 30 percent of the taxpayer 's AGI. If a taxpayer makes a contribution in one year that exceeds the applicable 50-percent or 30-percent limitation, the excess amount of the contribution may be carried over and deducted during the next five taxable years.

In addition to the percentage limitations imposed specifically on charitable contributions, present law imposes a reduction on most itemized deductions, including charitable contribution deductions, for taxpayers with adjusted gross income in excess of a threshold amount, which is adjusted annually for inflation. The threshold amount for 2001 is $132,950 ($66,475 for married individuals filing separate returns). For those deductions that are subject to the limit, the total amount of itemized deductions is reduced by three percent of AGI over the threshold amount, but not by more than 80 percent of itemized deductions subject to the limit.

[56] Early distribution of converted amounts may also accelerate income inclusion of converted amounts that are taxable under the four-year rule applicable to 1998 conversions.

The effect of this reduction may be to limit a taxpayer 's ability to deduct some of his or her charitable contributions.

HOUSE BILL

Increase in annual contribution limits

The House bill increases the maximum annual dollar contribution limit for IRA contributions from $2,000 to $3,000 in 2002, $4,000 in 2003, and $5,000 in 2004. The limit is indexed in $500 increments in 2005 and thereafter.

Additional catch-up contributions

The House bill accelerates the increase of the IRA maximum contribution limit for individuals who have attained age 50 before the end of the taxable year. The maximum dollar contribution limit (before application of the AGI phase-out limits) for such an individual is increased to $5,000 in 2002 and 2003. In 2004 and thereafter, the general limit applies to all individuals.

Deemed IRAs under qualified plans

No provision.

Tax-free IRA withdrawals for charitable purposes

No provision.

Effective date.—The provision is effective for taxable years beginning after December 31, 2001.

SENATE AMENDMENT

Increase in annual contribution limits

The Senate amendment increases the maximum annual dollar contribution limit for IRA contributions from $2,000 to $2,500 for 2002 through 2005, $3,000 for 2006 and 2007, $3,500 for 2008 and 2009, $4,000 for 2010, and $5,000 for 2011. After 2011, the limit is adjusted annually for inflation in $500 increments.

Additional catch-up contributions

The Senate amendment provides that individuals who have attained age 50 may make additional catch-up IRA contributions. The otherwise maximum contribution limit (before application of the AGI phase-out limits) for an individual who has attained age 50 before the end of the taxable year is increased by $500 for 2002 through 2005, $1,000 for 2006 through 2009, $1,500 for 2010, and $2,000 for 2011 and thereafter.

Deemed IRAs under employer plans

The Senate amendment provides that, if an eligible retirement plan permits employees to make voluntary employee contributions to a separate account or annuity that (1) is established under the plan, and (2) meets the requirements applicable to either traditional IRAs or Roth IRAs, then the separate account or annuity is deemed a traditional IRA or a Roth IRA, as applicable, for all purposes of the Code. For example, the reporting requirements applicable to IRAs apply. The deemed IRA, and contributions thereto, are not subject to the Code rules pertaining to the eligible retirement plan. In addition, the deemed IRA, and contributions thereto, are not taken into account in applying such rules to any other contributions under the plan. The deemed IRA, and contributions thereto, are subject to the exclusive benefit and fiduciary rules of ERISA to the extent otherwise applicable to the plan, and are not subject to the ERISA reporting and disclosure, participation, vesting, funding, and enforcement requirements applicable to the eligible retirement plan.[57] An eligible retirement plan is a qualified plan (sec. 401(a)), tax-sheltered annuity (sec. 403(b)), or a governmental section 457 plan.

Tax-free IRA withdrawals for charitable purposes

The Senate amendment provides an exclusion from gross income for qualified charitable distributions from an IRA: (1) to a charitable organization (as described in sec. 170(c)) to which deductible contributions may be made; (2) to a charitable remainder annuity trust or charitable remainder unitrust; (3) to a pooled income fund (as defined in sec. 642(c)(5)); or (4) for the issuance of a charitable gift annuity. The exclusion applies with respect to distributions described in (2), (3), or (4) only if no person holds an income interest in the trust, fund, or annuity attributable to such distributions other than the IRA owner, his or her spouse, or a charitable organization.

In determining the character of distributions from a charitable remainder annuity trust or a charitable remainder unitrust to which a qualified charitable distribution from an IRA is made, the charitable remainder trust is required to treat as ordinary income the portion of the distribution from the IRA to the trust which would have been includible in income but for the Senate amendment, and as corpus any remaining portion of the distribution. Similarly, in determining the amount includible in gross income by reason of a payment from a charitable gift annuity purchased with a qualified charitable distribution from an IRA, the taxpayer is not permitted to treat the portion of the distribution from the IRA that would have been taxable but for the Senate amendment and that is used to purchase the annuity as an investment in the annuity contract.

A qualified charitable distribution is any distribution from an IRA that is made after age 70 ½, that qualifies as a charitable contribution (within the meaning of sec. 170(c)), and that is made directly to the charitable organization or to a charitable remainder annuity trust, charitable remainder unitrust, pooled income fund, or charitable gift annuity (as described above).[58] A taxpayer is not permitted to claim a charitable contribution deduction for amounts transferred from his or her IRA to a charity or to a trust, fund, or annuity that, because of the Senate amendment, are excluded from the taxpayer's income. Conversely, if the amounts transferred are

[57] The Senate amendment does not specify the treatment of deemed IRAs for purposes other than the Code and ERISA.

[58] It is intended that, in the case of transfer to a trust, fund, or annuity, the full amount distributed from an IRA will meet the definition of a qualified charitable distribution if the charitable organization's interest in the distribution would qualify as a charitable contribution under section 170.

otherwise nontaxable, e.g., a qualified distribution from a Roth IRA, the regularly applicable deduction rules apply.

Effective date.—The Senate amendment is generally effective for taxable years beginning after December 31, 2001. The provision relating to deemed IRAs under employer plans is effective for plan years beginning after December 31, 2002. The provision relating to tax-free IRA withdrawals for charitable purposes is effective for taxable years beginning after December 31, 2009.

CONFERENCE AGREEMENT

Increase in annual contribution limits

The cônference agreement increases the maximum annual dollar contribution limit for IRA contributions from $2,000 to $3,000 for 2002 through 2004, $4,000 for 2005 through 2007, and $5,000 for 2008. After 2008, the limit is adjusted annually for inflation in $500 increments.

Additional catch-up contributions

The conference agreement provides that individuals who have attained age 50 may make additional catch-up IRA contributions. The otherwise maximum contribution limit (before application of the AGI phase-out limits) for an individual who has attained age 50 before the end of the taxable year is increased by $500 for 2002 through 2005, and $1,000 for 2006 and thereafter.

Deemed IRAs under employer plans

The conference agreement follows the Senate amendment.

Tax-free IRA withdrawals for charitable purposes

The conference agreement does not include the Senate amendment.

Effective date.—The conference agreement is generally effective for taxable years beginning after December 31, 2001. The provision relating to deemed IRAs under employer plans is effective for plan years beginning after December 31, 2002.

Appendix 6

Select Text of Pension Protection Act of 2006

SEC. 824. ALLOW DIRECT ROLLOVERS FROM RETIREMENT PLANS TO ROTH IRAS.

(a) IN GENERAL.—Subsection (e) of section 408A of the Internal Revenue Code of 1986 (defining qualified rollover contribution) is amended to read as follows:

"(e) QUALIFIED ROLLOVER CONTRIBUTION.—For purposes of this section, the term 'qualified rollover contribution' means a rollover contribution—

"(1) to a Roth IRA from another such account,

"(2) from an eligible retirement plan, but only if—

"(A) in the case of an individual retirement plan, such rollover contribution meets the requirements of section 408(d)(3), and

"(B) in the case of any eligible retirement plan (as defined in section 402(c)(8)(B) other than clauses (i) and (ii) thereof), such rollover contribution meets the requirements of section 402(c), 403(b)(8), or 457(e)(16), as applicable.

For purposes of section 408(d)(3)(B), there shall be disregarded any qualified rollover contribution from an individual retirement plan (other than a Roth IRA) to a Roth IRA.".

(b) CONFORMING AMENDMENTS.—

(1) Section 408A(c)(3)(B) of such Code, as in effect before the Tax Increase Prevention and Reconciliation Act of 2005, is amended—

(A) in the text by striking "individual retirement plan" and inserting "an eligible retirement plan (as defined by section 402(c)(8)(B))", and

(B) in the heading by striking "IRA" the first place it appears and inserting "ELIGIBLE RETIREMENT PLAN".

(2) Section 408A(d)(3) of such Code is amended—

(A) in subparagraph (A), by striking "section 408(d)(3)" inserting "sections 402(c), 403(b)(8), 408(d)(3), and 457(e)(16)",

(B) in subparagraph (B), by striking "individual retirement plan" and inserting "eligible retirement plan (as defined by section 402(c)(8)(B))",

(C) in subparagraph (D), by inserting "or 6047" after '408(i)",

(D) in subparagraph (D), by striking "or both" and inserting "persons subject to section 6047(d)(1), or all of the foregoing persons", and

(E) in the heading, by striking "IRA" the first place it appears and inserting "ELIGIBLE RETIREMENT PLAN".

(c) EFFECTIVE DATE.—The amendments made by this section shall apply to distributions after December 31, 2007.

SEC. 829. ALLOW ROLLOVERS BY NONSPOUSE BENEFICIARIES OF CERTAIN RETIREMENT PLAN DISTRIBUTIONS.

(a) IN GENERAL.—

(1) QUALIFIED PLANS.—Section 402(c) of the Internal Revenue Code of 1986 (relating to rollovers from exempt trusts) is amended by adding at the end the following new paragraph:

"(11) DISTRIBUTIONS TO INHERITED INDIVIDUAL RETIREMENT PLAN OF NONSPOUSE BENEFICIARY.—

"(A) IN GENERAL.—If, with respect to any portion of a distribution from an eligible retirement plan of a deceased employee, a direct trustee-to-trustee transfer is made to an individual retirement plan described in clause (i) or (ii) of paragraph (8)(B) established for the purposes of receiving the distribution on behalf of an individual who is a designated beneficiary (as defined by section 401(a)(9)(E)) of the employee and who is not the surviving spouse of the employee—

"(i) the transfer shall be treated as an eligible rollover distribution for purposes of this subsection, H. R. 4–223

"(ii) the individual retirement plan shall be treated as an inherited individual retirement account or individual retirement annuity (within the meaning of section 408(d)(3)(C)) for purposes of this title, and

"(iii) section 401(a)(9)(B) (other than clause (iv) thereof) shall apply to such plan.

"(B) CERTAIN TRUSTS TREATED AS BENEFICIARIES.—For purposes of this paragraph, to the extent provided in rules prescribed by the Secretary, a trust maintained for the benefit of one or more designated beneficiaries shall be treated in the same manner as a trust designated beneficiary.".

(2) SECTION 403(a) PLANS.—Subparagraph (B) of section 403(a)(4) of such Code (relating to rollover amounts) is amended by inserting "and (11)" after "(7)".

(3) SECTION 403(b) PLANS.—Subparagraph (B) of section 403(b)(8) of such Code (relating to rollover amounts) is amended by striking "and (9)" and inserting ", (9), and (11)".

(4) SECTION 457 PLANS.—Subparagraph (B) of section 457(e)(16) of such Code (relating to rollover amounts) is amended by striking "and (9)" and inserting ", (9), and (11)".

(b) EFFECTIVE DATE.—The amendments made by this section shall apply to distributions after December 31, 2006.

SEC. 1201. TAX-FREE DISTRIBUTIONS FROM INDIVIDUAL RETIREMENT PLANS FOR CHARITABLE PURPOSES.

(a) IN GENERAL.—Subsection (d) of section 408 (relating to individual retirement accounts) is amended by adding at the end the following new paragraph:

"(8) DISTRIBUTIONS FOR CHARITABLE PURPOSES.

"(A) IN GENERAL.—So much of the aggregate amount of qualified charitable distributions with respect to a taxpayer made during any taxable year which does not exceed $100,000 shall not be includible in gross income of such taxpayer for such taxable year.

"(B) QUALIFIED CHARITABLE DISTRIBUTION.—For purposes of this paragraph, the term 'qualified charitable distribution' means any distribution from an individual retirement plan (other than a plan described in subsection (k) or (p))—

"(i) which is made directly by the trustee to an organization described in section 170(b)(1)(A) (other than any organization described in section 509(a)(3) or any fund or account described in section 4966(d)(2)), and

"(ii) which is made on or after the date that the individual for whose benefit the plan is maintained has attained age 70½.

A distribution shall be treated as a qualified charitable distribution only to the extent that the distribution would be includible in gross income without regard to subparagraph (A).

"(C) CONTRIBUTIONS MUST BE OTHERWISE DEDUCTIBLE.—For purposes of this paragraph, a distribution to an organization described in subparagraph (B)(i) shall be treated as a qualified charitable distribution only if a deduction for the entire distribution would be allowable under section 170 (determined without regard to subsection (b) thereof and this paragraph).

"(D) APPLICATION OF SECTION 72.—Notwithstanding section 72, in determining the extent to which a distribution is a qualified charitable distribution, the entire amount of the distribution shall be treated as includible in gross income without regard to subparagraph (A) to the extent that such amount does not exceed the aggregate amount which would have been so includible if all amounts distributed from all individual retirement plans were treated as 1 contract under paragraph (2)(A) for purposes of determining the inclusion of such distribution under section 72. Proper adjustments shall be made in applying section 72 to other distributions in such taxable year and subsequent taxable years.

"(E) DENIAL OF DEDUCTION.—Qualified charitable distributions which are not includible in gross income pursuant to subparagraph (A) shall not be taken into account in determining the deduction under section 170.

"(F) TERMINATION.—This paragraph shall not apply to distributions made in taxable years beginning after December 31, 2007.".

Appendix 7

Sample Client Letter

August 18, 2009

Mr. and Mrs. Harold Benson 1222 Osius Street
Adell, WI

Re: Your IRAs and the Inherited IRA Strategy

Dear Harold and Amanda:

I think that you should consider adopting a strategy that would allow the large balance in your IRAs to be inherited intact by your children at the time the surviving spouse dies. The key advantage of this strategy is that it allows your children to keep the qualified assets in an income tax-deferred environment (an inherited ERA) and to take withdrawals from the inherited IRA over their own life expectancies. Through proper planning, which requires the execution of documents and providing funding for the strategy, you can create substantial wealth transfer opportunities for your family.

Ordinarily, an IRA distribution strategy that provides the greatest benefit to your family is one that provides the greatest possible tax deferral. By delaying withdrawals from the IRA as long as possible, the amount of wealth that can be transferred is maximized. There is one exception, however, to this general rule. The exception comes into play when funds are withdrawn from an IRA to purchase life insurance that will permit the IRA to remain *intact* beyond the surviving spouse's death. The insurance proceeds will provide the necessary liquidity to pay any estate taxes due following the death of the surviving spouse.

Typically, at the death of the first spouse to die, the surviving spouse rolls over the IRA assets into a roll-over IRA. When this step is taken, any estate taxes are deferred until the death of the surviving spouse. At the surviving spouse's death, estate tax is due on the total taxable estate and the tax must be paid within nine months of the death. Unless the estate tax can be paid from sources other than the IRA, the IRA will have to be *invaded* to pay the tax. If it is necessary to invade, the opportunity for tax deferral on the funds invested in the IRA comes to an end.

When funds have to be withdrawn from an IRA to pay an estate tax liability, those withdrawn funds become subject to income tax. This results in the so-called *negative tax spiral* and could ultimately result in a total tax loss of up to 60 to 70 percent of the original IRA balance. Here are some numbers that will show you this massive tax erosion, which leaves only 30 to 40 percent of the IRA to your heirs.

Balance in your IRA	$ 2,000,000
Less: Projected Estate Tax	(900,000)
Projected Income Tax	$ (315,000)
Net to Heirs	$ 785,000
Percentage to Heirs	39 percent
Percentage to Taxes	61 percent

To prevent this devastating depletion of wealth, the funds to pay the taxes must come from sources outside of the IRA. It is possible, when we review your personal balance sheet, that you may have enough liquid assets available to pay any projected estate taxes due. But because your IRAs represent such a large portion of your estate, you should consider the strategy of buying life insurance to provide the necessary liquidity.

Generally this strategy is implemented by establishing an irrevocable life insurance trust with your family as beneficiaries. Once the trust is created, you would make gifts of cash to the trust. The trustees would then use the cash to purchase a survivorship life insurance policy covering both of you. Then at the second death, when the trust receives the life insurance proceeds, those funds are used to purchase estate assets (usually nonliquid assets) or are loaned to the estate. An alternative to consider is to distribute trust assets directly to the beneficiaries so they can pay the estate tax. Whichever way you might choose to proceed, you have provided the funds to pay any estate tax liability while at the same time eliminating the need to invade the IRA.

In a related step, your heirs can begin to receive distributions from the IRA over their life expectancies following the second death. (There are special rules for determining the amount of the distributions to the heirs related to the life expectancy of the oldest beneficiary—the beneficiary with the shortest life expectancy.) I think that this strategy deserves to be considered as part of your retirement and estate planning. I will call in a few days to answer any questions you have about putting the strategy outlined above to work for you and your family.

With kindest personal regards.

Sincerely,

Robert S. Keebler, CPA, MST